THE POLITICS OF UNSUSTAINABILITY

Two decades after its launch by the UN Brundtland Commission, the paradigm of sustainability seems to have reached its limits. Whilst the concept figures more prominently in public debate and policy making than ever before, the ecological footprint of advanced liberal consumer societies continues to grow, and the forceful economic development of countries such as China and India reinforces concerns that the world is moving further away from, rather than closer towards the ideal of sustainability.

Given the proven failure of ecological modernisation strategies to secure sustainability, the traditional question "How may our established lifestyles and socio-economic practices be made more sustainable?" needs to be supplemented by a second, equally important, question: "How do advanced modern consumer democracies try and manage to sustain what is known to be unsustainable?" Put differently, traditional research into the *politics of sustainability* needs to be supplemented by a new line of research into the *politics of unsustainability*. Exploring the recent transformation of eco-political discourses and a variety of ways in which the unfolding paradox of sustaining the unsustainable is being managed, the present volume pioneers this new research agenda.

This book was previously published as a special issue of *Environmental Politics*

Ingolfur Blühdorn is Reader in Politics and Political Sociology at the University of Bath, UK. His work connects aspects of political sociology, social theory, eco-political theory and environmental sociology. He has published widely on social movements, Green Parties and processes of societal modernisation.

Ian Welsh is Reader in Sociology in the Cardiff School of Social Sciences. He has worked on the interface between science, environment and social movements. His most recent work addresses the social and political implications of complexity theory.

Environmental Politics/Routledge Research in Environmental Politics
Edited by Matthew Paterson, University of Ottawa and Graham Smith, University of Southampton

Over recent years environmental politics has moved from a peripheral interest to a central concern within the discipline of politics. This series aims to reinforce this trend through the publication of books that investigate the nature of contemporary environmental politics and show the centrality of environmental politics to the study of politics per se. The series understands politics in a broad sense and books will focus on mainstream issues such as the policy process and new social movements as well as emerging areas such as cultural politics and political economy. Books in the series will analyse contemporary political practices with regards to the environment and/or explore possible future directions for the 'greening' of contemporary politics. The series will be of interest not only to academics and students working in the environmental field, but will also demand to be read within the broader discipline.

The series consists of two strands:

Environmental Politics addresses the needs of students and teachers, and the titles will be published in paperback and hardback. Titles include:

Global Warming and Global Politics
Matthew Paterson

Politics and the Environment
James Connelly & Graham Smith

International Relations Theory and Ecological Thought
Towards Synthesis
Eric Laferrière & Peter Stoett

Planning Sustainability
Edited by Michael Kenny & James Meadowcroft

Deliberative Democracy and the Environment
Graham Smith

EU Enlargement and the Environment
Institutional change and environmental policy in Central and Eastern Europe
Edited by JoAnn Carmin and Stacy D. VanDeveer

The Crisis of Global Environmental Governance
Towards a New Political Economy of Sustainability
Edited by Jacob Park, Ken Conca and Matthias Finger

Routledge Research in Environmental Politics presents innovative new research intended for high-level specialist readership. These titles are published in hardback only and include:

1. The Emergence of Ecological Modernisation
   Integrating the Environment and the Economy?
   Stephen C. Young

2. Ideas and Actions in the Green Movement
Brian Doherty

3. Russia and the West
Environmental Cooperation and Conflict
Geir Hønneland

4. Global Warming and East Asia
The Domestic and International Politics of Climate Change
Edited by Paul G. Harris

5. Europe, Globalization and Sustainable Development
Edited by John Barry, Brian Baxter and Richard Dunphy

6. The Politics of GM Food
A Comparative Study of the UK, USA and EU
Dave Toke

7. Environmental Policy in Europe
The Europeanization of National Environmental Policy
Edited by Andrew Jordan and Duncan Liefferink

8. A Theory of Ecological Justice
Brian Baxter

9. Security and Climate Change
International Relations and the Limits of Realism
Mark J. Lacy

10. The Environment and International Politics
International Fisheries, Heidegger and Social Method
Hakan Seckinelgin

11. Postmodern Climate Change
Leigh Glover

12. Contemporary Environmental Politics
From margins to mainstream
Edited by Piers H.G. Stephens, with John Barry and Andrew Dobson

13. Sustainable Consumption, Ecology and Fair Trade
Edited by Edwin Zaccaï

14. Environmental Governance in China
Edited by Neil Carter and Arthur P.J. Mol

15. Global Justice and Neoliberal Environmental Governance
Ethics, Sustainable Development and International Cooperation
Chukwumerije Okereke

16. Beyond Borders
Environmental Movements and Transnational Politics
Edited by Brian Doherty and Timothy Doyle

17. The Politics of Unsustainability
Eco-Politics in the Post-Ecologist Era
Edited by Ingolfur Blühdorn amd Ian Welsh

THE POLITICS OF UNSUSTAINABILITY

ECO-POLITICS IN THE POST-ECOLOGIST ERA

Edited by
Ingolfur Blühdorn and Ian Welsh

LONDON AND NEW YORK

First published 2008 by Routledge
2 Park Square, Milton Park, Abingdon, Oxfordshire OX14 4RN

Simultaneously published in the USA and Canada by Routledge
711 Third Avenue, New York, NY, 10017, USA

First issued in paperback 2014

Routledge is an imprint of the Taylor & Francis Group, an informa business

© 2008 Taylor & Francis

Typeset in Times by KnowledgeWorks Global Limited, Chennai, India

All rights reserved. No part of this book may be reprinted or
reproduced or utilised in any form or by any electronic,
mechanical, or other means, now known or hereafter
invented, including photocopying and recording, or in any
information storage or retrieval system, without permission in
writing from the publishers.

British Library Cataloguing in Publication Data
A catalogue record for this book is available from the British Library

ISBN 13: 978-1-138-88233-1 (pbk)
ISBN 13: 978-0-415-46620-2 (hbk)

CONTENTS

1. **Eco-politics beyond the Paradigm of Sustainability: A Conceptual Framework and Research Agenda**   **1**
   INGOLFUR BLÜHDORN & IAN WELSH

2. **Changing Public Discourse on the Environment: Danish Media Coverage of the Rio and Johannesburg UN Summits**   **22**
   LARS KJERULF PETERSEN

3. **Participation and Sustainable Development: The Post-ecologist Transformation of Citizen Involvement in Denmark**   **47**
   JEPPE LÆSSØE

4. **Sustaining the Unsustainable: Symbolic Politics and the Politics of Simulation**   **67**
   INGOLFUR BLÜHDORN

5. **Symbolic Environmental Legislation and Societal Self-Deception**   **92**
   JENS NEWIG

6. **Sustainable Development as Symbolic Commitment: Declaratory Politics and the Seductive Appeal of Ecological Modernisation in the European Union**   **113**
   SUSAN BAKER

7. **Dissolving the Nation: Self-deception and Symbolic Inversion in the GM Debate**   **134**
   EMMA HUGHES

8. **The Post-ecologist Condition: Irony as Symptom and Cure**   **153**
   BRONISLAW SZERSZYNSKI

9. **In Defence of Civilisation: Terrorism and Environmental Politics in the 21st Century**   **172**
   IAN WELSH

   Index   **193**

Eco-politics beyond the Paradigm of Sustainability: A Conceptual Framework and Research Agenda

INGOLFUR BLÜHDORN & IAN WELSH
*Department of European Studies, University of Bath, Bath, UK, **Cardiff School of Social Sciences, Cardiff University, Wales, UK

ABSTRACT *This contribution sketches a conceptual framework for the analysis of the post-ecologist era and outlines a research agenda for investigating its politics of unsustainability. The article suggests that this new era and its particular mode of eco-politics necessitate a new environmental sociology. Following a review of some achievements and limitations of the paradigm of sustainability, the concept of post-ecologism is related to existing discourses of the 'end of nature', the 'green backlash' and the 'death of environmentalism'. The shifting terrain of eco-politics in the late-modern condition is mapped and an eco-sociological research programme outlined centring on the post-ecologist question: How do advanced modern capitalist consumer democracies try and manage to sustain what is known to be unsustainable?*

A Watershed in Eco-politics?

This volume is devoted to exploring the stakes associated with entry into an era in which the historically radical and transformative elements of environmental movements and eco-political thought are blunted through mainstreaming and have been reconfigured by comprehensive cultural change. We are proposing to call this the *era of post-ecologism* and its eco-politics the *politics of unsustainability*. Furthermore, we are suggesting that this new era and its particular mode of eco-politics necessitate a new environmental sociology. We are aware that these propositions will trigger responses of intuitive caution not only within the academic community. Given the prominence of key

2 The Politics of Unsustainability

eco-political issues in current public debate and the overpowering declaratory commitment of leading societal actors to the goals of sustainable development and global justice, terms like *hyper-ecologism* might intuitively seem more appropriate. Also, the notion of post-ecologism is reminiscent of diagnoses of the 'end of nature' (e.g. Carson, 1962; Merchant, 1980; McKibben, 1990) and earlier announcements of 'post-environmentalism', the 'fading of the Greens' and the 'death of the environmental movement' (Young, 1990; Bramwell, 1994; Shellenberger & Nordhaus, 2005). Such announcements have always been around – and they have always proved premature. Are things really going to be different with the *post-ecologist era* and its *politics of unsustainability*? Is it really appropriate to speak of a *watershed in eco-politics*? Is there really a need for a new environmental sociology?

We believe so! As the reassuring belief in the compatibility and inter-dependence of democratic consumer capitalism and ecological sustainability has become hegemonic, different and perhaps counter-intuitive lines of enquiry are not particularly popular. They appear disturbing, even counter-productive. As faith in technological innovation, market instruments and managerial perfection is asserted as *the* most appropriate means for achieving sustain-ability, empirical experience reveals the limitations of such approaches. This insistence on the capabilities of these strategies; the denial that the capitalist principles of infinite economic growth and wealth accumulation are ecologically, socially, politically and culturally unsustainable and destructive; the pathological refusal to acknowledge that western 'needs' in terms of animal protein, air travel or electric energy, to name but three examples, simply cannot, i.e. *can not*, be satisfied in ecologically and otherwise sustainable ways, is itself a syndrome that deserves close sociological attention. But more generally, an environmental sociology that opportunistically refrains from pursuing potentially inconvenient lines of enquiry and instead confines itself to serving and enabling the prevailing techno-economic hegemony fails in terms of both academic and eco-political integrity. For these reasons, a new sociological effort to grasp and address what we are calling the post-ecologist era and its politics of unsustainability is in fact imperative.

It is 27 years since André Gorz likened ecology to the movement for universal suffrage and the campaign for a 40 hour working week, movements initially dismissed as 'anarchy and irrationality' until accumulating 'factual evidence and popular pressure' made 'the establishment suddenly give way' (Gorz, 1980/1987: 3). 'What was unthinkable yesterday becomes taken for granted today', Gorz noted, but ironically, 'fundamentally nothing changes': democratic consumer capitalism assimilates 'ecological necessities as technical constraints, and adapt[s] the conditions of exploitation to them' (Gorz, 1980/ 1987: 3). Today, the ascendancy of neo-liberal free market principles and the 'metaphysics of efficiency' (Blühdorn, 2007a: 80–5) renders Gorz's insights tangible amidst discussion of the 'inexorable growth of environmentalism' (Jordan & Maloney, 1997: 7). Indeed, the environment has acquired a position of unprecedented prominence within economics and international politics

Eco-politics beyond the Paradigm of Sustainability   3

(witness the UK Treasury's *Stern Review on the Economics of Climate Change* (Her Majesty's Treasury, 2006)). An abundance of eco-political measures are being considered and implemented. Yet the key principles governing western practices of production, circulation, exchange and consumption remain immutable. The key principles of consumer capitalism, i.e. infinite economic growth and wealth accumulation, which ecologists have always branded as fundamentally unsustainable, remain fully in place.[1] Over the past few decades there has been a steady build-up of work that is fascinated by this resilience of democratic consumer capitalism and is setting itself against both the hegemony of eco-economic 'win–win thinking' and the ongoing flow of eco-apocalyptic doomsday literature. This literature pays particular attention to symbolic stakes, rhetorical forms and the enactment of forms of societal self-deception in eco-political matters. It explores the ways in which the formalisation, declaration, communication and absorption of ecological politics take place within the context of wider social, political and economic transformation beyond the confines of traditional modern politics. It is exactly this agenda which we are seeking to formalise around the notions of the *post-ecologist era* and the *politics of unsustainability*.

The transformation of communication and other technologies since the 1980s (Thompson, 1995) has significantly changed what it is possible to know about the environment, how quickly this knowledge can be accessed and how it is disseminated and socially distributed (Adam *et al.*, 1999). The knowledge economy and the information society are widely depicted as increasingly reflexive, adaptive and innovative compared to a previous corporatist era which had been constrained by the dead hand of the state. Social movements are portrayed as critical social forces scrutinising 'every individual speck of cement in the structure of civilization for the potential of self-endangerment' (Beck, 1992: 176). They are said to be capable of constraining the 'juggernaut' of modernity (Giddens, 1990: 151). Public–private partnerships are advanced as dynamic means of innovation to meet the challenges of globalisation including ecological ones. Yet amidst this technological and managerial optimism western consumer democracies are experiencing a metamorphosis that does indeed qualify as something like a paradigm shift in eco-politics. Indicators include *inter alia*:

- the normalisation of the environmental crisis, with reports about the worst ever floods, droughts, forest fires, famines, species extinction rates, desertification, deforestation, shrinking of ice caps, etc. becoming a standard feature of daily news coverage;
- the globalisation-induced reinforcement of the fixation on economic growth, international competitiveness, consumer spending, material accumulation, etc., which are radically incompatible with the *ecological virtues* (Blühdorn, 2007a) constitutive of a sustainable society;
- the acceptance by environmental figureheads such as Jonathon Porritt of capitalism as an integral ingredient of the solution to deepening problems of unsustainability (Porritt, 2005);

4   *The Politics of Unsustainability*

- the alignment of traditionally radical non-governmental organisations (NGOs) like Friends of the Earth and Greenpeace with regulatory initiatives and commercial partnerships consistent with ecological modernisation;
- the transformation of Green parties across Europe and their struggle to redefine and reposition themselves in a radically changing political landscape;
- the rebranding of nuclear energy as green energy, inverting its symbolic status and historic founding role for eco-politics as the iconic symbol of an unsustainable form of civilisation.

This list of indicators could easily be extended;[2] they signal entry into what we are calling the era of post-ecologism. But of course none of this means that environmental issues have disappeared from either political agenda(s) or the public sphere. What we are describing as the politics of unsustainability is not simply the denial of environmental problems; nor must it be understood as an anti-environmentalist backlash. If anything media coverage and mainstream party political commentary on environmental issues have increased as debates over climate change intensify amidst incessant commentary on 'the war on terror'. Indeed climate change and terrorism compete in terms of which represents the greater threat to established patterns of western life, with *energy security* having emerged as the key concern connecting the two. So ecology and the environment have moved centre stage within formal politics, but at the same time, a combination of structural and contingent phenomena leaves established eco-politics in something of a hiatus. Commenting on the US, Cohen notes that the eco-political trajectory that had its origins in the 1970s has 'come to an end' marking the start of a protracted period of 'foraging' to 'find a new path forward' (Cohen, 2006: 77). This assessment is *mutatis mutandis* also applicable to the European context. The causes and wide-ranging implications of this reconfiguration of eco-political stakes and remedial strategies need to be investigated.

The objective of this contribution is to sketch a conceptual framework for the analysis of the post-ecologist era and outline a research agenda for investigating its politics of unsustainability. As a preliminary exercise, the next section will review some achievements and limitations of the paradigm of sustainability. This paradigm was instrumental in obtaining the status of a 'non-controversial public concern' for the environment (Eder, 1996: 183), and without it, it would not make sense to speak of an eco-politics *beyond* the paradigm of sustainability. The third section will then be devoted to some of those observers who have talked about the 'end of nature', the 'green backlash' and the 'death of environmentalism'. A review of their work will help to establish a conceptual framework for the exploration of the post-ecologist era. Building on this framework, the fourth section will sketch the research agenda into the politics of unsustainability. We will conclude with an overview of the contributions which are assembled here and with some pointers as to how these

Eco-politics beyond the Paradigm of Sustainability   5

analyses fit into the much larger research project that this volume is hoping to launch.

The Limitations of the Sustainability Paradigm

Whilst the notion of sustainable development (SD) has been central for establishing environmentalism as an 'ideological masterframe' (Eder, 1996: 183), sustainability remains a contested concept in academic and political circles, giving rise to practical policy approaches to which broader publics find it difficult to relate. It is now a commonplace to distinguish between different forms of sustainable development and sustainability (e.g. Dobson, 1998: 33–61; Jacobs, 1999). The prime distinction between 'strong' and 'weak' forms involves differences in emphasis placed on inter-generational equity, North–South equity and the importance attached to precaution within regulatory and legislative institutions (Baker, 2006). Furthermore, the question of what is to be sustained and how is a critical issue. If this is first and foremost the established economic system, or cherished western practices of individualised, consumption-oriented identity formation, then this is a far cry from the demand to sustain planetary ecological integrity and the intrinsic value of nature. Carruthers (2001) argues that the continued primacy of economic growth within SD, reinforced by World Bank and International Monetary Fund approaches, represents the effective subversion of any radical counter-hegemonic programme. Meadowcroft (2000), in contrast, sees SD as a cumulative process with long term positive consequences, even though it may in the short term contain unsustainable practices and technologies. Key commentators over the lifetime of the SD debate now argue that even actors which are widely perceived as adopting a pro-active stance – such as the European Union (EU) – have prioritised economic and commercial dimensions of sustainability at the expense of ecological and social dimensions (Baker, 2006 and in this volume).

At the societal level conditions are no more favourable. The culture of mass consumption remains fundamentally incompatible with the principles of sustainability. Furthermore, as the axiom of individual self-responsibility cascades down through societies via the institutions of market-oriented governance, citizens find their capacities stretched by rising levels of complexity and precariousness (Chesters & Welsh, 2006; Ilcan, 2006). For individuals struggling to confront the multiple challenges of late-modern *'life in fragments'* (Bauman, 1995), adopting lifestyles consistent with strong sustainable development adds further to the escalating burden of 'self-responsibility', compromising their capacity for personal competitiveness (Bauman, 2004). Against this backdrop, environmental issues are delegated to political actors and regulatory regimes. In line with the principles of both representative democracy and the service society, such actors and regimes are keenly providing reassurance that appropriate action is being taken. Yet, strong sustainable development in terms of individual lifestyles, inter-generational equity, North–South redistribution of wealth and the long-term preservation of

6 *The Politics of Unsustainability*

eco-system integrity remain distant prospects, whilst traditional economic growth remains prominent. The *ecological footprint* of western consumer societies (and their emulation around the world) continues to grow dramatically, and so does the size of what researchers of societal metabolisms and global material flows are describing as the *ecological debts* and *ecological rucksacks* of western societies (e.g. Sustainable Europe Research Institute (SERI)/Friends of the Earth Europe, 2005; Giljum, 2006). Such metaphorical terms aim to illustrate the increasingly visible and deepening unsustainability of 'Northern' lifestyles, the geographical imbalance in resource extraction and consumption and the unequal distribution of environmental degradation around the globe.

The centrality afforded to the 'categorical imperatives' of globalisation implies that the social, cultural and political dimensions of sustainability which figure prominently within Agenda 21 and Local Agenda 21 are almost invariably subordinated to economic growth, competitiveness and innovation. As labour market participation rates and hours worked rise amidst increasingly 'flexible', precarious and often poorly paid forms of employment, social, cultural and political activities dependent upon free time and resources are eroded. The performative demands of the 'only game in town', globalisation, necessitate the reconfiguration – more often than not into more *unsustainable* directions – of the traditional family, residence and mobility patterns, education practices, work, leisure and the construction and articulation of identity. Local Agenda 21 had envisaged public engagement with the long term, inter-generational dimensions of sustainable development to devise action programmes with extensive (if not consensual) societal support. Little of this has materialised, not least because of escalating demands upon time in dual income, sometimes multi-occupation households. Roundtables, public consultation exercises and other participatory initiatives open up new circuits of communication, but structurally cannot stimulate the envisaged degree of public (re)engagement. Whilst material living standards continue to rise, western societies exhibit multiple faultlines. Britain, a widely celebrated example of successful economic modernisation (e.g. Jun, 2007), aptly illustrates how the enforcement of market liberal reform agendas directly augments social unsustainability as manifested in excessive individualisation, social inequality, political disengagement, family breakdown, anti-social behaviour, alcohol and drug abuse, high crime rates and prison populations, and so forth.

As social responses to policy initiatives in pursuit of sustainable development (e.g. household waste recycling or road pricing) exhibit confounding complexity – because situated publics respond to progressive measures in unanticipated and contradictory ways – two responses can be discerned. First, initiatives requiring social participation begin to be accompanied by surveillance and compulsion. Second, the balance between social and political initiatives, on the one hand, and technological fixes, on the other, has begun to tip decisively towards the latter *irrespective* of public alignment. The preference of politicians and policy makers for the apparent certainty of techno-managerial solutions

Eco-politics beyond the Paradigm of Sustainability 7

reflects a *reciprocal* withdrawal of trust. Whilst public trust in political parties declines amidst historically low electoral participation rates and collapsing party membership figures, politicians and policy makers increasingly distrust 'innovation-resistant' publics. Innovation and reform need to be imposed on refractory publics, legitimised by the superior wisdom of *responsible* rather than *representative* governments. Public resistance against genetically modified (GM) crops or the expansion of nuclear energy, to name but two prominent examples, is perceived as the 'irrational' rejection of 'inevitable' modernisation by an 'innovation-resistant' public (Welsh, 2000a, 2000b, 2006; Blühdorn, 2007a; Hughes, this volume). As reciprocal trust between publics, political representatives and officials of state is diminishing, the tacit bedrock of liberal democratic theory has entered a particularly corrosive conjuncture (Blühdorn, 2007b), and the tensions between 'the game' and viable eco- and social systems begin to play out across multiple sites. This is the shifting terrain upon which post-ecologist politics is situated.

Whilst ecological modernisation had been widely praised as a win–win path to aligning economic and environmental goals in realising sustainable development, 21st century politics tacitly accepts environmental crises such as climate change, including their consequential outcomes, as an inescapable given. This does not mean to say that any attempts to control such developments have been abandoned, but the novelty in the politics of unsustainability is the shift of emphasis from trying to *avert* such crises to *managing* their implications and consequences. States are familiar with crises as operational modes which legitimate extraordinary security measures, the suspension of democratic safeguards and the uncoupling of checks and balances. The extension of terror tropes to contemporary movement radicals utilising direct action tactics and the creation of offences relating to 'economic terrorism' underlines the importance that state authorities attach to containing post-1990s activism (Chesters & Welsh, 2006; Welsh, this volume). By framing the implications of the bio-economy or new nuclear build in terms of the sustainable development and modernisation agendas, any challenge to the hegemony of techno-managerialism and economic efficiency can be portrayed as a threat to both environmental reform and societal progress (Welsh, 2007). Addressing the 2006 Labour Party Conference former US President Bill Clinton acknowledged that the contemporary epoch could be characterised as 'unequal, unstable and unsustainable' (BBC Radio 4, *World at One*, 27 September 2006). The responsible way forward, he suggested, was the creation of more wealth, North–South redistribution, a resolute stance against terror and the pursuit of ecological modernisation consistent with economic growth. The electoral appeal of such leadership statements is considerable, yet they seamlessly endorse substantial public subsidies to the 'creative, dynamic and innovative' corporate sector, the erosion of civil liberties and the renunciation of the emancipatory project. Thus the pervasive sense of environmental crisis becomes another means of reinforcing state authority and citizens' com-pliance with future-fitness programmes orientated towards 'sustaining the

8   *The Politics of Unsustainability*

unsustainable' (Blühdorn, this volume). Post-democratic and neo-authoritarian tendencies are an important dimension of the politics of unsustainability.

So sustainable development has been appropriated by established political parties and re-spun in such a way that the state/corporate sector nexus, operating through deepening public–private partnerships, emerges as the central means of delivering sustainability. George W. Bush's investment initiative to spur technological innovation and Tony Blair's underwriting of the accumulated costs of nuclear waste and reactor decommissioning are examples of the re-engineering of sectors which were formerly closely associated with environmental destruction as agents of a sustainable future. The return to nuclear power, backed by the International Energy Agency, as a key ingredient of energy security and climate change policy consistent with perceived economic interests illustrates the firm resolve to *defend* and *continue* rather than *review* and *change* the established path. Critics of the discourse of sustainable development have always argued that this paradigm does not envisage a genuine departure from the trajectory of material growth, social inequality and ecological deterioration. But if it ever did (e.g. Baker, this volume), the ongoing process of modernisation has taken western consumer democracies *beyond* the politics of sustainability and into a realm where *the management of the inability and unwillingness to become sustainable* has taken the centre ground. Thus, environmental sociology is confronted with a categorically new constellation to which it must respond. Yet the conceptual and strategic tools which it has accumulated so far are not sufficient for this purpose.

Green Backlash, End of Environmentalism and Post-ecologism

What then are the constitutive ingredients of post-ecologism, and when and how did the era of post-ecologism emerge? A detailed answer to these questions exceeds present confines and will be provided later in this volume (e.g. Blühdorn). At this stage we want to point to some important milestones in the accompanying academic debate. This will, at the same time, help to clarify the relationship between our notion of post-ecologism and earlier diagnoses of *anti-environmentalism*, the *end of nature* or the *end of environmentalism*. In 1990, at the time when globalisation began to emerge as a major paradigm within the social sciences, two books articulated central dimensions of what we are formalising here as the era of post-ecologism and its politics of unsustainability: John Young's *Post Environmentalism* and Bill McKibben's *The End of Nature*. Young argued that the advent of post-industrial society would lead to a political consensus on the environment, with ideological environmentalism giving way to a pragmatic diversity of practices, and 'all parties' offering 'sensible long-term environmental policies' (Young, 1990: 165–7). McKibben pointed to the disappearance of nature as an external pristine domain uninfluenced by human culture and civilisation. As the markers of human activity are increasingly apparent even in the heart of wilderness areas,

Eco-politics beyond the Paradigm of Sustainability   9

he noted, we are entering a 'post-natural world' (McKibben, 1990: 55).[3] McKibben also realised that with the 'end of nature' ecological movements – and modern societies at large – are losing an important normative standard and source of meaning. The loss of *naturalness* as an extra-societal and therefore reliable normative category triggers the rampant growth of negotiability, decideability and responsibility, and hence McKibben's end of nature leads straight into Bauman's (1999) *political economy of uncertainty*. Yet, McKibben himself did not follow this through by questioning the concept of nature, which was in fact drawn into a maelstrom of political contestation. Towards the end of the 1990s, Eder's (1996) *The Social Construction of Nature* and MacNaghten & Urry's (1998) *Contested Natures* formalised and consolidated this area, establishing that in the discursive realm of eco-politics there is no single and stable phenomenon called nature but an unlimited number of competing and ever changing conceptions of 'nature' each of which has its own perspective on what ought to be valued, protected or recognised as an environmental problem or good. By implication, this work at the same time reconfirmed that eco-politics is in fact most closely connected to the politics of individual and social identity (Inglehart, 1977; Blühdorn, 2000).

The recognition of the inescapably social character of nature and the social constructedness of environmental consciousness, problems and concerns had major repercussions on eco-political thought. For a long time ecologists had implicitly assumed that nature could be a functional equivalent or substantive grounding of transcendental reason, but it now transpired that whatever environmentalists may regard as ecologically necessary or desirable are projections of their ethical and political values into the supposedly external Other of society, i.e. into nature. Whilst anthropogenic change of the natural environment including the wide range of empirically measurable consequences is undeniable, ubiquitous, accelerating and probably irreversible, categorical ecological imperatives do not exist.[4] There are no political values or prescriptions which can be read off nature. The political ideology of *ecologism* as it had emerged in the 1980s had been the most comprehensive and consistent articulation of eco-political thought (Dobson, 1990; Goodin, 1992; Hayward, 1995). Yet the diversity of ways in which the environment, environmental crises and environmental consciousness are conceived frustrated the attempt to create a unified ecologist ideology and severely moderated the political impact of the ecological critique.

Sociological work, inspired by systems theory, then led to the announcement of the 'abdication of the ecologist paradigm' (Blühdorn, 1997, 2000). Central in this was, in particular, the belief that for the analysis of the late-modern condition the traditionally modern concept of the *autonomous subject* needs to be replaced by the late-modern concept of the *autopoietic system*. More specifically, the suggestion that the idealist notion of the subject has run its course not only as the central category of sociological analysis, but also as the dominant ideal of late-modern identity construction,[5] implied that the *subjectivisation* of eco-politics and the *differentiation* of its value base were

10 The Politics of Unsustainability

supplemented by an important third development which is the *identification of the Self with the system*, i.e. the collapse of traditional modernity's central dualism of the *Self* and its *Other*. Together these three dimensions paved the way for the 'post-ecologist constellation' or the 'post-ecologist condition' (Blühdorn, 2000, 2004). In a number of respects, eco-politics now turned into a politics 'without identity' (Blühdorn, 2000: 151–72).

Whilst sociological and eco-political theory were trying to get a conceptual grip on the changing ways in which advanced modern societies frame and address their eco-political problems, the policy-oriented paradigm of ecological modernisation further accelerated this *post*-ecologist transformation. The proponents of ecological modernisation reframed environmental problems primarily in technological, economic and managerial terms. While there are different varieties of the ecological modernisation approach (e.g. Christoff, 1996; Barry, 2005), the overarching effect of this paradigm was the softening of the tension between (a) technology and ecology, (b) economic growth and ecology and (c) the competitive market and ecology (e.g. Mol & Sonnenfeld, 2000). The undeniable successes of ecological modernisation strategies and the promise that the full potential of 'new environmental policy instruments' (e.g. Jordan *et al.*, 2003) is only just being discovered spread considerable eco-political optimism. The paradigm of ecological modernisation thus challenged a range of established ecologist beliefs. In particular, it rehabilitated the 'ecologist enemies' and made technological innovation, economic growth, capital accumulation and consumerism in principle acceptable[6] – if only they were of the correct, i.e. the 'green', variety. The paradigm of ecological modernisation thus offered reassurance, disempowered radical ecologist movements and helped to pacify eco-political conflicts whilst bolstering the argument that radical system change is not actually required as environmental goals can be realised through the modification of existing structures.

Around the turn of the century, this message was powerfully reinforced by Bjørn Lomborg's best-selling *The Skeptical Environmentalist*, which set out to fully debunk the ecologist 'litany' (Lomborg, 2001: 3–42). Whilst putting much emphasis on how genuinely he 'care[d] for our Earth and...for the future health and wellbeing of its succeeding generations' (Lomborg, 2001: 3), Lomborg suggested that 'if we want to leave a planet with the most possibilities for our descendants', it is 'imperative that we focus primarily on the economy' (Lomborg, 2001: 324). He wanted to see the 'spotlight on securing economic growth', and this should be pursued 'within the framework of the World Trade Organization' (Lomborg, 2001: 324). Just like the proponents of ecological modernisation, Lomborg was responding to an implicit societal demand.[7] The overwhelming popularity of their message reflected a *Zeitgeist* which insists on the official acknowledgement and incorporation of environmental concerns and at the same time desires a *green light* signalling the continuation – if in a modified form – of established practices and principles. This green light was exactly what Lomborg and the paradigm of ecological modernisation – each in their particular ways – delivered, and in doing so, they paved the way for the

Eco-politics beyond the Paradigm of Sustainability   11

pacification of eco-political conflicts surrounding the assumed incompatibility of consumer capitalism and ecological sustainability. The transformation this implied for eco-movements and eco-politics in western consumer democracies has been described and discussed as the 'end of environmentalism' (Wissenburg & Levy, 2004).

This 'end of environmentalism' through the selective mainstreaming and post-ecologist reframing of environmental concerns displays specifically European features. Its American counterpart, the hotly debated 'death of environmentalism' (Shellenberger & Nordhaus, 2005), bears markedly different characteristics. Shellenberger & Nordhaus's (2005) influential article focused on the institutionalised environmental movement, i.e. the major environmental NGOs of the US, and argued that this movement is no longer able to connect to the concerns and aspirations of mainstream society. The American eco-movement's 'slide into death' (Cohen, 2006: 76) is widely explained by the fact that the 'movement is overwhelmingly preoccupied with . . . wildlife protection and landscape preservation' and has consistently neglected an equally important dimension of environmental activism: 'the well-being of people' (Cohen, 2006: 75).[8] Furthermore, the 'death of environmentalism' in the US has been portrayed as effected by a powerful 'anti-environmental movement' which in terms of 'grassroots organizing' and grassroots mobilisation has 'beaten the environmentalists at their own game' (Rowell, 1996: 373). The corporate counter-attack on US environmentalism detailed in Rowell's *Green Backlash* (1996) also included extensive use of law suits, heralding the wider use of legal intimidation (Donson, 2000). The rise of neo-conservatism and the 'far right' then brought to completion what Buell (2004) terms the transition *From Apocalypse to Way of Life*. Indeed Buell regards neo-conservatism as 'the most important explanation' (2004: 3) for the demise of American environmentalism. Along with Shellenberger and Nordhaus, he points to the 'strong and enormously successful anti-environmental disinformation industry' (Buell, 2004: 3) in the US, which was 'not simply spontaneous' but 'carefully crafted' by the neo-conservative movement (Buell, 2004: 7; also see Brulle & Jenkins, 2006; Devall, 2006).

Comparison to the US illuminates what exactly the transition to an era of post-ecologism is supposed to imply. The phenomena described by Rowell, Buell, Shellenberger and Nordhaus and many others are undoubtedly highly relevant, but they neither capture nor explain the metamorphosis of environmental politics that is the topic of the present volume. European societies and their eco-movements have not been affected by factors similar to those that have reshaped environmentalism in the US.[9] And for the US, too, the observation that 'a sense of unresolved, perhaps unresolvable, environmental crisis has become part of people's normality today' and 'part of the uncertainty in which people nowadays dwell' (Buell, 2004: xvii and following) points well beyond explanations in terms of *anti-environmentalism*. An appropriate and more nuanced understanding of the late-modern transformation of eco-politics requires more complex approaches. What

12   The Politics of Unsustainability

European–American comparison reveals is the important difference between established varieties of *anti-environmentalism* and the new phenomenon of *post-ecologism*. Whilst the American situation – at least in the somewhat reductionist account by Shellenberger and Nordhaus – seems to be, first and foremost, one of the *marginalisation* and *exclusion* of *environmentalist* demands, the European experience is more than anything one of the *exhaustion* and *reframing* of *ecologist* concerns amidst overwhelming adoption and absorption. In this sense, the European condition is much more literally *post-ecologist*, and the distinction between *anti-environmentalism* and *post-ecologism* is crucially important for any research into what we are calling the politics of unsustainability.

The Politics of Unsustainability: A Research Agenda for Environmental Sociology

The diagnoses of the *death of environmentalism*, the *end of nature* and the *post-ecologist turn* have triggered at least five different objections:

- demands for empirical verification with calls to 'Show us the data' (Dunlap, 2006);
- arguments that surveys and opinion polls provide no evidence of any social movement decline (Rootes, 1999, 2003) and that indeed environmental activism represents a growing part of 'civil society on a global scale' (Dalton, 2005: 453);
- the rejection of the *end of nature* in McKibben's sense on the grounds that 'a lot of external nature remains' and paradigms of naturalness continue to be available (Yearley, 2006: 17);
- the denunciation of the theory of post-ecologism as 'profound conservatism' (Barry, 2004: 184) equivalent to 'US President George W. Bush's denial of global warming' (Barry, 2004: 183);
- attempts to 'reverse these trends' (Cohen, 2006: 75) and to 'resurrect environmentalism' (Dunlap, 2006: 95ff.), either by reconstituting major NGOs as a 'progressive vanguard' (Cohen, 2006: 75) or by going 'back to the grassroots' (Devall, 2006: 171).

Reflecting on these different critical responses helps to avoid potential misunderstandings and to clarify what the sociological investigation of the politics of unsustainability involves. Each of these responses can be addressed firstly at the level of the substantive argument they make, and secondly at the level of the underlying question they raise. Looking at the substantive level first, it is important to understand that polls and surveys indicating that despite 'the current political impotence' of the eco-movement (Dunlap, 2006: 90), the public 'continue to support values of the environmental movement' (Devall, 2006: 167) do not constitute an argument against what is engaged with here as the post-ecologist turn. Similarly, empirical evidence of stable and perhaps

Eco-politics beyond the Paradigm of Sustainability   13

even rising levels of environmental activism can be entirely consistent with the formal politics of unsustainability (e.g. Blühdorn, 2007c). The surveys which Dunlap, Devall, Dalton and many others are referring to tend to have an undifferentiated understanding of environment-related values, concern and activism, and are insensitive to the qualitative transformation of such values and activism. This transformation also escapes Yearley, who reassures us that there is still plenty of nature and naturalness around and that, anyway, the end of nature is not a singular event but a continuous process of ending and (re)creation (2006: 20). Exactly this transformation, however, i.e. the reframing and repackaging of environmental concerns and commitment, is at the centre of the paradigm of post-ecologism. The new forms of expression adopted by movement-based, party-political and other actors are of critical importance. In party-political terms strange bedfellows are emerging highlighting the shifting ground upon which environmental politics stands. In the UK Zac Goldsmith, editor of the radical journal the *Ecologist,* is now advising the Conservative Party, whose leader introduced the slogan 'Vote Blue Go Green'. Across Europe major political parties need to (re)position themselves in relation to 'the green vote', not simply because of Green parties – which are themselves engaged in a process of repositioning – but because of the environmental posture of other mainstream parties. In terms of movement-based actors, such realignments and the absence of any radical ecologist content are equally striking.

Attempts to 'reverse' the post-ecologist turn and 'resurrect' what is supposedly 'dead' overlooks the question of whether it is actually *possible* to resuscitate particular forms of eco-political thought and action once their historical context has passed away (see Blühdorn, 2006; Welsh, 2007). According to the account provided here, these older forms of thought and activism have become exhausted because in the process of ongoing modernisation their specific social and cultural foundations have been superseded by very different constellations. Problem perceptions and priority lists have changed and do not allow for a simple resuscitation of older movements. Beyond this, a revival based on major environmental organisations becoming a vanguard would have a top-down ethos of social engineering. Clearly any genuine rejuvenation could only emerge from the bottom up, but the potential for radical renewal from within the movement milieux is constrained, firstly, by the fact that the late-modern condition is much more conducive to populist right-wing than emancipatory left-wing mass mobilisation; secondly, by the growth of self-experience and self-interest movements (Blühdorn, 2006; McDonald, 2006), which reflects a wider decline in collective identity movements. And thirdly, the networking of diverse activist communities that consolidated into the misnamed anti-globalisation movement constituted a 'unity in diversity' actor (Chesters & Welsh, 2006) that *de-centres* traditional environmental movements rather than infusing them with new energy.[10] Thus established environmentalism has been incorporated from above at the same time as being superseded and emasculated from below. The

14 *The Politics of Unsustainability*

defiant insistence that diagnosing this fundamentally new condition is profoundly conservative or outright reactionary is unlikely to reverse the post-ecologist turn and is, anyway, based on a confusion of the categories of academic description and analysis with those of political campaigning.[11]

So each of these responses can and ought to be contested at the level of their substantive content, but in the present context this is actually less important than recognising that none of them raises the really important questions. If the objective is to understand the specific conditions and constellations which determine the ways in which late-modern societies are framing and processing their environmental problems, the question is not:

- whether environmental issues and concerns in the most general sense are still present in the public sphere;
- whether the number of eco-political actions and the membership of environmental groups is rising or falling;
- whether there are residues of nature and naturalness 'out there';
- how the post-ecologist turn may be reversed and the eco-movement resuscitated;
- or whether tentative conceptualisations of the ongoing shift in late-modern society's eco-politics are ideologically acceptable or politically helpful for ecologist activists.

All of these questions are valid and important in their own right, but they are all missing the point that is at the centre of our research agenda into the eco-politics of the post-ecologist era. As we have argued above the politics of unsustainability is unfolding amidst the simultaneity of, on the one hand, a general acceptance that the achievement of sustainability requires radical change in the most basic principles of late-modern societies and, on the other hand, an equally general consensus about the non-negotiability of democratic consumer capitalism – irrespective of mounting evidence of its unsustainability. It is this tension and the multiple ways in which it materialises in contemporary politics that need to be researched in much more detail. For environmental sociology to embrace this agenda, something like a paradigm change is required. So far environmental sociology has predominantly served as a 'handmaiden' (Welsh, 1996: 407) helping to resolve environmental problems and paving the way towards an ecologically more benign modernity. This work has been important and remains indispensable, but in the era of post-ecologism it needs to be supplemented by a second line of enquiry. Given the continuing addiction of western(ised) societies to consumer capitalism and the proven failure of ecological modernisation strategies to secure sustainability, it is no longer enough to ask how technological and managerial efficiency revolutions may help to secure, further improve and spread the lifestyles associated with that system. Another equally important line of research will have to focus on the question: *How do advanced modern capitalist consumer democracies try and manage to sustain what is known to be unsustainable?* This is the politics and

Eco-politics beyond the Paradigm of Sustainability 15

sociology of unsustainability. Questions figuring prominently on this research agenda include *inter alia*:

- How has the progressive project that some environmentalists would like to *resurrect* instead been *recast*?
- What were the factors that triggered this process of recasting, and which parameters are shaping it?
- How does this recasting affect political actors historically associated with agendas of radical change? To what extent can they reinvent and reposition themselves in a political landscape that has fundamentally changed?
- By what mechanisms are advanced consumer democracies sustaining simultaneous discourses of radical change and uncompromising defence?
- Why are both discourses being sustained at the same time, and who benefits?
- How does this simultaneity of discourses affect established understandings and institutions of representative democracy?

Asking these questions in no way implies the justification or approval of late-modern society's unsustainability or the assertion that things cannot be different. It is true, however, that research into the politics of unsustainability is not immediately about building ecological consciousness, revealing eco-political implementation deficits or devising new policy suggestions. Instead it first of all focuses on detecting and investigating the strategies by which late-modern societies are trying to cope with the awareness and the apparent inescapability of their unsustainability and the full range of its ecological, social, cultural, political and economic consequences. The paradox of post-ecologist politics is that whilst embracing ecological modernisation and elements of progressive social movement agendas, contemporary democracies are failing to provide the 'level playing field' fundamental to developing environmental economies. It is only by beginning to unpick this paradox and the tensions highlighted above that the transformation of eco-political (and wider social movement) agendas through selective accommodation within political systems and their recasting in terms of modernisation and progressive politics can be unpacked. With this volume we cannot do more than sketch a conceptual framework and a research agenda for this post-ecologist environmental sociology. But the contributions assembled here at least begin to make tangible what the ambitious and at times counter-intuitive investigation of the politics of unsustainability might entail.

An Itinerary for This Collection

The two contributions by Petersen and Læssøe focus on Denmark, in eco-political terms one of the most ambitious and advanced European countries. Both pieces investigate how, since the early 1990s, environmental issues and policy have been reframed in Denmark. Lars Kjerulf Petersen compares

16   *The Politics of Unsustainability*

Danish terrestrial television news coverage of the 1992 and 2002 Earth Summits and analyses the interpretive themes used in the portrayal of climate change and wider environmental issues. He argues that within this coverage, between 1992 and 2002, the framing of the environment as a collective good threatened by consumption and economic growth had been replaced by the portrayal of the environment as an economic cost needing to be balanced against other opportunities and priorities. He suggests that the master frame of the early 1990s in which environmentalism was depicted as a common and integrating concern had in the 2002 reportage been replaced with a frame that emphasises the contested nature of environmentalist claims, depicting nature as resilient and questioning the wisdom of prioritising climate change as an area requiring action. Adopting a somewhat wider temporal horizon, Jeppe Læssøe focuses on the reframing of citizen participation in Danish environmental politics from the 1970s to the present. He investigates how in Denmark the relationship between citizen involvement and environmental policy has changed over the decades. Based on empirical research on *the mediating agents*, i.e. those who have tried to involve citizens in environmental issues and sustainable development, Læssøe identifies a number of stages through which a *post-ecologist* approach to participation has gradually taken shape. This transformation, Læssøe argues, has not been strategically promoted by particular actors, but has come about in an inclusive process in which environmentalists themselves have played an active part.

These two pieces are followed by a set of three contributions which focus on different varieties of symbolic politics. Stirred by the contradiction between the mainstreamed castigation of *merely symbolic* eco-politics and the firm resolve of advanced consumer democracies to defend the core principles of democratic consumer capitalism, Ingolfur Blühdorn undertakes a meta-critique of the critical discourse of symbolic politics. He argues that a comprehensive cultural shift which he conceptualises as the *post-ecologist turn* is responsible not only for a fundamental transformation of the ways in which late-modern societies frame and process their environmental problems, but also for the exhaustion of *authentic* eco-politics which, by implication, renders the critique of *merely symbolic* politics questionable. Blühdorn develops the concept of *simulative politics* as a more appropriate conceptualisation of late-modern eco-politics and suggests that practices of simulative politics are a key strategy by which late-modern societies are trying to sustain what is known to be unsustainable.

Further elaborating on the issue of symbolic politics, Jens Newig focuses on symbolic environmental legislation, which is widely held responsible for the absence of really effective environmental policy. Using two pieces of environmental legislation in Germany as empirical case studies, Newig identifies a series of external factors which are conducive to the production of primarily symbolic laws, and argues that such legislation must not be understood as wilfully deceiving citizens, but can also be read as reflecting a certain readiness of citizens to be deceived. Thus, the incidence of symbolic legislation is

Eco-politics beyond the Paradigm of Sustainability 17

indicative of practices of societal self-deception. Susan Baker in turn looks at symbolic politics at the EU level, highlighting the discrepancy between the EU's declared commitment to the goal of SD and its policy practice which is determined by the paradigm of ecological modernisation (EM). Baker elaborates on the distinction between SD and EM and suggests that the EU's symbolic commitment to SD contributes to the construction of the Union's identity and external image as a green global actor whilst permitting economic considerations to subordinate eco-political interests.

Emma Hughes then analyses print media coverage of the GM debate in the UK through a combination of textual analysis of press coverage and interviews with editors, campaigners and GM companies. Her contribution traces how these multiple circuits of communication symbolically structure the GM debate around traditional notions of the nation despite widespread knowledge of trans-boundary gene flows. The persistence of the modernist notion of the nation as a closed system maintains established notions of British identity rather than the renegotiation of identity central to theories of reflexive modernisation. This societal self-deception is co-constructed by all the parties to this issue, including Friends of the Earth campaigners, suggesting that the creation of *apparent* certainty is preferable to acknowledging global complexity.

Bron Szerszynski focuses on the potentials for moving beyond the paradigm of post-ecologist politics. He argues that irony is a necessary means of both engaging with and overcoming the post-ecologist predicament. Irony is presented as an indispensable means of transcending the familiar juxtaposition of enlightenment rationality and romanticism associated with environmental debates. Szerszynski posits a cultural modernism which acknowledges the contributions of both conscious human action and forces beyond conscious control in structuring both the human condition and human–environment relationships. Irony, mounted from this perspective, becomes both a resource for environmental campaigning and a means of redefining an environmental politics which neither over-rationalises nor over-romanticises human natures.

Ian Welsh finally examines the re-emergence of *civilisation* and *terror* as central rhetorical categories within political discourse in the post 9/11 era. He argues that this represents both a resurrection and an extension of previous uses. Through a consideration of US and UK measures to defend civilisation against external and internal enemies, Welsh argues that sections of the environmental movement aligned with the alternative globalisation movement become subjects of this discourse. This enemy within is targeted by security services because of the mobilisation of symbolic stakes corrosive of both global and national institutions orchestrating the neo-liberal axiomatic central to unsustainability.

Thus the contributions to this volume are a first attempt to capture very different dimensions of the politics of unsustainability. They are beginning to map out the tasks an environmental sociology for the post-ecologist era might have to perform, but more than anything, they are an invitation to

18   The Politics of Unsustainability

environmental sociologists to reach beyond the dominant service provider mentality and embark on a research programme that restores the discipline's academic and eco-political integrity.

Notes

1. Note that even the Brundtland Report (World Commission on Environment and Development, 1987) identified the recognition of limits to growth and a shift of focus away from the insatiable needs of western consumers and towards the fundamental needs of human beings worldwide as the constitutive principles of sustainable development.
2. See Blühdorn in this volume for a much more comprehensive version.
3. McKibben was referring to North America. In Europe the last areas of *wilderness* had obviously been conquered at a much earlier point in time. But the significance of McKibben's book was that it facilitated the reflection on the end of nature within a context sensitised by a broad societal discussion of environmental deterioration.
4. The same argument can obviously be made for environmental problems which are widely believed to be *objectively existing out there*. The recognition that these problems always have the status of social constructions rather than ontological realities can, of course, easily be misinterpreted as the denial of major anthropogenic environmental change, but it remains a fact that what environmental politics negotiates are issues which *appear* as problematic from particular social perspectives, but which are not problematic *in themselves* (Blühdorn, 2000: 40–8; 2004: 41–3).
5. Late-modern identity construction arguably takes place first and foremost *within* the confines of the system of consumer capitalism and largely relies on the means this system holds available (primarily acts of consumption). This contrasts sharply with the modernist – and the ecologist – tradition which saw identity construction as a matter of creating and developing spaces *outside* the established system. It was only in *opposition* to the *wrong modernity* that authentic identity and life and the categories of the natural could be acquired or reinstated.
6. In the sense that they are turning into central tools of ecological modernisation, technological innovation, green consumerism, etc. are in fact regarded as indispensable.
7. This comparison does not mean to brush over the obvious differences between Lomborg's project of denying any eco-political urgency and the project of ecological modernisation to use technological and managerial innovation in order to make environmental improvement economically profitable.
8. This rather reductionist perspective on and assessment of US environmentalism clearly ignores the wide spectrum of environmental and environment-related movements which are not represented by the mainstream environmental NGOs.
9. It could however be argued that eco-political movements in certain European countries like the UK encountered aggressive neo-conservatism in the late 1980s and early 1990s, and that this encounter was central in the following reconfiguration of radical grassroots movements.
10. The associated networks include environmentally orientated initiatives but environmentalism as a prioritised movement is not credible within this constellation.
11. Of course, any attempt to make a watertight distinction between these categories will remain subject to inescapable limitations, but for environmental sociology it is still imperative to at least try to separate the two.

References

Adam, B., Allan, S. & Carter, C. (1999) *Environmental Risks and the Media* (London: Routledge).
Baker, S. (2006) *Sustainable Development* (London: Routledge).
Barry, J. (2003) 'Ecological modernisation', in E. Page & J. Proops (eds.), *Environmental Thought*, pp. 191–213 (Cheltenham: Edward Elgar).

Eco-politics beyond the Paradigm of Sustainability 19

Barry, J. (2004) 'From environmental politics to the politics of the environment. The pacification and normalization of environmentalism?', in M. Wissenburg & Y. Levy (eds.), *Liberal Democracy and Environmentalism. The End of Environmentalism?* pp. 179–92 (London: Routledge).

Barry, J. (2005) 'Ecological modernisation', in J. Dryzek & D. Schlosberg (eds.), *Debating the Earth*, pp. 303–21 (Oxford: Oxford University Press).

Bauman, Z. (1995) *Life in Fragments: Essays in Post-modern Morality* (Cambridge: Polity).

Bauman, Z. (1999) *In Search of Politics* (Cambridge: Polity).

Bauman, Z. (2004) *Wasted Lives: Modernity and its Outcasts* (Cambridge: Polity).

Beck, U. (1992) *Risk Society. Towards a New Modernity* (London: Sage).

Blühdorn, I. (1997) 'A theory of post-ecologist politics', *Environmental Politics* 6(3): 125–47.

Blühdorn, I. (2000) *Post-ecologist Politics. Social Theory and the Abdication of the Ecologist Paradigm* (London: Routledge).

Blühdorn, I. (2004) 'Post-ecologism and the politics of simulation', in M. Wissenburg & Y. Levy (eds.), *Liberal Democracy and Environmentalism. The End of Environmentalism?* pp. 35–47 (London: Routledge).

Blühdorn, I. (2006) 'Self-experience in the theme park of radical action? Social movements and political articulation in the late-modern condition', *European Journal of Social Theory* 9(1): 23–42.

Blühdorn, I. (2007a) 'Democracy, efficiency, futurity: contested objectives of societal reform', in I. Blühdorn & U. Jun (eds.), *Economic Efficiency – Democratic Empowerment*, pp. 69–98 (Lanham, MD: Rowman & Littlefield/Lexington).

Blühdorn, I. (2007b) 'The third transformation of democracy: on the efficient management of late-modern complexity', in I. Blühdorn & U. Jun (eds.), *Economic Efficiency – Democratic Empowerment*, pp. 299–331 (Lanham, MD: Rowman & Littlefield/Lexington).

Blühdorn, I. (2007c) 'Self-description, self-deception, simulation. A systems-theoretical perspective on contemporary discourses of radical change', *Social Movement Studies* 6(1) (forthcoming).

Bramwell, A. (1994) *The Fading of the Greens. The Decline of Environmental Politics in the West* (New Haven, CT: Yale University Press).

Brulle, R. & Jenkins, C. (2006) 'Spinning our way to sustainability', *Organization & Environment* 19(1): 1–6.

Buell, F. (2004) *From Apocalypse to Way of Life. Environmental Crisis in the American Century* (London: Routledge).

Carruthers, D. (2001) 'From opposition to orthodoxy: the remaking of sustainable development', *Journal of Third World Studies* 18(2): 93–122.

Carson, R. (1962) *Silent Spring* (London: Penguin).

Chesters, G. & Welsh, I. (2006) *Complexity and Social Movements: Multitudes on the Edge of Chaos* (London: Routledge).

Christoff, P. (1996) 'Ecological modernisation, ecological modernities', *Environmental Politics* 5(3): 476–500.

Cohen, M. (2006) 'The death of environmentalism. Introduction to the symposium', *Organization & Environment* 19(1): 74–81.

Dalton, R. (2005) 'The greening of the globe? Cross-national levels of environmental group membership', *Environmental Politics* 14(4): 441–59.

Devall, B. (2006) 'The end of American environmentalism?', *Nature and Culture* 1(2): 157–80.

Dobson, A. (1990) *Green Political Thought* (London: Routledge).

Dobson, A. (1998) *Justice and the Environment. Conceptions of Environmental Sustainability and Dimensions of Social Justice* (Oxford: Oxford University Press).

Donson, F. (2000) *Legal Intimidation* (London: Free Association Books).

Dunlap, R. (2006) 'Show us the data. The questionable empirical foundations of the *death of environmentalism* thesis', *Organization & Environment* 19(1): 88–102.

Eder, K. (1996) *The Social Construction of Nature* (London: Sage).

Giddens, A. (1990) *The Consequences of Modernity* (Cambridge: Polity).

Giddens, A. (1991) *Modernity and Self-identity* (Cambridge: Polity).

20 The Politics of Unsustainability

Giljum, S. (2006) 'Global appropriation of environmental space. Past trends and future scenarios of natural resource use in different world regions'. Paper presented at the Heinrich Böll Foundation, Berlin, 9 October.

Goodin, R. (1992) *Green Political Theory* (Cambridge: Polity).

Gorz, A. (1980/1987) *Ecology as Politics* (London: Pluto).

Hayward, T. (1995) *Ecological Thought: An Introduction* (Cambridge: Polity).

Her Majesty's Treasury (2006) *Stern Review on the Economics of Climate Change*. Available at: http://www.hm-treasury.gov.uk (Last accessed 12 December 2006).

Ilcan, S. (2006) 'Global governing organisations: order-building and waste management', *Current Sociology* 54(6): 851–72.

Inglehart, R. (1977) *The Silent Revolution: Changing Values and Political Styles among Western Publics* (Princeton, NJ: Princeton University Press).

Jacobs, M. (1999) 'Sustainable development as a contested concept', in A. Dobson (ed.), *Fairness and Futurity. Essays on Environmental Sustainability and Social Justice*, pp. 21–45 (Oxford: Oxford University Press).

Jordan, A., Wurzel, R. & Zito, A. (eds.) (2003) *'New' Instruments of Environmental Governance? National Experiences and Prospects* (London: Frank Cass).

Jordan, G. & Maloney, W. (1997) *The Protest Business? Mobilizing Campaign Groups* (Manchester: Manchester University Press).

Jun, U. (2007) 'Radical reformers – defiant electorates? Reform policy and international competitiveness under Schröder and Blair', in I. Blühdorn & U. Jun (eds.), *Economic Efficiency – Democratic Empowerment*, pp. 31–67 (Lanham, MD: Rowman & Littlefield/Lexington).

Lomborg, B. (2001) *The Skeptical Environmentalist. Measuring the Real State of the World* (Cambridge: Cambridge University Press).

MacNaghten, P. & Urry, J. (1998) *Contested Natures* (London: Sage).

McDonald, K. (2006) *Global Movements: Action and Culture* (Oxford: Blackwell).

McKibben, Bill (1990) *The End of Nature* (London: Penguin).

Meadowcroft, J. (2000) 'Sustainable development: a new(ish) idea for a new century?', *Political Studies* 48(3): 70–87.

Merchant, C. (1980) *The Death of Nature. Women, Ecology and the Scientific Revolution* (San Francisco: Harper & Row).

Mol, A. & Sonnenfeld, D. (eds.) (2000) *Ecological Modernisation around the World: Perspectives and Critical Debates* (London: Frank Cass).

Porritt, J. (2005) *Capitalism as if the World Matters* (London: Earthscan).

Ridgeway, J. (1970) *The Politics of Ecology* (New York: E. P. Dutton).

Rootes, C. (1999) *Environmental Movements: Local, National and Global* (London: Frank Cass).

Rootes, C. (ed.) (2003) *Environmental Protest in Western Europe* (Oxford: Oxford University Press).

Rowell, A. (1996) *Green Backlash. Global Subversion of the Environmental Movement* (London: Routledge).

SERI/Friends of the Earth Europe (2005) *Europe's Global Responsibility. Environmental Space, International Trade and Factor X* (Vienna: Sustainable Europe Research Institute).

Shellenberger, M. & Nordhaus, T. (2005) 'The death of environmentalism. Global warming politics in a post-environmental world'. Available at: http://www.grist.org/ci-bin/printthis.pl (accessed 27 January 2005).

Thompson, J. (1995) *Media and Modernity* (Cambridge: Polity Press).

Welsh, I. (1996) 'Risk, global governance and environmental politics', *Innovation* 9(4): 407–20.

Welsh, I. (2000a) *Mobilising Modernity: The Nuclear Moment* (London: Routledge).

Welsh, I. (2000b) 'Desiring risk: nuclear myths and the social selection of risk', in B. Adam, U. Beck & J. Vanloon (eds.), *The Risk Society and Beyond: Critical Issues for Social Theory* (London: Sage).

Welsh, I. (2006) 'Values, science and the EU: bio-technology and transatlantic relations', in I. Manners & S. Lucarelli (eds.), *Values and Principles in EU Foreign Policy*, pp. 59–76 (London: Routledge).

Eco-politics beyond the Paradigm of Sustainability   21

Welsh, I. (2007) 'Participation, innovation and efficiency: social movements and the new genetics in Germany and the UK', in I. Blühdorn & U. Jun (eds.), *Economic Efficiency – Democratic Empowerment*, pp. 275–95 (Lanham, MD: Rowman & Littlefield/Lexington).

Wissenburg, M. & Levy Y. (eds.) (2004) *Liberal Democracy and Environmentalism. The End of Environmentalism?* (London: Routledge).

World Commission on Environment and Development (1987) *Our Common Future* (Oxford: Oxford University Press).

Yearley, S. (2006) 'How many *ends* of nature: making sociological and phenomenological sense of the end of nature', *Nature and Culture* 1(1): 10–21.

Young, J. (1990) *Post Environmentalism* (London, Belhaven).

Changing Public Discourse on the Environment: Danish Media Coverage of the Rio and Johannesburg UN Summits

LARS KJERULF PETERSEN
National Environmental Research Institute, University of Aarhus, Denmark

ABSTRACT *Environmental degradation and unsustainable development were addressed on a global scale at the UN summits in Rio de Janeiro in 1992 and Johannesburg in 2002. This contribution presents analyses of Danish television coverage of these two summits and related topics, viewing the media stories as exemplary cases of wider public conceptions of the environment. Over a decade rhetoric about the summits and the environment changed, the agenda changed, and key environmental issues were repackaged. These changes are interpreted in relation to ecological modernisation and discussed as a possible development towards post-environmentalism. Already ecological modernisation can be perceived as post-environmentalist, but the suggestion here is the transformation of ecological modernisation as a prominent discursive frame and thus a further shift in eco-political discourse.*

Introduction

Environmental concern and demands for sustainability are established as strong narratives and discourses in many sectors of society, and media coverage of environmental issues is a key factor in this mainstreaming. Yet, as this contribution demonstrates, the content of environmentalism as public discourse has changed over the past decades. Different issues have been at the centre of environmental concern, from wilderness conservation to global warming, and the diagnosis and handling of environmental problems have been associated with different visions of social order.

Ideas of *ecological modernisation* are among those environmentally concerned social orderings that have most successfully entered into logics of society at many levels: in administration and planning, in production and technological innovation, *and* in images and narratives of public media. Ecological modernisation seeks to combine economic growth with environmental protection and to integrate environmental concern into established society. In that respect it may already signify a *post-environmentalist* state, because it abandons beliefs constitutive to earlier environmentalism, such as limits to growth, restraints on consumerism, and the need for a break with established capitalist society. But in recent years there has arguably been a decline in the prominence of ecological modernisation leading to an entirely new level of *post-environmentalism*.

An understanding of a common global destiny has also been a recurrent theme in environmentalism and has been linked to notions of *sustainable development* – which differ from ecological modernisation in key ways (see Baker, this volume) but also share its idea of combining environmental concern and economic development. A *post-environmentalist* state can, *inter alia*, be defined in terms of a neglect of common destiny, i.e. as demarcations of public space and definitions of collective identity becoming less open and less inclusive.

Central questions are thus: (1) How has public discourse on the environment changed? (2) Do these changes signify a post-environmentalist turn, and do they signify a change in the status of ecological modernisation? (3) Do changes in environmental discourse also imply changes in the definition of collective identity as part of a post-environmentalist turn?

This contribution presents a case study of Danish television coverage of the Rio and Johannesburg UN summits in 1992 and 2002. It also includes coverage of some related environmental issues in the same period. This case is considered significant for several reasons: Denmark used to have a high environmental profile and was a frontrunner in the development of ecological modernisation. The UN summits on sustainable development treated the most serious and emblematic environmental problems, worked around a number of key concepts such as sustainability and biodiversity, established environmental problems as a global concern and attracted considerable media attention. Thus, the UN summits represented the essence and broadness of environmental discourse. The related issues to which this analysis also extends complete the picture by including (1) climate change, which has been a global environmental issue for more than two decades, and (2) news stories which, like the summits themselves, were about the environment in a comprehensive sense.

The analysis will proceed with a theoretical discussion, first on societal communication, then on the characteristics of ecological modernisation, its role in public discourse and its relation to post-environmentalism. This feeds into an outline of criteria for what constitutes different discursive orderings of the environment. The latter half of this contribution is devoted to presenting the case study.

Societal Communication

Telling news about nature and the environment in broadcast media is an act of societal communication. Mass-mediated societal communication can, as inspired by John B. Thompson, be defined as 'institutionalised production

24 *The Politics of Unsustainability*

and generalized diffusion of symbolic goods' via the fixation and transmission of information, knowledge and symbolic content across distances in space and time (Thompson, 1995: 26). Actors in this communication are tied together by participating in it – producing, reproducing, organising, interpreting and being audience to the same information and knowledge. And they participate in the same communication on the grounds of sharing societal relations at large, such as economic interaction, political institutions, location in the same geographical area, common language and a collective memory of mutual myths and histories.

'The media are not simply involved in reporting on a social world ... Rather, the media are actively involved in constituting the social world' (Thompson, 1995: 117). Or put differently, the social world is – in part – constructed through *discourses* fixed and diffused by mass media. The concept of discourse is here defined in line with Fairclough (following the tradition of Foucault). A discourse is not just a speech act or statement; it is a shared way of apprehending social phenomena, a specific ordering of the world, a *system of knowledge and belief*. 'Discourse is a practice not just of representing the world, but of signifying the world, constituting and constructing the world in meaning' (Fairclough, 1992: 64). Media texts, including images and non-verbal sound, are articulations of discourses, of discursive orderings of the world. Hence, the point of analysing a corpus of media texts, as is done later in this contribution, is to identify what sort of discourse is at work in these texts.

According to cultural sociologist James Carey, there are two dimensions or functions of societal communication – *control* and *ritual* – that constitute and order the social world through generalised dissemination of information and symbolic content (Carey, 1989: 13–36). One function of societal communication is 'the transmission of signals or messages over distance for the purpose of control' (Carey, 1989: 15). Environmental problems such as depletion of the ozone layer or long term toxic effects of chemicals are beyond personal and tactile experience. Hence, individual and collective knowledge about such dangers is only established through forms of societal communication. In dealing with environmental risks, the control aspect of communication can thus be seen as a matter of publicly establishing the existence and gravity of dangers, defining them and distributing information about their importance and how to deal with them.

However, the notion of 'control' embraces a much broader spectrum of communicative practices with regulatory potential. Apart from warning about imminent or long term dangers and information about how to deal with them, it may imply: (1) publication of laws and regulations to the affected populace; (2) public campaigns – emanating from a broad range of actors, not just governments – seeking to advance or prevent certain forms of behaviour; and (3) involvement of mass media in political *agenda setting*, i.e. the framing of social issues in public media, thereby defining what issues should attract attention and forming the perception of them.[1] Beyond this, 'control' also includes guidance and even education and enlightenment, through which templates for everyday practices are established, thereby forming these practices. Whilst lying outside the present remit it should also be emphasised that entertainment formats also contain templates for behaviour and thought.

This also points to the *ritual* dimension of societal communication. 'A ritual view of communication is directed not towards the extension of messages in space but towards the maintenance of society in time; not the act of imparting information but the representation of shared beliefs' (Carey, 1989: 18). Through the ritual of communication – particularly the ritual of *risk* communication – social cohesion is established and confirmed. In other words, risk communication is also a matter of ritualising dangers: providing comfort, interpreting unknown dangers through well known formulae and, very importantly, defining and confirming the community that shares these dangers.

If communication as ritual is a projection of a collectivity's cohesion, this is however not just a projection of the consensus that unites a social grouping, but also a projection of what divides it (Douglas, 1997: 129). *Dissent* can also be an integral part of collective and individual identity. It seems, for instance, that an ongoing disagreement over the issue of abortion has become a defining trait of the American public. Similarly, the analysis below suggests the development of a division between environmentalist and economistic world-views.

The point then is that news stories about the environment contribute to the formation of public spheres and collective identities. As Susan Baker demonstrates (this volume), environmental discourse can be a building block in the construction of an imagined community; more specifically in the construction of a European identity distinct from the American (Welsh, 2006). A similar point is presented in the work of Douglas & Wildavsky (1982). The selection of dangers and risks that are communicated publicly contribute to the construction of collective identity and differ according to cultural and social context. And vice versa: the choice of which danger society is more concerned with does not depend exclusively or even primarily upon an objective estimation of the precise urgency and scale of possible dangers. The choice of dangers, the selection of risks that become dominant issues for media attention and determine practices of individual and institutional actors, depends upon societal organisation, rationales of social cohesion and community structure at large and, it should be added, *shifting* ideological orientations.[2]

Ecological Modernisation

There are a number of different discursive orderings of nature and the environment (many of which are identified as ideal types in Dryzek (1997)). For present purposes only the discourse of ecological modernisation is discussed in detail, including a focus upon how it differs from more far-reaching forms of environmentalism (survivalism, ecologism) and its relation to post-environmentalism.

26   *The Politics of Unsustainability*

Ecological modernisation is basically about the integration of environmental concern in central institutions of society. As Hajer writes: 'ecological modernization can be defined as the discourse that recognizes the structural character of the environmental problematique but none the less assumes that existing political, economic, and social institutions can internalize the care for the environment' (Hajer, 1995: 25).

More radical forms of environmentalism understand the structural character of environmental problems as so profound that an actual break with industrial and capitalist society is required to effectively deal with environmental deterioration. The notion of *limits to growth* has also been a general understanding in more moderate versions of environmentalism. But the core of ecological modernisation is to combine economic growth with environmental protection, not just as end-of-pipe solutions for growing industry, but also through the incorporation of environmental protection within economic and planning practices concerning waste management, energy, transport, etc. (Hajer, 1995: 26, 1996: 248–9).

Moreover, in ecological modernisation economic growth is perceived as necessary for the development of new, non-polluting technologies, and environmental concern is prioritised as a potential source of future growth, driving both technological and economic innovation. The environment becomes a dynamic market. 'Capitalism is changing constantly, and [two] ... of the main triggers are environmental concerns and interests' (Mol & Spaargaren, 2002: 37).

Theories of ecological modernisation also point to institutional changes in government and administrative bodies. The integration of environmental concern into public planning and administration is linked to the development of policy styles that focus on voluntary and *communicative* measures, stressing the need to involve stakeholders and citizens in consultation and *co-production of collective images* (see the discussion of discursive control and ritual communication above). State agencies, private companies, researchers and environmental grassroots organisations are all framed as partners in ecological modernisation, contributing to proactive and preventive measures (Mol, 2000: 46).

Institutional changes also involve a transfer of capacities for environmental policy making from the nation state to international fora and institutions (Mol, 2001: 106). As Susan Baker demonstrates (this volume), ecological modernisation has become a central concept in European Union (EU) environmental management strategies. But the concept of *sustainability*, coined by the Brundtland Commission, in all its multiple meanings has also become a common frame of reference for international environmental discourse and regulation. Indeed, ideas of economic growth and environmental protection within sustainable development debates resemble those of ecological modernisation. Sustainable development has increasingly come to embrace economic growth, in both developing and developed nations, as vital to the reduction of direct environmental harm created by poverty and the creation of prosperity in the developing world (Dryzek, 1997: 121–2).

There are however important differences between sustainability and ecological modernisation. Definitions and theories of the two vary considerably. Hajer sees the international endorsement of the Brundtland report and the general acceptance of Agenda 21 as a paradigmatic example of ecological modernisation (Hajer, 1996: 249). But Langhelle argues that sustainability and ecological modernisation should not be conflated. Firstly, sustainable development attempts to address a number of issues, such as poverty and distribution of wealth, about which ecological modernisation has nothing to say. Secondly, and more importantly, the focus of attention for sustainable development is the future of the world, its population, its natural resources and its biosphere, whereas ecological modernisation has its focus set on optimisation of industry, management and government (Langhelle, 2000). For the purposes of this analysis, however, the point is that, despite competing interpretations, there are enough common denominators between ecological modernisation and sustainability – especially the combination of economic growth and environmental protection – to group them together when analysing different media framings of the environment. Ideas that may be separated in other spheres can be linked together in the public sphere.

The Common Good

While Mol basically relates his understandings of ecological modernisation to institutional changes in business corporations and administrative bodies, we need to understand more of its place in public discourse. German sociologist Klaus Eder discusses how environmental discourses shape the public sphere. In fact, he understands ecological *modernity* – rather than ecological *modernisation* – as related to a redefinition of the common good as it is established in public discourse. In the form of ecological modernity environmentalism becomes a master discourse amongst the general public.

Environmental concern may have developed through a series of marginal, specialist and mutually unconnected discourses stretching from protection of singular species to dismay over toxic chemicals and the tale of limits to growth, but across these differences it has developed into a master discourse in the public sphere, establishing environmental concern as a coherent project despite all differences. A master discourse operates with universal frames of reference pointing to the relationship between man and nature, not in terms of the inherent values of nature, but in terms of a just distribution of natural resources. Nature is defined and valued as common good, as both resource and recreational value (Eder, 1998: 247, 275) – which is similar to the Brundtland Commission's construction of environmental and developmental problems as mutual issues tying the world together in a common future.

Furthermore, the development of ecology/environmentalism as a new master discourse is connected to a significant change in modern societies: the explosion in the supply of media texts, and the formidable expansion of a media sector with its own logics.[3] Whereas other master discourses (of economic growth and

28   *The Politics of Unsustainability*

political economy, labour rights and national security) are firmly rooted in their own institutions – of market and state, of industry and mass organisations – the ecology discourse does not have its own mass sociality or an equivalent institutionalised sector. It has proliferated through discursive actions in the public arena of mass media from its origins in less coherent and less institutionalised groups of issue entrepreneurs. In that respect environmentalism is a master discourse of the media age (Eder, 1996).

On one hand, this makes environmental discourses more dependent upon and more vulnerable to shifting fashions in the public arena. On the other hand, the claim of environmentalism to speak for the *common good* corresponds with the media sector's status as *commonly* accessible. The environment is an issue which fosters the role of collective symbols and beliefs in the organisation of public discourses and which represents and establishes the need to 'protect common goods against the individual utilities that make demands on it' (Eder, 1996: 205). Or in other words, with environmentalism as a master discourse the ritual of communication establishes collective identity around the common good in humanity's relation with nature.

Post-environmentalism

In Eder's vision environmental concern has been fully integrated into the fabric of public discourse, thus re-establishing the rationality of the common good. There is however a reverse side to Eder's vision. There may have been an integration of environmentalist vocabulary into the core of public discourse, but environmentalist rhetoric remains detached from actual changes in societal practices towards sustainability. It also remains detached in the sense that environmental concerns do not represent a general rationality but are reserved to their own limited field.

Ingolfur Blühdorn understands post-environmentalism in a similar vein. His concept of *post-ecologism* (Blühdorn 2000, 2004 and this volume) sees the contemporary proliferation of environmentalist rhetoric, especially in terms of ecological modernisation, as part of a development towards *simulative politics*. In general what he calls the *politics of simulation* entails: (1) a reshaping of the core values of modernity, e.g. the struggle for freedom turns into the struggle for free markets and consumer choice, and the struggle for equality is turned into campaigns for equal access to the market; (2) implementation of policy instruments designed for the cost-effective management of the economic system's side-effects, like environmental deterioration and social marginalisation; and (3) integration of these policy instruments into reformist discourses such as those of ecological modernisation (Blühdorn, 2004: 45).

The discourse of ecological modernisation is part of this development in that it 'simulates the possibility and the political will to achieve environmental justice, integrity and sustainability, whilst at the same time ensuring that established lifestyles, privileges and patterns of economic development are maintained' (Blühdorn, 2004: 45). One could say that the ritual of environmental communication, constituting collective identity around environmentalist rhetoric, is detached from the controlling aspects of the same communication, which are not directed towards sustainability. Put concisely, the ritual of environmental communication carries contradictory messages and contradictory definitions of collectivity. Both environmental responsibility and boundless self-realisation are core values. Herein lies the simulation.

When Eder finds that 'The environment is the issue that brings collective rationality back into the theory and practice of modern societies' (Eder, 1996: 216), then Blühdorn contradicts that vision suggesting that the images and stories of environmental concern have become tied to the politics of individual self-realisation. A further interpretation of this might suggest that the focus of environmental concern will move to issues of personal health and regard nature as a site of amusement (see Blühdorn, this volume).

Another understanding of post-environmentalism sees it as a backlash against environmental claims and politics and the proliferation of *anti*-environmental claims. For instance, Frederick Buell tells how environmentalism has come under attack in the USA: 'The ozone hole was denied and trivialized, food and population crises were debunked, and global warming was hotly denied, doubted and dismissed as unproven' (Buell, 2004: 4; see also Lahsen, 2005). John Barry sees a similar development: 'Powerful actors have successfully emasculated the green critique by normalizing it as controversy', and 'attempts to galvanize democratic publics behind environmental change [have]...been blocked, delayed, watered down and otherwise prevented' (Barry, 2004: 181). Moreover, such attacks on environmentalism are inscribed in an overarching logic of 'economism' which sees:

> ... the earth/nature/environment as surrounded by and subordinate to the global...economy and free flow of capital, and the overarching imperative of economic growth at any cost, rather than the economy as a sub-system of the larger global ecosystem. (Barry, 2004: 190)

This logic is not uncontested; in fact Barry argues that radical environmentalism is alive and well, but it does signify a particular form of post-environmentalism, one where *anti*-environmentalist claims proliferate.

Eder makes it possible to conceive ecological modernisation/modernity not just as managerial adjustments, but also as a powerful public discourse with a unifying appeal emphasising the common good, even across national borders. In this understanding technological ingenuity is valued for its services to mankind rather than its services to personal self-realisation. The concept of *post-environmentalism* is in distinct contrast to this vision. It may signify the deterioration of environmental discourse into simulative politics, i.e. the rhetoric of sustainability combined with implicit and explicit acceptance of boundless growth and unsustainable practice – reflecting an inherent conflict in

30   *The Politics of Unsustainability*

ecological modernisation. Alternatively, post-environmentalism could also be seen as the shift of public and media attention away from all forms of environmentalism and towards other issues and public concerns which emerge in the context of changing ideological orientation and societal tensions.

Basis for the Case Study

The theoretical discussions above form the basis for the interpretation of a selection of news stories from Danish television. The case study examines changes in environmental discourses by analysing television news stories about the UN summits on sustainable development in Rio de Janeiro and Johannesburg, focusing on global warming, climate change and wider environment reportage. The material originally consisted of stories from prime time news programmes on both Danish national public service television channels, DR (Danish Radio) and TV2. Space constraints only permit the detailed presentation of material from TV2, but this provides an interesting and significant case.

DR began as a national radio broadcasting corporation in 1925. It started sending television in 1951 and had a national monopoly on television broadcasting until 1988 when TV2 started. Together, these two stations remain dominant in the Danish television landscape. TV2 is financially a hybrid channel with commercials funding approximately two-thirds of the budget and public licence fees – with accompanying public service obligations – constituting the remaining third. Only a few years after its start TV2 as a whole and its news programme *Nyhederne* became the larger of the two national television channels in terms of viewers. It has maintained this position to date (Hjarvard, 2000: 63).[4]

Proximity has consistently been the central feature in TV2's and *Nyhederne*'s profile: proximity as a criterion in news selection and in the choice of both story angle and narrative style. This priority follows from the general self-conception of TV2, which has 'made a conscious effort to form a contrast to the kind of "top-down" news reporting that brought messages to the people from on high – from the central institutions of Danish society'. Instead TV2 perceives itself as a voice of the people, a channel of communication from ordinary people to the corridors of power and to society at large (Hjarvard, 2000: 65). Politically the station has leaned towards the right, but primarily its position is populist and constructed around a contrast between common sense, ordinary people, the provinces and the individual on one side and 'the system' and the metropole on the other (Hjarvard, 2000: 76).

TV2 and *Nyhederne* constitute a significant case for several reasons. Not only has *Nyhederne* maintained a larger share of viewers compared to DR's *TV-Avisen*, throughout the 1990s and the early 2000s, but DR has gradually adopted more and more elements of *Nyhederne*'s editorial policy (Hjarvard, 2000: 63). In terms of the relationship between media discourses and societal logic, it is interesting how global and general environmental issues are covered in news programming which stresses proximity, individual stories, the popular and the homely. Such cases can show which understandings of environmental issues are constructed and communicated to the political-administrative system as approximating to the viewpoint of ordinary people and communicated to the general public as a concern for common people.

The media texts from TV2 have been taken through a number of basic analytic procedures scrutinising the stories for different features: (1) binary oppositions and other contrasts; (2) narrative development and actors; and (3) images and their denotative and connotative content.[5] All the meanings caught through these analyses are summarised in storylines following a set of questions asked of each story:

- What description and assessment of a problem – or, if not conceptualised as a problem, portrayal of reality – is expressed and implied in the news story?
- How are the state, the cause and the effect of the problem understood, and what sort of action to address the problem is presented?
- How is community delimited? Who are 'we' and who are 'them'? On what are collective cohesion and sense of identity based?

The content of the media texts is further interpreted in light of the theoretical considerations unfolded above. These can tentatively be summarised as a set of criteria for the constitution of different discursive orderings of the environment.

Survivalism and Ecologism

There are a number of environmental discourses that differ from ecological modernisation in terms of bleaker perceptions of the environmental crises and more radical visions of sustainability. In this context they will be pooled together and identified by how they differ from ecological modernisation.

- *Causes*: The way we live; society's basic structures; excessive consumption; population growth.
- *Present condition and future effect*: Massive and irreversible damage to nature and the environment; food supplies and health under threat; apocalyptic visions of environmental deterioration.
- *Addressing*: Insistence on limits to growth; radical changes of society; new practices in everyday life; new modes of production and government.
- *Community*: Man and nature are connected; common good is based in nature and the environment; grassroots against state and capital; solidarity across borders with those affected by environmental deterioration; solidarity with future generations.

32   *The Politics of Unsustainability*

Ecological Modernisation/Modernity and Sustainable Development

- *Causes*: Same kind of specific causes, but perceived in terms of problems of the past and inexpedient practices rather than profound structural malfunctioning.
- *Present condition and future effect*: Serious problems but not irreversible damage; further deterioration of the environment can be avoided.
- *Addressing*: Combination of economic growth and environmental protection; focus on technological and managerial solutions; decoupling of strains on the environment from economic activity.
- *Community*: A unifying appeal; an outlook beyond national borders; an inclusive definition of the common good related to environmental and developmental problems.

Simulation and Self-deception

Ecological modernisation can also be perceived as the simulation of environmental awareness, i.e. an unreflective co-existence between inconsistent messages about both environmental responsibility and the boundless expansion of markets and consumption.

- *Causes*: As above.
- *Present condition and future effect*: Discrepancy between messages about the benefits of boundless growth and the need for environmental concern; focus on health issues.
- *Addressing*: Environmentalism as lifestyle consumption and dynamic market.
- *Community*: Establish means for individual self-realisation; nature as amusement site.

Anti-environmentalism

Implies direct attacks on the relevance of environmental claims.

- *Causes*: Environmentalists have gained too much power.
- *Problem/present condition*: Environmental claims are damaging; too much money is wasted on environmental regulation; markets are distorted; development and progress are blocked.
- *Addressing*: Disintegration of environmental concern from logics of production, consumption and administration; economic logic: expenses for environmental protection are to be prioritised as all other expenses.
- Construction of community is not related to the environment.

On this basis we can now proceed with the case study. The stories from each year are presented, first with a list of all the items in the sample, and with a summary of their storylines.

1992: Limits to Growth and Ecological Modernisation

In 1992 there were 11 items on the selected topics:

- 26 April: UN report anticipates mass extinction due to climate change.
- 10 May: Climate convention reached.
- 28 May: Prince Charles is deeply engaged in environmental debate prior to Rio and points to the problem of overpopulation. He is met with criticism.
- 30 May: Indigenous peoples from around the world have met for an alternative summit.
- 1 June: USA refuses treaty on nature protection. Report about Danish forester in Brazil showing that the rainforest can be cultivated without disrupting nature.
- 2 June: The Rio summit has started.
- 10 June: USA refuses biodiversity treaty. Report about utilisation of the rainforest's resources and the common life in Belém, north-east Brazil.
- 11 June: Problems with the climate convention. Massive criticism of USA.
- 12 June: More than 100 heads of state meet. Protection of the rainforest; conflict between North and South; report about rainforest timber.
- 13 June: Disappointment with the results of the Rio conference. Interview with Danish tree merchant and consul to Belém: 'Danish environmentalists are pathetic'.
- 14 June: Interview with chairman of Danish people-to-people aid organisation; evaluation of the conference.

Problem descriptions and assessments expressed and implied in these news stories may be summarised as shown in Figures 1–3.

A tale of limits to growth is clearly present. Within this reporting a fear of overpopulation is prominent (26 April, 28 May, 14 June) and overconsumption in the rich countries is also mentioned several times as a problem in itself. 'The report from World Watch says that global warming, pollution, overconsumption and population increase will accelerate mass extinction of all those forms of life with which man shares the earth' (reporter, 26 April). The damage of overpopulation and overconsumption is thus lamented because nature has a value in and of itself, and mankind has a moral obligation to protect it, but also because material subsistence is threatened. 'There are places on earth where it is expected that global warming can lead to a catastrophe. The soil is at risk of being desiccated, because precipitation isn't sufficient to make up for increased evaporation due to higher temperatures' (engineer as expert witness, 26 April).

A sense of imminent environmental crisis is also established through the camera coverage. There are images of multi-lane motorways with endless rows of cars, energy plants with chimneys and wires and metal structures shrouded in smoke; and by contrast a humming bird (26 April). Similar pictures of roads and power plants are followed by the words: 'Industrialised countries must limit emissions of greenhouse gases' (10 May). And images of dense traffic on a

34   *The Politics of Unsustainability*

Greenhouse effect, global warming, climate change

Heavy motor traffic and fuming power plants. Ever-increasing consumption of fossil fuels. Massive timber felling in tropical forests.

Leads to climate change. Two understandings: Climate change is already happening and causing damage *or* Climate is still OK, preserve it as it is, prevent it running amok.

Future effects: Climate change will lead to irreversible damage: Mass extinction of all forms of life with which man shares the globe. Risk of scarcity in food supplies. Indefinite and immense damage.

Problem addressed through international climate convention. Two understandings: Characterised as weak with no binding commitments *or* Characterised as a start, a goal for global environmental politics. Proposal for global taxes and binding targets, but USA is blocking.

Figure 1. 1992 storylines, climate change

Biodiversity, preservation of rainforest

Background: Rainforests are an important part of the global climate. Timber and soil are valuable; local resources can be used in global industry.

Causes: Global warming, pollution, overconsumption, increase in population. Increasing demand for tropical wood. Bad agricultural techniques and ignorance.

Current situation: Rainforests of the world are threatened. Mass extinction of animal and plant species already under way; one species is disappearing every hour every day. Soil exhaustion and destruction of rainforest biomass.

Future effects: Mass extinction of all forms of life. No more mahogany 10 years from now. Climate change when rainforest is cut down.

Problem can be solved through sustainable forestry. It is possible to utilise rainforest resources without ruining nature. Address problem through convention on biodiversity: Shall protect animals and plants from extinction. Will preserve ordinary people's subsistence.

Figure 2. 1992 storylines, biodiversity

10-lane road are followed by the words: 'the cause of these [climate] changes is the ever-increasing consumption of fossil fuels, i.e. oil and petrol' (11 June). Images of car traffic and fossil energy plants are simply established and confirmed as the standard index for climate problems and the ensuing environmental crisis, and the contrast with the humming bird establishes the beauty that the earth is about to lose.

In the stories from Rio a sense of imminent disaster is maintained: 'The Secretary-General of the conference, Maurice Strong of Canada, says that the

Environment in general

Increase in population and overconsumption in the rich world.

Lead to environmental problems.

Assessment: Two opposing views (expressed in last story from the summit): (1) Developing countries don't want to address the problem of population growth; they just want to be showered with money. (2) Poverty is a cause of population increase, but the rich countries don't want to help with economic development in poor countries.

Developed countries, leaders and non-governmental organisations alike, are confused and not mentally prepared to protect the earth.

The globe is in crisis.

Indigenous peoples have alternative and sustainable technologies.

Problem: Danish environmentalists understand nothing about the rainforest in Brazil.

Addressing: The locals have experience in taking good care of the rainforest.

Figure 3. 1992 storylines, environment in general

summit is "Earth's last chance" if future generations shall enjoy its riches' (reporter's voice-over, 2 June). But, to some extent, the construction of an environmental crisis is supplemented and replaced with a conception of sustainable uses of nature's resources.

Two stories in particular express this sentiment. One is about a Danish forester who owns a piece of tropical rainforest on the Brazilian coast and runs a profitable farming business on the land (1 June). The journalistic framing of the story is that many rainforests have disappeared, but that it is possible, as the Danish forester shows, to 'exploit the rainforest in an ecologically sound way'. Accompanied by sounds and images from the rainforest – streaming water, chattering birds, forest-covered hills – the forester tells about proper agricultural methods in rainforests and how to avoid deforestation and erosion.

Another story is about life in Belém (10 June). First, the treaty on biodiversity is explained as 'a legal document that will ensure survival of the species – plants, animals and ultimately humans', and it is explained how various fruits from the rainforest can be used commercially. Second, this is followed by images of people working and a couple dancing by the river, and by the words: 'Nature provides work, but not always. Life here and in many other places could easily be better, especially if the rich gave something for using their resources'. In a third story it is stated that 'Brazilians are probably more aware of these dangers. Therefore sustainable forestry is becoming more and more common, and there is research as never before in rainforests and their survival' (12 June).

36   *The Politics of Unsustainability*

Community is established in different ways in the 11 items from 1992, but there is an overall tendency to include the whole world in a common destiny. There are even signs of seeing man and nature as connected (26 April, 10 June), but mainly sentiments of community revolve around notions of a common human destiny and thereby a global 'we'. This is expressed in reports about how we all will suffer from climate changes and other forms of environmental deterioration (26 April, 10 May, 2, 11 and 12 June). The threat that defines 'us' is the threat of global environmental crisis.

'We' is also established in terms of the rich countries/the northern hemisphere and as such endowed with responsibility and blame for the predicament in which earth finds itself mainly due to our overconsumption (26 April, 28 May), our demand for unsustainable products such as tropical timber (12 June) and our general confusion and lack of understanding for the earth (30 May). A form of eco-imperialism is also present in terms of rich countries calling on poorer nations to refrain from exploiting indigenous natural resources (30 May, 12 and 13 June).

Sentiments of community are also established through constructions of who the 'others' are. To the extent 'they' are the poor countries in general or local and indigenous people of Brazil; they are established both as victims of environmental deterioration and unjust trade – which 'we' are to blame for – and as carriers of the good, endowed with knowledge of a sustainable path. Sentiments of solidarity are also implied in this construction of the others (e.g. 10 June).

Seen as *ritual* the 11 stories express societal cohesion around the notion that we as society are threatened by climate change and loss of biodiversity, that we *care* about the environment, that we are responsible for its deterioration and that we are able to clear a path towards sustainability. The stories thereby seem to carry a unifying appeal across borders, and collective identity is established around notions of the common good in relation to environment and nature. Considering TV2's preference for proximity this inclusive definition of community and outlook to include the entire globe may seem remarkable, but it is consistently constructed around stories about individuals, the royals or ordinary people living in the provinces.

In terms of dissemination of knowledge and control there are no direct instructions in these 11 news stories. Any controlling potential lies in their agenda-setting – or agenda-*confirming* – capacities and in the templates for behaviour and thought that are implied by the collective images they produce. A public agenda is maintained around issues of environmental sustainability feeding into administration and politics. By showing and defining sustainable practice, the stories may serve as a potential basis for altering customs to protect the environment. It would, by implication from these stories, be meaningful for consumers to ask for sustainable products, e.g. when purchasing wood products.

The stories from 1992 of course show no complete match with any of the discourse types discussed above, but there are clear traces of both survivalism/ ecologism and ecological modernisation. Outlining massive and irreversible damage to the environment and finding the causes in population growth as well as in overconsumption and general lifestyle indicate a survivalist sentiment in the environmental reporting. But this is followed by depictions of how environmental protection can be achieved in unison with economic development and profitable business, and there is also a focus on research and technological solutions. This is supported by the ways community is constructed with a unifying appeal, a global outlook and an inclusive definition of the common good related to environmental problems. There is some criticism of environmentalists, but it is focused on grassroots organisations, not on environmentalism in principle. It thus appears that environmental concern is conveyed as a theme in news stories on behalf of the general public rather than as an expression of opinions from special interest groups, grassroots organisations or oppositional experts. Discourse on the environment moves from survivalism to ecological modernity.

2002: Environmentalism Contested

The material from 2002 includes the two last months of 2001, because there was a general election in Denmark on 20 November 2001 leading to a new government and immediate changes in environmental politics. In the period 1 November 2001 to 31 December 2002 there were 18 items on the selected topics:

- 10 December 2001: Confrontation with environmental politics. Government plans a new institute to assess benefits of public environmental spending.
- 24 December 2001: Giant ice floes break off from Antarctica.
- 26 February: The government has appointed Bjørn Lomborg as head of the new institute for environmental assessment.[6] New principles for environmental politics.
- 27 February: Junior partner in government criticises the appointment of Lomborg.
- 1 March: Discord about the Kyoto agreement. Denmark risks additional expenses.
- 4 March: Denmark's problems with additional Kyoto expenses postponed.
- 9 July: Report from World Wide Fund for Nature predicting that the earth will be exhausted in 50 years' time, but report is met with criticism.
- 19 July: EU ministers for the environment meet in Denmark
- 2 August: Danish climate is changing and new exciting species are introduced.
- 12 and 13 August: Cloudburst and flooding in Prague and central Europe. Causes of the unusual weather. Black cloud of pollution over Asia. (Three stories.)
- 26 August: World summit has started in Johannesburg. Danish artist in protest action against USA and its polluting.

38   *The Politics of Unsustainability*

- 28 August: Lomborg provokes again: Politicians should address poverty rather than greenhouse effect.
- 1 September: Prime Minister Anders Fogh Rasmussen arrives at the summit. Agrees with Lomborg. Plus: Report about the summit proceedings.
- 2 September: Disagreement at the Johannesburg summit about reduction of air pollution and greenhouse gas emissions; criticism of USA. Plus: Report about Prime Minister Rasmussen's visit in Soweto; calls for concrete action instead of just words.
- 3 September: Criticism of agreement on sustainable development. Plus: Reporter's assessment of the conference as both success and failure.
- 4 September: Protests against USA. Reporter's assessment of conference results: Lomborg was right.

These stories revolved to some extent around similar topics to those in 1992, but conveyed different messages and introduced some new topics, especially in terms of priorities and the expense of environmental politics and administration. Problem descriptions and assessments expressed and implied in these news stories can be summarised as shown in Figures 4–7.

In 2002 there are several stories on global warming and the greenhouse effect, but contesting it is now an integral part of framing this issue. Both the seriousness and the causes of the problem are contested. For instance a story about a World Wide Fund for Nature (WWF) report (9 July) was introduced as follows: 'And from the humdrum of everyday life to something that

---

Greenhouse effect, global warming, climate change

Causes: Two positions: Natural variation *versus* human activity and emission of greenhouse gases *may* cause global warming, which *may* cause extreme weather.

Current situation: Ice is melting in Antarctica. Extreme weather in Europe, massive precipitation, flooding in Prague and all over central Europe, people evacuated. Two understandings: Climate is changing, earth is getting warmer, the planet is exhausted *versus* Scare mongering and publicity stunt; no need to fear global change.

Advantages of climate change: Nice warm summers, interesting new species, good conditions for the beech trees (a national symbol).

Problems: Uncertainty, loss of landscape types and species, more incidents of extreme weather.

Addressing: Waste of money to act against greenhouse effect; faster and more effective to provide clean water than to mitigate global warming *versus* Greenhouse effect is a game of uncertainty, no one knows what might go wrong and how dire the consequences will be.

Figure 4. 2002 storylines, climate change

Climate politics

Denmark got a bad deal in the Kyoto agreement due to unfair calculation principles.

Tough negotiations in EU about the implementation of Kyoto.

Denmark faces additional expenses of €333 million in meeting the Kyoto protocol.

Denmark must stand up for its rights and insist on a fairer deal.

Figure 5. 2002 storylines, climate politics

The Johannesburg summit

Description and assessment: Impossible to make decisions in such a large forum; summit is marked by pompous declarations and airy resolutions.

Concrete action is better than endless negotiations.

Problem: Poverty and underdevelopment.

Addressing: Poor countries must have opportunities to make money for themselves. Plus: Economic growth is more important than environmental protection *or* Economic growth will provide more means and better technology to lift people out of poverty and also protect the environment *or* Economic growth is not enough to mitigate poverty.

Problem: Reducing greenhouse gas emissions is a waste of money.

Faster and more effective to provide clean water than to mitigate global warming.

Figure 6. 2002 storylines, UN summit

Environmental problems and politics in general

Current problem: We spend too much money on the environment, good sense and balance has disappeared, activists and tree-huggers have taken control. We make decisions and prioritise with closed eyes. Plus: Experts disagree about the state of the environment; their dispute is inaccessible to most people.

Two understandings: We need to develop a sound economic basis for making decisions *versus* The 'number people' (i.e. economists) are taking over the environmental cause; only what pays will be accepted.

Figure 7. 2002 storylines, environment in general

resembles a prophecy of doom. The World Wildlife Fund has figured out that in 50 years' time our planet will be exhausted. Fortunately, one could say, there is some disagreement on the matter'. Later in the story it is claimed that

40   *The Politics of Unsustainability*

WWF's motive for publishing such scary reports is only 'to get publicity', and 'change is natural, it is unnatural to expect that everything remains the same' (economist as expert witness).

Other examples: 'Here on Antarctica giant icebergs are breaking off. Some see it as a result of man-made climate changes, others as whims of nature' (presenter, 24 December). 'Tropical nights and rain; the Danish climate is changing, and with these changes follow new exciting animals and plants' (presenter, 2 August) followed by images with connotations of the good life in a warmer climate, such as bikini-clad young women jumping from a pier. Although limits to growth was one prominent theme in stories from 1992 it was entirely absent in 2002, whilst coverage of criticisms of the high cost and irrational priorities in environmental politics made an appearance.

A 3-minute-long story about confrontation with previous environmental politics (10 December 2001) is introduced as follows: 'What are we really getting from all the billions we spend on the environment? The new government will try to straighten that out by setting up an *independent* institute'. Images of environment inspectors and their equipment are accompanied by the reporter telling that '*Brush prowlers*[7] are getting ready for another day of *control*. There are thousands of them with their measuring equipment and speed boats', and they burden us with taxes. This is followed by a contributor given credibility by reference to his environmental commitment: 'In fact we have to choose between greenhouse effect and how many hips we want to operate, we have to find a way to talk about priorities'.

Where images of aesthetically appealing nature are used in stories about sustainable productions (in rainforests) or as an illustration of what we are losing (a humming bird) in 1992, that kind of imagery is used to establish that nature is doing fine in 2002: images of a pond encircled by trees and plants, low sun, a grebe swimming on the water, a swarm of insects caught in the sunlight, accompanied by a reporter's voice-over: 'Lomborg says that maybe things aren't so bad on earth, and money for the environment could often be used much more sensibly, he thinks' (10 December 2001).

Coverage of the Johannesburg summit starts with a story about Lomborg, who 'provokes again' by stating that we should concentrate not on fighting the greenhouse effect but rather on fighting poverty: 'We must not just do what *feels* right in Europe, we must make sure that what we do in Johannesburg is that which *is* right for *all* the world' (28 August). This story focuses on protest against Lomborg's statements, including those from government representatives. But already in the next story ... Lomborg's views are supported: 'I think it has been entirely relevant of Lomborg to single this problem out ... sustainable development is also about poor countries getting the opportunity to earn their own money' (Denmark's prime minister, 1 September). In the last story from the summit the reporter concludes in a similar way: 'Possible conclusion: clean water helps faster and more effectively than windmills and solar cells. As Lomborg said before the meeting' (4 September). Rhetorically, concern with climate change is aligned with feelings, and concern with clean

Danish Media Coverage of the Rio and Johannesburg UN Summits 41

water supply is aligned with good sense. Lomborg's role seems to have developed according to mythic tales like that of Galileo (or that of Numbskull Jack in Hans Christian Andersen's fairy tale): First his opinions are met with disbelief and protest, but eventually he is vindicated.

This also points to a new understanding of the relation between environment and development. It is explained that 'on one side you have the USA and the developing countries who focus on economic growth and development, which is also the Danish prime minister's approach, and on the other side you have the EU in general who focus more on the environment' (reporter, 1 September). And the overall frame for it – the frame that is marked out by the development of the summit coverage from Lomborg's provocation to his vindication – is that addressing environmental problems and addressing poverty are alternatives to each other. A choice has to be made between them.

Community is constructed in several different ways, but tends to be limited to the national Danish 'we' rather than including the whole world. In reports from Johannesburg the Danish 'we' is foregrounded through accounts of the summit as airy and pompous in relation to the statements of the Danish prime minister, who sets things straight and calls for concrete action (1–2 September) – this is Danishness in action – or the reporter's assessments of the summit as an event (1–4 September). A Danish 'we' is also constructed in opposition to the rest of Europe in two stories about Denmark's problems with the Kyoto protocol (1 and 4 March).

The Danish 'we' thus constructed in 2002 is not set in consensus. The ritual setting of 'we' is in most of the stories characterised by disagreement and established around dissent between what might be called environmentalist and economist worldviews, a division between the alarm over climate change and environmental degradation on one side and scepticism towards environmentalism on the other. This is the case where an alarming WWF report is set up against an economic expert's reassurances (9 July), where a need to develop a sound economic basis for environmental regulation is set up against a critique of economic rationality, and when opponents and supporters of Lomborg are pitched against each other (10 December, 27 February, 28 August, 1 and 4 September). To the extent that reports seem to resolve these differences 'we' is constructed around a sentiment of ordinary common sense dismissing alarmist reports and environmental bureaucracy. As part of such delimitations of community 'the others' are defined, not as carriers of the good, but as world leaders indulging in useless negotiations, or 'brush prowlers' wasting tax payers' money.

As in 1992 the controlling potential of the 18 news stories in 2002 lies in their agenda setting and practice-modelling capacities. An agenda of financial and economic consideration when dealing with environmental issues is foregrounded and an agenda of scepticism towards environmental claims advanced. The urgency of environmental concerns is questioned and the isuue moves away from the centre of the public sphere. The stories may consequently contribute to the framing of practices ignoring environmental concern,

42   The Politics of Unsustainability

scepticism towards environmental authorities and a focus on economic considerations.

In comparison with 1992 the stories from 2002 convey quite different messages. Overconsumption is no longer defined as the cause of environmental problems; it is the waste of money on environmental regulation that is defined as a problem, the causes of which are scaremongering from interest groups and a dominance of environmentalists in politics and administration. These are traits of an *anti*-environmentalist discourse, whereas ideas of ecological modernisation seem to be absent.

Handling environmental problems does not appear as an *integral* part of economic development, which is the message that was conveyed in 1992. Environmental protection is rather conceived as an extra cost, only affordable if economic growth is up and running, and provided that more important considerations have been given higher priority. Such a separation of environmental concern from the rationales of production, consumption and administration is precisely one of the criteria mentioned above for a *post*-environmentalist turn; a turn that goes beyond the simulative politics of ecological modernisation and resembles open anti-environmentalism.[8]

Another indication hereof is that the 2002 stories to a large extent are framed as controversies between economic considerations and environmental concern, between the struggle against the greenhouse effect and a struggle against poverty and between scary prophecies from the WWF and a rejection of them. With John Barry (2004) it could be said that a green critique is turned into controversy and thereby normalised. Environmentalism seems to have lost its empowering 'inclusive' link within the TV2 coverage perhaps reflecting wider media sector realignment. The link between the environment and the common good is substantively replaced by a reflection of the common good which is preoccupied with expense levels or locked in conflict of priorities.

Comparison and Conclusion: The Demise of Ecological Modernisation?

This analysis set out to examine how Danish public discourse on the environment expressed in television news programming changed from the early 1990s to the early 2000s. From the analysis presented here it is clear that major changes did indeed take place. In 1992 there are clear traces of a survivalist framing of the environment with indications of limits to growth, bleak predictions of environmental disasters to come and perceptions of man and nature as connected. Contrary to the discourse of ecological modernisation and sustainability the issue of increase in population is framed as an important problem for the environment. But the bleak perceptions of serious environmental crisis lead to understandings of how environmental problems can be handled by applying the proper methods and technologies and at the same time building profitable businesses. Thus, there is a development from a survivalist discourse to a discourse of ecological modernisation, the former leading to the latter. Furthermore, environmental problems become the central concern in a unifying appeal which tends to include the whole world in a common destiny.

In 2002 ecological modernisation no longer seems to be prominent, or more to the point, it has become invisible. Rather than a development of survivalist positions leading to ecological modernisation, environmentalist positions of a survivalist character are pitched against open anti-environmentalism with the latter established as good sense. Furthermore, it appears that an economistic discourse has become more prominent in framing environmental questions. Environmental concern is not construed as integral to economic growth; rather the earth is subordinate to the global economy. Protection of the environment no longer occupies the same position as a foundational common good. On the contrary, the rationality and priority of environmentalism are directly attacked. There are no traces of a discourse of ecological modernisation in the sample from 2002.

Eder's vision of a new ecological modernity centred around a common good rooted in humanity's relationship with nature finds little support within the coverage analysed here. On the contrary it rather signifies a post-environmentalist turn. Post-environmentalism can be conceived in terms of an inherent inconsistency in ecological modernisation between boundlessness of economic growth and the limits imposed by environmental concern; an inconsistency that leads to a detachment of environmental symbols and rhetoric from actual ecologically sound practice. Perceived in these terms, traces of a post-environmentalist development might be imminent already in 1992, where the idea of sustainable growth is explicitly advanced, though at that point it is still also substantiated with distinct examples of how sustainable practices can be combined with economic development, and ideas of sustainability are linked to a unifying appeal and an inclusive definition of the common good centred on man's relationship with nature – rather than images of individual self-realisation.

A decade later, the detachment of environmental considerations from economic development amounts to more than a simulation of environmentalism; it resembles a distancing from it. Post-environmentalism simply means that the relevance of environmental claims is pulled into doubt, that environmental issues leave the centre ground of public concern, that they are no longer foundational in defining the common good being overshadowed by other dominant discourses – an economist discourse for instance – and other topics for public worry.

This turn is not necessarily permanent; in fact there are strong signs that an environmental outlook is becoming more prominent again – albeit with a significant element of simulation and built-in discrepancy between environmental concern and the desire for boundless growth – and the timing of these shifting media sentiments may be specific to Denmark. But the character of anti-environmentalism is not specifically Danish, and the fact that it turns up in Denmark with its previously high environmental profile suggests that environmentalism still has a long way to go in establishing a global presence.

44 *The Politics of Unsustainability*

Ecological modernisation or other and more radical forms of environment-alism may rise again (in the Danish public). But one lesson from this development could be that the discourses of environmentalism in general and ecological modernisation specifically are not vehicles for or defining elements in a new modernity. They are just discourses, or even master discourses, that are in contrast, strife and alliance with other (master) discourses as part of socio-cultural and ideological changes and the pursuit of vested interests.

Notes

1. The agenda-setting role of general public media has been widely theorised, e.g. by Dearing & Rogers (1996) defining it as a political process 'in which the mass media play a crucial role in enabling social problems to become acknowledged as public issues' (p. 22, here quoted from Ørsten *et al.*, 2005), a process that is facilitated by issue entrepreneurs from power institutions as well as public campaigners (on issue entrepreneurs and environmental issues see also Anderson, 1997).
2. Douglas & Wildavsky's analysis does however run counter to theories of ecological modernisation (see next paragraph) since they understand environmental concern as belonging to a sectarian rationality at the borders of society rather than in the centre.
3. See for instance Luhmann (2000), who opens his theory of mass media by noting that: 'Whatever we know about our society, or indeed about the world in which we live, we know through the mass media' (p. 1).
4. In the relevant weeks, and a few randomly selected additional weeks, shares were on average in 1992 34% for *Nyhederne* at 19:00 (26–39%) and 21% for *TV-Avisen* at 19:30 (20–37%). In 2002 average share was 19% for *Nyhederne* at 19:00 (15–21%) and 16% for *TV-Avisen* at 21:00 (13–22%), not counting the two weeks there was a strike). Despite the significant drop in shares for both news programmes from 1992 to 2002, they remain the biggest national television news programmes, if not the only ones. DR and TV2 had a combined total share of 80% on average in the selected weeks in 1992 and 68% in 2002 (Gallup TV-Meter online weekly press releases http://tvm.gallup.dk/tvm/pm/, 8 May 2006).
5. There is a point to applying a broad selection of analytic procedures, in order to discern which discourses are at work in the text sample, because even a short format like news stories constructs meaning in many different ways. (1) Systems of knowledge and belief can be ordered in binary oppositions, so identifying such binaries gives an insight into the discourse. What categories are set in opposition to each other, and which qualities are they aligned with, e.g. when the economy is set in opposition to the environment and the first is aligned with sense and the latter with feelings (cf. Harland, 1993)? (2) Much news reporting is organised as narrations in which knowledge and belief are ordered in relation to the course of events and the actors involved. What follows from what? What are the initial state, the moving force and the consequences? To whom and what are the roles of acting subject (hero), pursued object, helper, opponent (villain), etc. ascribed? For example, when 'sensible priorities in environmental politics' is the pursued object, Lomborg is the hero, and environmentalists are the opponent (cf. Greimas, 1974). (3) On television much of the meaning is carried by images – by their denotative and connotative content established in connection with spoken words and narrative and rhetoric developments of the story. What is shown, what surplus meanings might the images carry and which meanings are settled in the combination of images, words and sounds (cf. Barthes, 1990)? Particular images can serve as an *index* of wider phenomena, which means that the image as sign carries traces of what it signifies (cf. Peirce, 1994). A picture of a fuming chimney can for instance be an index of economic activity as well as environmental deterioration; it carries traces of and can signify both.
6. The same Lomborg who became internationally renowned for his disregard of environment-alism in his book *The Skeptical Environmentalist* (2001) and countless media appearances.

Danish Media Coverage of the Rio and Johannesburg UN Summits   45

7. A direct translation of the Danish word 'kratluskere'.
8. In fact there seems to be a disclosure of the summit's simulative character a couple of times in the Johannesburg coverage when it is characterised as airy and pompous (2 and 3 September), but only to carry simulations into a new field when the prime minister's call for concrete action is followed by a report that focuses on the *statement* he gives while visiting Soweto rather than on the specifics of the concrete project he visits.

References

Anderson, A. (1997) *Media, Culture and the Environment* (London: University College London Press).
Barry, J. (2004) 'From environmental politics to the politics of the environment', in M. Wissenburg & Y. Levy (eds.), *Liberal Democracy and Environmentalism*, pp. 179–92 (London: Routledge).
Barthes, R. (1990) 'Rhetoric of the image', in R. Barthes *Image, Music, Text*, 6th edn (London: Fontana Press).
Blühdorn, I. (2000) *Post-ecologist Politics. Social Theory and the Abdication of the Ecologist Paradigm* (London: Routledge).
Blühdorn, I. (2004) 'Post-ecologism and the politics of simulation', in M. Wissenburg & Y. Levy (eds.), *Liberal Democracy and Environmentalism*, pp. 35–47 (London: Routledge).
Buell, F. (2004) *From Apocalypse to Way of Life. Environmental Crisis in the American Century* (New York: Routledge).
Carey, J. W. (1989) *Communication as Culture* (Boston, MA: Unwin Hyman).
Dearing, J. W. & Rogers, E. M. (1996) *Agenda Setting* (London: Sage).
Douglas, M. (1997) 'The depoliticization of risk', in R. J. Ellis & M. Thompson (eds.), *Culture Matters. Essays in Honor of Aaron Wildavsky*, pp. 121–32 (Boulder, CO: Westview Press).
Douglas, M. & Wildavsky, A. (1982) *Risk and Culture* (Berkeley, CA: University of California Press).
Dryzek, J. S. (1997) *The Politics of the Earth. Environmental Discourses* (Oxford: Oxford University Press).
Eder, K. (1996) 'The institutionalisation of environmentalism: ecological discourse and the second transformation of the public sphere', in S. Lash, B. Szerszynski & B. Wynne (eds.), *Risk, Environment and Modernity. Towards a New Ecology*, pp. 203–23 (London: Sage).
Eder, K. (1998) *Natur och samhälle. Om det praktiska förnuftets evolution* (Göteborg: Daidalos). (English edition: (1996) *The Social Construction of Nature. A Sociology of Ecological Enlightenment* (London: Sage).).
Fairclough, N. (1992) *Discourse and Social Change* (Cambridge: Polity).
Greimas, A. J. (1974) *Strukturel semantik* (Copenhagen: Borgen). (English edition: (1983) *Structural Semantics* (Lincoln, NB: University of Nebraska Press).).
Hajer, M. A. (1995) *The Politics of Environmental Discourse. Ecological Modernization and the Policy Process* (Oxford: Clarendon Press).
Hajer, M. A. (1996) 'Ecological modernisation as cultural politics', in S. Lash, B. Szerszynski & B. Wynne (eds.), *Risk, Environment and Modernity. Towards a New Ecology*, pp. 246–68 (London: Sage).
Harland, R. (1993) *Beyond Superstructuralism* (London: Routledge).
Hjarvard, S. (2000) 'Proximity. The name of the ratings game', *Nordicom Review* 21(2): 63–81.
Lahsen, M. (2005) 'Technocracy, democracy, and US climate politics: the need for demarcations', *Science, Technology and Human Values* 30(1): 137–69.
Langhelle, O. (2000) 'Why ecological modernization and sustainable development should not be conflated', *Journal of Environmental Policy and Planning* 2(4): 303–22.
Lomborg, B. (2001) *The Skeptical Environmentalist* (Cambridge: Cambridge University Press).
Luhmann, N. (2000) *The Reality of the Mass Media* (Cambridge: Polity).
Mol, A. P. J. (2000) 'The environmental movement in an era of ecological modernisation', *Geoforum* 31: 45–56.

46 The Politics of Unsustainability

Mol, A. P. J. (2001) *Globalization and Environmental Reform. The Ecological Modernization of the Global Economy* (Cambridge, MA: MIT Press).

Mol, A. P. J. & Spaargaren, G. (2002) 'Ecological modernization and the environmental state', in A. Mol & F. H. Buttel (eds.), *The Environmental State under Pressure*, pp. 33–53 (Oxford: Elsevier Science).

Peirce, C. S. (1994) *Semiotik og pragmatisme* (Copenhagen: Samlerens Bogklub).

Thompson, J. B. (1995) *The Media and Modernity* (Cambridge: Polity).

Welsh, I. (2006) 'Values, science and the EU: bio-technology and transatlantic relations', in I. Manners & S. Lucarelli (eds.), *Values and Principles in EU Foreign Policy*, pp. 59–76 (London: Routledge).

Participation and Sustainable Development: The Post-ecologist Transformation of Citizen Involvement in Denmark

JEPPE LÆSSØE
Department of Curriculum Research, The Danish University of Education, Copenhagen, Denmark

ABSTRACT *Since the 1970s, citizen participation has always been regarded as a crucial condition of successful eco-political change. However, the relationship between democracy and environmentalism is not unproblematic. How has this relationship transformed since the early days of modern environmentalism? This contribution investigates this question focusing on one particular country: Denmark. Based on empirical research on the mediating agents, i.e. those who have tried to involve citizens in environmental issues and sustainable development, a number of stages are identified through which a post-ecologist approach has taken shape. It is marked by an orientation towards consensus and* laissez-faire *and has marginalised any conflicts around the values implied in sustainable development. This transformation, it is argued, has not been strategically promoted by particular actors, but has come about in an inclusive process in which environmentalists themselves have played an active part.*

Introduction

Participation has been a key topic of environmental policy since the rise of modern environmentalism. However, the way in which participation is conceived and approached in practice has changed considerably over time. In this contribution I will use the case of Denmark to illustrate the transformation that has occurred. Denmark has a long tradition of active participation of the population in democratic processes and participation has been a crucial part of environmental policy since the new environmental movement emerged at the end of the 1960s (Jamison & Læssøe, 1990). As outlined by Petersen (this volume) and many others, Denmark was one of the European frontrunners in environmental policy making during the 1990s, but

48   *The Politics of Unsustainability*

the efforts were rolled back when a new right-wing government took over in 2001. Every particular country has its own unique trajectory, and generalisations cannot easily be made on the basis of just one case study. Nevertheless, the Danish endeavour to take a pioneering stance and the subsequent political backlash makes Denmark a good example to study and illustrate the rise and the characteristics of what Blühdorn and others have called 'the post-ecologist era'.[1]

In the Danish case, I will argue, citizen participation in environmental issues has changed dramatically from the 1970s to the present: from a grassroots movement to professionally – indeed even commercially – mediated involvement; from contestation of values and political ideology to dealing with household technologies; from confrontation to consensual actions. This transformation has led to the eclipse of any aspect bearing the potential for conflicts, including the ever-present tension between private (individual) and collective (general) interests. Interestingly, this marginalisation of conflict potentials has *not* come about through conscious and strategic top-down efforts to replace the heroic bottom-up grassroots movement with mainstreamed participation. Instead there has been an incremental realignment process promoted not least by relatively open-minded governmental initiatives that have actively engaged environmentalists. This has been a process of *inclusion* or *levelling* that has narrowed the scope of citizen participation on sustainable development. Thus, the change of government in 2001 was by no means the starting point of the *post-ecologist turn*; it rather marked the beginning of a new phase in this transformation.

In order to elaborate this argument in more detail, three specific phases are distinguished and analysed: first the environmental grassroots movement from 1969 to 1980; second the government-supported involvement of citizens from 1989 to 2001; and third the increasing use of commercial mediators since 2001. Given present confines, this is a tall order. I will therefore place the main emphasis on the second phase with the first and third phases receiving slightly less detailed attention.

The material on which this analysis is based stems from a number of empirical research projects focusing on movers and shakers initiating participatory processes related to the environment and sustainable development (Jamison & Læssøe, 1990; Larsen & Læssøe, 1991; Læssøe, 1991, 1993, 2001; Gram *et al.*, 1992; Gram-Hanssen, 1998; Kofoed & Læssøe, 1995). I use the concept *mediators* for these actors. In *Mediating Sustainability* Blauert & Zadek (1998: 10) describe mediation as 'a process of *coming between* different social interests with a view to finding a way forward from what is, or is in danger of becoming, a cul-de-sac of conflict or inertia'. Thus *networking* and *facilitation* are key aspects of mediation. A further dimension should be added: mediation is not only about social relations but also about the relationship between the involved actors and a particular topic. Mediators are organising participatory processes in order to bring a case to the people and people to the case. In this sense *interpretation* is another key aspect of mediation (Dekker *et al.*, 1998). Mediators are transforming knowledge into a form that they find useful for facilitating participatory processes. Historically, different social actors have adopted the role of mediators of public participation in environmental issues or sustainable development: grassroots movements, trained educators, public officers, professional consultants and so forth. By focusing on these different mediating agents it is possible to reveal changes in the conceptions and approaches prevalent among those who actually organise these processes.

Participation and sustainable development are both ambiguous concepts. In this analysis participation does not refer to every kind of stakeholder involvement but only to the involvement of lay people – non-professionals – in political processes. In Danish political culture all kinds of efforts to promote citizen participation in this sense are traditionally referred to as *folkeoplysning*. Translated literally, this concept means *people's enlightenment*, but it should more accurately be translated as *empowerment of the people to reflect on life and participate in democracy* (Borish, 1991; Dupont & Hansen, 1998).

Sustainable development, for the purposes of this contribution, is understood as a general and open term. Since the Brundtland Commission introduced the concept, it has been interpreted and defined in several different ways (Dobson, 1996; Baker, 2006). Rather than supporting any specific definition or approaching it as a distinct environmental discourse (Dryzek, 1997) I am using sustainable development here as an encompassing term for human endeavours to address environmental change and environmental risks. I am regarding it as a comprehensive display of diverse interpretations, and my interest is to explore how these interpretations are changing – not in terms of verbally articulated definitions, but as manifested in actual participatory approaches.

The next section briefly reflects on the relationship between participation and sustainable development. Following this, I will embark on the analysis of the three phases of transformation as outlined above. The contribution concludes by summarising the characteristics of the Danish path towards a post-ecologist approach to participation in sustainable development.

The Relationship between Participation and Sustainable Development

Citizen participation as a constitutive part of democracy is one of the strongest positive values in modern societies. Sustainable development is another ideal that is hard to reject. But how do these two ideals fit together?

From the perspective of democracy it can be argued that ordinary citizens should be able to control their own lives. As Frank Fischer puts it: 'If we are to take seriously a *strong* form of democracy ... all citizens need to deliberate at least some of the time on the decisions that affect their lives' (Fischer, 2000: 2). This is important not least when environmental risks are at issue. However, the complicated problems related to technological development and the associated environmental implications grant experts and technocrats considerable power

50   *The Politics of Unsustainability*

to influence political decisions that have major consequences for the lives of ordinary citizens (Nelkin, 1975). Thus, without citizen participation, attempts to achieve sustainability are, as André Gorz (1981) once put it, always in danger of bringing about 'an eco-fascist society'.

From the perspective of sustainable development, however, it is not obvious that participation of ordinary citizens promotes the goal of sustainability (cf. Dryzek, 2002: 141ff.; Smith, 2004). Back in the 1970s Heilbroner famously argued that liberal democracy and market systems have no incentives to care about long term environmental quality and human well-being, and he proposed a form of government that combines religious orientation and military discipline (Heilbroner, 1974). Arguing along similar lines, Ophuls (1977) recommended the establishment of a class of 'ecological mandarins' which would impose ecological principles. Ophuls's eco-authoritarianism was based on the assumption that citizens, having been reduced to passive consumers of biased information conveyed by the mass media, are unable to critically assess environmental risks and adopt appropriate strategies. This expertocratic policy approach understands citizen involvement first and foremost as top-down information and behavioural adjustment.

The same applies to contemporary technocratic and state-centric versions of environmental policy which in terms of their reliance on expertocratic approaches are not that far away from Ophuls's eco-authoritarianism (Barry, 1999: 195ff.; Bäckstrand, 2004). Such contemporary expertocratic approaches have furthermore been criticised for ignoring the uncertainty of scientific knowledge, and for marginalising the experience-based knowledge of citizens (cf. Irwin, 1995; Wynne, 1996; Fischer, 2000). Citizen involvement understood as bottom-up deliberation and participation has been suggested as a more appropriate alternative, yet there is little evidence that within prevailing societal conditions such strategies are really practicable (see Blühdorn & Welsh, this volume) nor that they are beneficial with regard to environmental objectives.[2]

The important point here is that there are no simple and obvious ways in which the tension between democracy and sustainable development may be resolved. In fact, the project of sustainability accentuates the basic tension between republican and liberal theories of democracy, i.e. the tension between citizenship as a matter of rights and citizenship as a matter of duties (Dobson, 2003). The objective of sustainable development places unprecedented emphasis on 'the common good' and thus heightens tensions with the private and personal. As the Danish environmentalist Claus Heinberg puts it:

> The core of the matter is that if you want to put sustainability on the agenda, it implies a radically new kind of policy: a kind of policy where the basic consideration is dealing with the fact that the consequences of a given practice here and now will affect someone at another time and in another place. Thus: what I am doing here to take care of myself, my family, my time, and my world, has consequences – not for me, but for

The Post-ecologist Transformation of Citizen Involvement in Denmark 51

someone else, not here, but in a another place, not now, but in another generation. (Heinberg, 2003)

So how do mediating agents with a brief to enhance public participation in environmental policy deal with this tension? Do they regard participation as an emancipatory effort to help people influence sustainable development? Or do they see it as a way to support people's ethical and practical adaptation to the imperatives of a common good? Or do they perhaps understand exercises of participation as a way of coping with the many concrete dilemmas and conflicts which emerge from this tension? Sustainable development is, as Blühdorn and Welsh note in the introduction, a contested concept with 'strong' versions emphasising ecology, the limits of materialism, inter-generational equity and global redistribution and 'weak' versions with a continued primacy of economic growth and high tech development. The question is whether the conflicts between these understandings of sustainable development should be highlighted as the key issues to be negotiated through citizen participation in sustainable development or whether the significance of such conflicts should be downplayed in order to promote consensus-based actions within the existing socio-cultural framework?

The Rise and Decline of the Environmental Grassroots Movement

During the 1970s and the early 1980s the Danish environmental movement rose and became a relatively powerful actor that, among other things, forced the government to drop their plans for nuclear power plants, and created space for the production and use of renewable energy and organic farming. How then did the environmental non-governmental organisations (NGOs) in that period approach participation and sustainable development, and how did this approach change during this period?[3]

It was not until 1969 that the new environmentalism gained an organisational foundation in Denmark. In that year a group of students formed the anti-pollution group NOAH[4], which in subsequent years became the key actor in informing and mobilising people to take part in the environmental struggle. They soon shifted the emphasis from protesting against pollution and demanding government regulation and the installation of filter systems towards political ecology arguments and the societal organisation of production and consumption. Thus, from fighting against pollution NOAH expanded their aim to include fighting against the causes of pollution.

This political ecology approach was developed whilst the organisational base of the movement evolved from a single group of students into a national network-based organisation with local groups all over the country. People were invited to establish their own groups and to choose the environmental problems they found important and wanted to campaign about. No leaders told the local activists what they should do, but they could join the common discussions and get advice from the other members. The objective was to

52 *The Politics of Unsustainability*

establish an alternative public sphere outside the mainstream institutions where ordinary people could collectively address specific issues and develop their own experiences. Participation in this setting simultaneously meant organising public opposition to concrete official policies, putting pressure on decision makers and stimulating generic learning for participants. The shared experiences jointly acquired at specific campaigning sites facilitated critical reflection on environmental values, societal structures and politics in a more general sense. Hence, participation became part of a process of social emancipation. Environmental destruction and the oppression of environmental values were regarded as just another dimension of the suppression of ordinary people in the capitalist system. In this perspective there was no contradiction between participation and the struggle for environmental improvements.

From the mid-1970s NOAH and the political ecology debates were pushed into the background by the new focus of attention on nuclear power. The resistance against nuclear power was organised by only one organisation: OOA (Organisation for Information about Nuclear Power). OOA emulated NOAH's decentralised structure without leaders and with autonomous local grassroots groups, but they introduced a new strategy that in a sense reversed the relationship between means and ends that had been characteristic of the NOAH approach. For OOA, the primary objective was to win the political case. Against this background, participation was no longer a value in itself, no longer a matter of campaign-based learning about environment and society, but purely a means of mobilising public pressure in the struggle against nuclear power. The political situation required OOA to mobilise public concern as quickly as possible to postpone the policy suggestions of the government and the electricity companies. Thus, OOA became 'tactical' and emphasised establishing as many alliances as possible, rather than stimulating controversial debates about materialist value orientations or igniting discussions about conflicting political and economic interests.[5] Speaking in Habermasian terms (Habermas, 1984), this was a move from creating case-specific spaces for *communicative action* towards a perspective of *strategic action* geared to the mobilisation of public support for a single issue. OOA succeeded in the sense that the government and electricity companies dropped their plans. But the change from value orientation to success orientation seriously changed the political ecology visions of the movement and the approach to participation (Jamison & Læssøe, 1990).

During the 1980s the environmental grassroots movement almost disappeared. In part this was because the struggle against nuclear power was over. Another reason was that public debate about environmental issues became increasingly professionalised. Experts from scientific institutions, public administration and big companies took over responsibility for the environment. While the old grassroots organisations were unable to catch up with the professional experts different types of environmental organisation shifted into the centre ground. These were international organisations like Greenpeace and

The Post-ecologist Transformation of Citizen Involvement in Denmark 53

the World Wide Fund for Nature, as well as national organisations like the revitalised Danmarks Naturfredningsforening (Danish Society for Nature Conservation) and LØJ, the Organic Farmer Organisation. These organisations were all as professional as their counterparts in scientific institutions and public administration, and thus they were able to represent environmental interests in the mass media and in negotiations with bureaucrats and politicians. This professional turn had serious consequences for the direct involvement of citizens. Rather than trying to empower ordinary citizens to participate, the professional environmental NGOs adopted the role of representative actors *on behalf of* the people and the environment. In a sense this was a success as many people responded positively and became supporting members of the environmental NGOs. However, this delegation of responsibility and activism left little room for alternative approaches aiming to create public spaces for direct citizen involvement in eco-political reflections and activity (Jamison & Læssøe, 1990).

The Government-supported Involvement of Citizens

While the environmental movement during the 1970s and the beginning of the 1980s was able to challenge established environmental policy in several fields, the situation became quite different at the end of the 1980s. The systems of environmental control and regulation were now well institutionalised and the government was ready to adopt a more proactive approach to environmental policy making targeting established practices of production and consumption. The focus shifted away from the earlier reactive policies to mobilising the potential of eco-technological development. 'Cleaner technology' and 'urban ecology' turned into key concepts (Remmen, 1998; Gram-Hanssen & Jensen, 2004). This change was very much in accordance with the basic ideas of *ecological modernisation*, including its promise of a win–win situation where ecological improvement and techno-economic development coincide (Hajer, 1995; Dryzek, 1997; Barry, 2005).[6] Furthermore, it was a political attempt to meet the challenge of global sustainable development, introduced by the UN Brundtland Commission on Environment and Development (World Commission on Environment and Development, 1987).

In direct response to the Brundtland report the Danish government decided at the end of 1988 to supplement its production-oriented, eco-technological strategy with two new initiatives supporting citizen participation in relation to sustainable development. Whilst the NGOs had almost abandoned any effort to involve citizens as active participants, the government now began to emphasise citizen engagement and devised strategies for this purpose. What consequences did this shift have for the organisation of participation in sustainable development? In a process that can best be described as a co-production involving government bodies, a variety of other actors and discourses and environmentalists, a new approach evolved. A review of this process from 1989 to 2001 makes visible how the understanding of citizen

54 *The Politics of Unsustainability*

participation was recast as a matter of adopting eco-technical practices at the individual level.

The two government schemes aimed at promoting citizen participation in sustainable development were the national Our Common Future campaign and the Green Municipality scheme. Both were launched in 1989 and lasted until 1992. They were based on the same approach to participation (Larsen & Læssøe, 1991; Gram *et al.*, 1992; Miljøministeriet, 1992) which emerged from interaction between different actors and the amalgamation of two different discourses.

- First, it reflected the perceived need for educational tools that could help to inform and convince people to buy and make use of new green technologies and products. This information and education was part of the ecological modernisation of everyday household practices.
- Second, it reflected the influence of people with a strong relation to the Danish *folkeoplysning* (empowerment) tradition, not least the Minister of Environment and Energy, Lone Dybkjær, who appointed Elsebeth Gerner Nielsen, who had a job with centre for Development of Adult Education and Folkeoplysning, to the chair of the Our Common Future campaign. Nielsen and others argued that a modern kind of *folkeoplysning* should not teach adults in schools but take its point of departure in people's everyday life settings and encourage local co-operation and action by providing support for community-based and community-oriented problem-solving projects (Albret & Brems, 1989). The objective was to pursue both social change and community learning as integrated dimensions of the same processes, and to create showcases that would attract attention and inspire fellow citizens (Balle-Petersen, 1986).

The Our Common Future campaign and the Green Municipality scheme were constructed in accordance with this approach, i.e. they provided top-down resource support for bottom-up action-oriented co-operative citizen projects focusing on environmental improvements in the local community.[7] Elsebeth Gerner Nielsen articulated the intentions of the two initiatives by asking:

> How do we ensure that citizens have the opportunity to contribute to the formulation of messages and to relate to the problems and possibilities confronting society? How do we re-establish the dialogue between popularly elected politicians and citizens? How do we reinstate democracy as a management tool? (Nielsen, 1989)

In line with these objectives, the terms of reference for the Our Common Future campaign stated that the objectives were to 'support the idea: think globally – act locally; develop the concept of sustainable development; communicate knowledge on ecological, economic and other societal relations'. At first glance this may look like a project of consciousness-raising or public

The Post-ecologist Transformation of Citizen Involvement in Denmark 55

education. However, the interpretation of the campaign committee also contains formulations that directly contradict this focus on knowledge and political dialogue:

> The task is not to get people to know. The task is now to get them to act. Only action creates change. Thus the personal involvement of the common people is a precondition for the lasting success of the campaign. (*Handlingsplan for kampagnen vor fælles fremtid* (Action plan for the Our Common Future campaign), 1989)

This strong emphasis on action may have been inspired by the experiences gained in earlier local social development projects, but they may also reflect the technical–instrumental ambition of informing people about how to act in an environmentally friendly way. The way in which the priorities are formulated makes visible that the intention of supporting political participation and dialogue is mixed with a focus on changing individual behaviour and civic life world activities, the latter being particularly evident in the statement that the campaign should be 'targeted at those who do not yet think and act in a sustainable way' and that it should 'demonstrate the opportunities for action for the individual' (Gram *et al.*, 1992: 8).

The ambiguity disappeared when the executive committee defined the criteria for giving financial support to local projects. These criteria further narrowed the approach. They did not say anything about the content or about dialogue related to political decision making, but they stipulated that in order to receive funding the activity had to be based on 'mutual exchange and co-operation between different groups', that it had to be 'related to practical action' and that it had to 'involve a dimension of dissemination' of good practice (Gram *et al.*, 1992: 9). These criteria were still open to interpretation by the applicants, but the way in which the applicants tended to interpret them in their projects turned the campaign even more into a tool for changing individual practices at the life world level. 'Think globally – act locally' was not what happened. The final evaluation concluded that 'whenever they act locally, people think locally' (Gram *et al.*, 1992: 143).[8] This local orientation was further narrowed down to the sphere of personal practices of green consumption and environment-related activities. Action was interpreted in different ways including *inter alia*: an activity that is part of an educational process; an activity from which participants can gain practical experience; games and competitions; demonstration projects; happenings and other kinds of artistic expression; experiments; or various development projects.[9] Only in very few cases, however, was action interpreted as participation in political democratic processes.

So the original idea of empowerment in the Our Common Future campaign and in the Green Municipality project gradually metamorphosed into a restricted conception of sustainable development as something that should take place in the private life world, and towards an informational approach

56   *The Politics of Unsustainability*

involving the use of action techniques and grassroots advisors. This narrowing of the approach was confirmed when in the spring of 1994 the Danish government established the Green Foundation, which was supposed to further strengthen the involvement of citizens in sustainable development (Gram-Hanssen, 1998). The aims, priorities and criteria for support through the Green Foundation were focusing on local guidance on matters of individual consumption and resource protection. However, when in 1996 the Green Foundation established the Green Guide Scheme (GGS) it created a new opening. This GGS received the same amount of money from the state as the rest of the activities supported by the Green Foundation (DKK25 million per year). The basic idea of the scheme was to offer local stakeholders the opportunity to join forces and get support to employ on a full-time basis for a period of three to six years a qualified and competent person, a *green guide*, whose remit was to facilitate the process of citizen involvement in local sustainable development.

As with previous government initiatives, the Green Foundation did not try to determine or control the nature of the local *green guide* activities. The only restriction was that they had to focus on the interrelation of the environment and social practices, and as in the earlier schemes, the green guides were expected to inspire, activate, co-ordinate and work in an action-oriented manner. Their remit was to promote co-operation between the different local stakeholders and, rather than focusing on single issues, they were expected to develop a holistic approach (Læssøe, 2001). These were only guidelines, and the Green Foundation stressed that they would give priority to different types of green guide projects, both in order to adapt to specific local conditions and in order to learn from past experience. Basically, the idea was to promote a new type of agency – the green guides – as third-party mediators between citizens, the municipality and other local actors. Thus, the green guides and their steering groups of local actors had good opportunities to design their own approaches to the involvement of citizens in sustainable development.

From 1996 to 2001 approximately 100 green guide projects were supported and an enormous number of activities were carried out. To a certain extent the green guides used the relative openness of the scheme to develop different strategies and roles as mediators. After a few years many of the guides became well integrated into the existing social networks and assumed the role of 'free agents' who were able to move and mediate between the different local actors (Læssøe, 2001: 181–9). Yet, as with previous initiatives most of their activities were focused on disseminating behavioural and technical advice aiming to help private households, local institutions and companies to act in more environmentally friendly ways without disturbing their everyday life practices or challenging their established values or priorities.

With a view to the post-ecologist transformation of citizen involvement, the important point to note here is that although the green guides enjoyed a considerable degree of autonomy and were encouraged to explore innovative and experimental avenues, they have not challenged the dominant framing of sustainable development in terms of the ecological modernisation approach. Instead, they have contributed to reconfirming and promoting this frame. There were examples providing evidence that the green guides could have used their 'free player' position to facilitate social change and learning by identifying and focusing on value-based tensions or structural problems, and by creating spaces for negotiating the relationship between local development and sustainability. However, such examples were rather scarce.

How can this be explained? Evidence from my evaluations of the GGS suggests that an explanation will incorporate three different aspects.

- *The selection of the green guides*: Each green guide project was designed and implemented by a group of different local stakeholders. These stakeholders selected, as their green guide, individuals who were enthusiastic about promoting green solutions and who had proven competence in environmental matters, but not necessarily in social matters and as facilitators of social change.[10] Thus the orientation of the green guides has been predominantly 'environment-centred' and 'mission-oriented'. They tended to adopt the role of promoting particular kinds of environmental practice rather than acting as mediators facilitating deliberation between citizens and other actors about contentious matters of sustainable development in a broader sense.
- *The pressure for success*: As is the case in many other kinds of externally funded projects, the steering groups of the green guide projects tended to make big promises in their applications to the Green Foundation. This put considerable pressure on the green guides forcing them to deliver quantifiable outputs. In order to legitimate themselves they became narrowly focused on producing measurable successes whereby the yardstick of success was, in accordance with the general ambitions of the green guide scheme, that they contacted and involved as many people as possible thus promoting active citizen participation and supporting citizens in making environmental improvements, preferably visible ones. Against this backdrop it is understandable that the green guides focused on tangible, achievable, small scale environmental improvements rather than on stimulating debates that would challenge established preferences, values, interests and lifestyles. A minority of green guides were trying to resist this focus on uncontentious deliverables and to put pressure on local authorities to take Local Agenda 21 more seriously. Such attempts, however, proved to be problematic and hence remained exceptions.
- *Consensus orientation*: The GGS had been designed from the perspective of the ecological modernisation discourse. The strategy of guiding citizen-consumers towards more environmentally benign practices fitted in with the 'anticipate-and-prevent' approach and with the effort to familiarise consumers with new eco-efficient products and technologies. The expectation of a double dividend, i.e. of the simultaneous achievement of environmental and economic gains, put the emphasis on consensus-based

58   *The Politics of Unsustainability*

co-operation and rendered it difficult to conceive of other ways of approaching participation in sustainable development.

Summarising the analysis so far it may thus be noted that in the period under investigation the approach to participation in sustainable development had undergone a major shift towards a narrow focus on individual consumer practices or local technological fixes. Yet, this transformation did not come about through government strategies of top-down manipulation. In fact, reflecting the *folkeoplysning* tradition, no specific political intentions had originally been attached to the government schemes. As the schemes evolved, emergent ideas about the activation of local communities fused with the way in which proponents of ecological modernisation typically understand sustainable development. The assessment criteria applied to projects seeking support, as well as the specific parameters conditioning the practices of green guides, led to a further narrowing in the interpretation of citizen participation in sustainable development. But as the official rhetoric of public engagement and sustainability remained unchanged, this incremental transformation occurred largely without being critically reflected upon.

From State-funded to Commercial Mediators

The situation changed dramatically when in 2001 Denmark got a right-wing government. The Ministry of Environment and Energy Affairs was split up and reduced in size and influence. An expert board that had been established to watch over the sustainable use of Denmark's natural resources was replaced by an environmental assessment institute led by the controversial Bjørn Lomborg. A number of environmental research and development programmes were stopped, including the Green Foundation and the GGS. As shown by Petersen (this volume), this change in policy happened simultaneously with a change in the mass media's coverage of sustainable development issues. The era of ecological modernisation had been innovative and affirmative at the same time. It had moved Danish environmental policy forward firstly in the sense that it had placed some emphasis on the regulation of production and consumption, and secondly in that it had provided co-operation and support regarding the development and implementation of green technologies. But it was also affirmative in the sense that important aspects of sustainable development such as the continuing growth in material consumption and the need for global redistribution of resources were excluded (Røpke, 2006; Baker, this volume; Blühdorn & Welsh, this volume). To put it differently: compared with the ecologist visions of a sustainable society, the ecological modernisation approach implied a major transformation of the sustainability paradigm. Yet, to some it was still perceived as overly radical. Amongst liberals, neo-classical economists and parts of the business community it was seen as relying on increasing government regulation beneath the surface of consensus, prompting growing resistance.

The Post-ecologist Transformation of Citizen Involvement in Denmark 59

This was facilitated, as Jamison (2004) emphasises, by the fact that there are still two competing political cultures in Denmark: one that has its roots in the cities and one that is related to the countryside. For many years these political cultures have co-existed and, unlike many other countries where the urban, industrial political culture is dominant, Denmark has retained and given equal consideration to both cultures, not least because of the economic significance of agriculture. What happened after the election in 2001 was that the co-operative relationship between the two was replaced by a much more confrontational stance, facilitated by the first straight right-wing majority in modern Danish history. As Jamison points out, 'the strong tendency in the previous government to turn the pursuit of sustainable development into an overly ideological greening of society contributed to the making of an aggressive counter-reaction' (Jamison, 2004: 176). Deviating from the ecological modernisation approach of the previous years, the new government pursued the retrenchment of environmental politics, emphasising environmental economic calculations *à la* Lomborg, and a liberal economic policy aimed at promoting private consumption. This amounted to a further move away from the ecologist values and visions for a sustainable society, and it was a further stage in the post-ecologist transformation of citizen participation in sustainable development.

Bjørn Lomborg has indeed played a significant part in this process, but not as the one-man army he is often presented as.[11] In 1998 one of the main Danish daily newspapers, *Politiken*, published the first articles by Lomborg and in subsequent years he became the main exponent of opposition against what he called the environmental 'litany'. His role became, as Blühdorn and Welsh correctly note in the introduction to this volume, to give a voice to an implicit societal demand. However, ascribing the remarkable change in environmental policy towards a neo-classical economic orientation to Lomborg alone would mean giving him too much credit. As Blok (2007) points out, this shift had already begun during the previous government when programmes for environmental economic research were established as the ecological modernisation approach created new openings for dialogue between ecology and economy. Lomborg utilised the arguments and findings of environmental economists to support what he described as a scientifically based scepticism *vis-à-vis* environmentalists. But despite the claim to scientific objectivity, his argument obviously makes a number of tacit political and ethical assumptions. From a public participation point of view his contribution could have been a good opportunity to open a discussion on the different political and ethical opinions about sustainable development, but what happened was almost the opposite. One reason for this was that in the mass media the debate narrowed to the discussion of scientific findings. Another reason was that the Danish government made use of Lomborg to disarm rather than stimulate the debate about sustainable development. Lomborg's Institute of Environmental Assessment, which was established immediately after the elections, had the official brief to secure better environmental returns for the public investments

60 *The Politics of Unsustainability*

made, but in practice Lomborg used the institute as a powerful platform for spreading his belief that the money spent on environmental issues should rather be spent on other issues.[12] Thus, through Lomborg, the Danish government sent a powerful signal to the public that there is no reason to be concerned about the environment and that other projects should have priority.

In terms of citizen participation, too, the years after the change in government can be described as a further move into the post-ecologist era. While the first step had been characterised by the *integration* of citizen involvement into the ecological modernisation approach, and by its *adaptation* to this paradigm, the second step was characterised by the opposite type of pacification: *marginalisation* and *exclusion*. All the state-funded efforts to support local environmentalists as mediators of participatory green activities were stopped, resulting in a sharp decrease in the level of activities. Yet, as in many other places around the world, all municipalities in Denmark are still required to devise and implement Local Agenda 21 action plans and, as an inherent part of these, to encourage citizen participation. There are major differences in how seriously this task is actually taken, but some municipalities, especially those governed by left-wing or centre parties, make a genuine commitment. Some of them still have green guides, who are now entirely paid for by the municipality. However, in line with the neo-liberal trend the role and structural embedding of the mediators are changing once again. Whereas the first shift had been the one from grassroots activists working in the civic sphere to professional agents funded by the state, the next move embedded the mediators into the market sphere. Some of these mediators are now employed by planning advisory firms while others have established their own small businesses. In the course of this second shift, a number of new actors have emerged. There are consultancy firms whose founders had previously worked as green guides. Furthermore, big advisory companies formerly offering only technical advice have begun to hire academics with a humanities and social science background. Opinion poll agencies have widened their activities from doing traditional surveys to offering focus group interviews as well as arranging public hearings and workshops. Beyond this, a demand for commercially available mediators appears to be developing among municipalities which find it too expensive to permanently employ their own green guides and find it problematic to let their own staff organise participatory processes. This privatisation of mediation reflects both the declining trust of citizens in public sector officers and the general trend towards outsourcing public services to private firms.

There is no research to date about the implications of this shift from state-funded mediators like the green guides to commercial mediators. On the one hand, the professional competences of external third-party mediators may help to promote critical dialogue and social learning about the wide range of sensitive and contentious issues inherent in the ideal of sustainable development. On the other hand, there are good reasons to doubt that such a politicisation will indeed occur.

The Post-ecologist Transformation of Citizen Involvement in Denmark   61

- First, the mediators are dependent on those who pay them, and the municipalities are first and foremost interested in achieving social consensus on specific matters. Will this objective be pursued in ways that facilitate regular deliberations and learning? Limited preliminary research indicates that the preferred approach is the use of new creative workshop methods, which professional consultants have been using for years as a tool for organisational development in enterprises. Rather than opening spaces for genuine deliberation, these workshops favour a combination of a brainstorming phase and a subsequent selection process that aims at identifying those elements on which everybody agrees. These types of workshops can make sense if they are part of a long term process, but as one-off events, managed by a mediator who comes from outside and disappears immediately afterwards, they are promoting a sense of consensus rather than being arenas for sustained deliberation.
- Second, the fact that the mediator is brought to the case from the outside implies that there is limited time for setting up the process and following it through. External mediators will lack knowledge about the specific local conditions and interest constellations. Their third-party position may bear a potential for facilitating dialogue across lines of conflict, but it also implies the risk that they lack commitment to the specific case and are not responsible for further developments once they have delivered their service.
- Third, there is a risk that they will give priority to workshop formats which emphasise elements of entertainment rather than the thorough analysis of issues and the debate of controversial questions. As commercial agents the mediators need to sell their products, i.e. they need to apply methods that yield results and are experienced by attendees as worthwhile and pleasurable. Hence such mediators may be more concerned about techniques than about didactic issues related to participation and sustainable development.

The trend towards commercial mediators and the exclusion of authentic deliberation might be expected to give rise to a new wave of mobilisation and organisation of grassroots protests. Around the turn of the century the anti-globalisation movement seemed to revitalise the social movement sector. More recently, however, this new movement has almost disappeared from the public space. In particular, Denmark has not experienced a revival of radical activism as it has been observed in other European countries. In his study of environ-mental protest in western Europe, Rootes concludes that the anti-nuclear and the animal rights movements, in particular, have recently re-radicalised and at times adopted tactics of violence (Rootes, 2003: 245). In Denmark the situation is different in that, following the exit from nuclear power back in 1980, an anti-nuclear power movement no longer exists, and the animal rights movement has not been radicalised even though the mass media regularly report the mistreatment of animals in the industrialised livestock factories. Considering the relatively high proportion of violent animal rights protests in Sweden and

62   The Politics of Unsustainability

Finland, the lack of such activism in Denmark is remarkable (Jamison, 2001: 168). It might be explained by the close relations between parties, movements and government agencies in Denmark (Jamison, 2004). The professional NGOs can still exert considerable pressure through the mass media and through direct negotiations with politicians and public officers. In the campaign against genetically modified organisms (GMOs) this is done by Greenpeace, the Organic Farmer Organisation and the Danish Consumer Council. They have been rather successful in this matter and, for this reason, do not leave much space for more radical grassroots-based actions. Thus, the role of the citizens is to follow the struggles in the mass media and to act as political consumers, for example by rejecting GMO products. Whilst there is little indication that new 'militant' movements may emerge in Denmark, this type of 'personal' environmentalism seems to be the preferred option (Jamison, 2001: 164ff.).

Post-ecologist Participation and Beyond

Summarising the results of this analysis it is now time to address the following three questions: What characterises the post-ecologist approach to participation in relation to sustainable development? What are the characteristics of the process through which this approach has replaced that of the early period of the environmental movement? What are the prospects for a further reinterpretation of participation in relation to sustainable development? A brief answer to the first question would be that the dominant interpretation of participation has silently and incrementally become very *narrow*. As the new understanding has established itself through a process of *incorporation* and *co-production* involving government bodies, environmentalists and, most recently, professional mediators, it is, secondly, reasonable to speak of a process of *evolution* rather than *imposition*. If compared to the way in which grassroots environmentalists in the early 1970s conceptualised participation, the post-ecologist transformation implies a narrowing in four different meanings:

- *from* a strategy focused on exposing and attacking the socio-cultural dynamics of environmental risk production – *to* a technical–functionalistic approach restricted to optimising the use of resources with little or no attention being paid to social and cultural dimensions;
- *from* social mobilisation that highlights the value-based and structural conflicts which any serious sustainability policy needs to address – *to* a consensus orientation that narrows the scope to those solutions that all parties involved can easily agree upon;
- *from* an understanding of action that implies political engagement and collective empowerment – *to* an approach that avoids politicisation and promotes small technical fixes;
- *from* an emphasis on issue-based learning about society at large – *to* a local perspective that eclipses any awareness that the problems to be addressed may require more encompassing strategies.

The Post-ecologist Transformation of Citizen Involvement in Denmark   63

In accordance with Blühdorn's suggestion that post-ecologist politics is not a matter of top-down imposition and conspiring elites (Blühdorn, 2004), the Danish case could be described as a kind of *societal self-seduction* that has involved the state, environmentalists and professional mediators. In its first phase, this was a process of *inclusion* and *levelling*: the first important move took place within the environmental movement as the deliberative political ecology approach was given up in favour of an orientation towards strategic action. When in the next phase the state adopted responsibility for involving citizens in sustainable development policies there were still a variety of discourses at play and the approach was still relatively open to interpretation and experiments. Environmentalists understood this as a positive invitation and opportunity, and as mediators and local green citizens they actively contributed to the co-production of a new approach to participation in sustainable development consistent with the paradigm of ecological modernisation. Following this process of inclusion, however, environmentalists were finally *excluded* by the new government. Commercial agents increasingly moved in as mediators facilitating environmental policies and promoted consensus- and entertainment-oriented varieties of citizen involvement.

As outlined in the second section of this contribution, the relationship between democracy and sustainable development has never been simple and harmonious. In the Danish case there has been a remarkable move from an encompassing notion of sustainability that emphasises the collective good and inter- and intra-generational equity to a liberalist, *laissez-faire* approach that focuses on the private good in the *here and now*. The problem with the first strategy is that it may easily turn into a paternalistic top-down process. The problem with the *laissez-faire* approach is that it easily brushes over fundamental tensions and conflicts and ends up with the self-deceptive simulation of sustainable development. This underlying tension between paternalism and populism has never been a subject that mediators of participation in sustainable development in Denmark have been aware of. Yet, the consensual path to sustainability that has been favoured by the proponents of ecological modernisation has been put in doubt not least by Lomborg's mechanical economism, the government's declared 'value struggle' and the heavy increase in material consumption. Perhaps this might lead to the recognition that a different approach is urgently required. Rather than being brushed over, the many ambivalences, dilemmas, unpleasant choices and social conflicts which are inherent in the notion of sustainable development might eventually become the subject-matter for a participatory process of social learning on sustainable development.[13] Borrowing the words of Joan Martinez-Alier one might stress 'the focus should not be on *environmental conflict resolution* but rather (within the Gandhian limits) on *conflict exacerbation* in order to advance towards an ecological economy' (Martinez-Alier, 2002: 257). The old Danish tradition of *folkeoplysning* could serve as an inspiration for such an approach because in this tradition participation is not limited and governed by the imperatives of the

64   *The Politics of Unsustainability*

parliamentarian decision-making process, but creates its own public space for socio-cultural learning.

Notes

1. See Blühdorn (2002, 2004), as well as Blühdorn & Welsh (this volume). According to Blühdorn the transition to *post-ecologist politics* implies, *inter alia*, that commitment to sustainability is emphasised at the level of declaratory politics, but in political and social practice the ecologist diagnoses, values and strategies are superseded by neo-materialist orientations and policy approaches consistent with the paradigm of ecological modernisation. I regard this as a plausible hypothesis that needs further research, and the case study presented below ought to be seen as a contribution to this project.
2. See Cooke & Kothari's (2001) attack on the 'participatory orthodoxy' among development researchers.
3. The summary provided here is based on the work of Jamison & Læssøe (1990) and Baark (1997). Both volumes offer a comparative perspective showing rather similar phases of development of environmentalism in a number of European countries. However, whilst the shift of emphasis from pollution control to movements against nuclear power, and then to professionalisation and institutionalisation, has taken place in similar periods, differences between the respective political cultures have influenced the knowledge, interests and political strategies. Hence, the Danish case illustrates a more general pattern, but does so in its own unique way.
4. Even though spelled with capital letter NOAH is not an abridgement but refers to the biblical myth about 'the first environmental activist who fought for the survival of the species'.
5. Welsh (2000) describes a rather similar transformation of activism in the UK.
6. Ecological modernisation has been conceived in different ways and can be divided into 'weaker' and 'stronger' versions (Christoff, 2000). In Denmark elements of both can be discerned. Yet in the present context the important point is not *which version* of ecological modernisation was adopted, but the *general shift* towards discourses and policies consistent with the ecological modernisation approach.
7. In the Our Common Future campaign the resource support was of a financial nature, whereas in the Green Municipality scheme support primarily took the form of co-operation between local officers and citizen groups.
8. The weak link to the global aspects and the emphasis on the local sphere are not exclusive to this particular campaign but seem to be a part of a general trend in Danish political culture (see also Petersen's contribution to this volume).
9. Of the 620 supported projects, 200 were focused on private consumption (recycling, waste, water saving, product packaging, detergents, etc.). Another group of projects (53) were about energy saving and the use of windmills and solar power; 121 projects were about nature excursions, birds, planting trees, animal parks, etc. (Gram *et al.*, 1992: 155ff.).
10. The majority of the green guides were educated as biologists, engineers, environmental planners, environmental technicians, laboratory workers or the like. Only 14% of them had an educational background in the social sciences, communication or educational studies (Læssøe, 2001: 223).
11. For a detailed discussion of Lomborg's rise and political impact see Jamison (2004).
12. After two years Lomborg quit his position as director of the Institute of Environmental Assessment and this institute was later closed down. However, Lomborg is now director of Copenhagen Consensus Conferences, which undertake cost–benefit analyses comparing investment in directly environmental projects with investment in other projects. This work is still supported by the Danish government.
13. Thinking along similar lines, Scott & Gough (2003: 30, 125) have stressed that social learning, rather than being regarded as a tool for the implementation of sustainable development, should itself be regarded as an integral part of the process of sustainable development.

The Post-ecologist Transformation of Citizen Involvement in Denmark   65

References

Albret, P. & Brems, J. (1989) 'Folkeoplysning er nærmest modsat fritidsaktivitet', *Information*. Interview in the daily newspaper 'Information' the 16th of January, 1989.

Baark, E. (1997) 'Environmental technology policy in a consensus mode. The case of Denmark', in A. Jamison (ed.), *Public Participation and Sustainable Development. Comparing European Experiences*, pp. 45–69 (Aalborg: Aalborg Universitetsforlag).

Bäckstrand, K. (2004) 'Precaution, scientization or deliberation?', in Y. Levy & M. Wissenburg (eds.), *Liberal democracy and environmentalism – the end of environmentalism?*, pp. 100–12 (London, New York: Routledge).

Baker, S (2006) *Sustainable Development* (London: Routledge).

Balle-Petersen, M. (1986) *At overskride grænser. Første melding om den landsdækkende erfaringsindsamling fra folkeoplysningens udviklingsarbejde under 10 punkts programmet* (Copenhagen: Udviklingscenter for folkeoplysning og voksenundervisning).

Barry, J. (1999) *Rethinking Green Politics. Nature, Virtue and Progress* (London: Sage).

Barry, J. (2005) 'Ecological modernisation', in J. S. Dryzek & D. Schlosberg (eds.), *Debating the Earth. The Environmental Politics Reader*, 2nd edn, pp. 303–21 (Oxford: Oxford University Press).

Blauert, J. & Zadek, S. (eds.) (1998) *Mediating Sustainability. Growing Policy from the Grassroots* (West Hartford, CT: Kumarian Press).

Blok, A. (2007) 'Naturkapitalens kultur – om strategisk miljøforskning og miljøøkonomi i danmark', in C. J. Hansen, J. Læssøe, L. K. Petersen & A. Remmen (eds.), *Miljøet i samfundet – udviklingen i diskurser og politik på miljøområdet i danmark* (Copenhagen: Frydenlund) (in press).

Blühdorn, I. (2002) 'Unsustainability as a frame of mind – and how we disguise it: the silent counter-revolution and the politics of simulation', *Trumpeter* 18(1): 59–69.

Blühdorn, I. (2004) 'Post-ecologism and the politics of simulation', in Y. Levy & M. Wissenburg (eds.), *Liberal Democracy and Environmentalism*, pp. 35–47 (London: Routledge).

Borish, S. M. (1991) *The Land of the Living* (Nevada City, NV: Blue Dolphin).

Christoff, P. (2000) 'Ecological modernisation, ecological modernities', in Young (ed.), pp. 476–500.

Cooke, B. & Kothari, U. (eds.) (2001) *Participation – The New Tyranny?* (London: Zed Books).

Dekker, K., Diani, M., Jamison, A. & Kvande, L. (1998) 'Representing the public: new roles for environmental organizations', in A. Jamison (ed.), *Technology Policy Meets the Public*, vol. 2, pp. 49–79 (Aalborg: Aalborg University Press).

Dobson, A. (1996) 'Environmental sustainabilities: an analysis and a typology', *Environmental Politics* 5(3): 401–28.

Dobson, A. (2003) *Citizenship and the Environment* (Oxford: Oxford University Press).

Dryzek, J. (1997) *The Politics of the Earth. Environmental Discourses* (Oxford: Oxford University Press).

Dryzek, J. S. (2002) *Deliberative Democracy and Beyond. Liberals, Critics, Contestations* (Oxford: Oxford University Press).

Dupont, S. & Hansen, F. T. (1998) *Eksistenspædagogik. På vej mod en ny voksenpædagogik?* (Roskilde: FOFU).

Fischer, F. (2000) *Citizens, Experts, and the Environment – The Politics of Local Knowledge* (Durham, NC: Duke University Press).

Gorz, A. (1981) *Økologi og frihed* (Copenhagen: Politisk Revy).

Gram, S., Jeppesen, T. & Sørensen, T. P. (1992) *Evaluering af brundtlandkampagnen, vor fælles fremtid* (Copenhagen: CASA).

Gram-Hanssen, K. (1998) *Evaluering af den grønne fond, hovedrapport* (Copenhagen: Den Grønne Fond, c/o Miljø- og Energiministeriet, Miljøstyrelsen).

Gram-Hanssen, K. & Jensen, J. O. (2004) 'Green buildings in Denmark. From radical ecology to consumer-oriented market approaches?', in S. Guy & S. Moore (eds.), *Sustainable Architectures*, pp. 165–75 (London: Spon Press).

66 The Politics of Unsustainability

Habermas, J. (1984) *The Theory of Communicative Action* (London: Polity).

Hajer, M. A. (1995) *The Politics of Environmental Discourse* (Oxford: Clarendon Press).

Heilbroner, R. (1974) *An Inquiry into the Human Prospect* (New York: W. W. Norton).

Heinberg, C. (2003) 'Det begynder med hinanden', *Nyhedsbrevet Øko-Net*, 2. Available at: http://www.eco-nfo.dk/art/detail.asp?id=106&arttext=Det%20begynder%20med%20hinanden (accessed 2 December 2006).

Irwin, A. (1995) *Citizen Science – A Study of People, Expertise and Sustainable Development* (London: Routledge).

Jamison, A. (2001) *The Making of Green Knowledge. Environmental Politics and Cultural Transformation* (New York: Cambridge University Press).

Jamison, A. (2004) 'Learning from Lomborg: or where do anti-environmentalists come from?', *Science as Culture* 13(2): 173–95.

Jamison, A., Eyerman, R., Cramer, J. & Læssøe, J. (1990) *The Making of the New Environmental Consciousness. A Comparative Study of the Environmental Movements in Sweden, Denmark and the Netherlands* (Edinburgh: Edinburgh University Press).

Kofoed, J. & Læssøe, J. (1995) *Kulturbyens grønne centre. Om udviklingen af 13 socialøkologiske initiativer i hovedstadsregionen* (Lyngby: Danmarks Tekniske Universitet).

Larsen, J. H. & Læssøe, J. (1991) *Midtvejsrapport. Erfaringsindsamling og evaluering af kampagnen vor fælles fremtid* (Lyngby: Danmarks Tekniske Højskole).

Læssøe, J. (1991) *Borgerdeltagelsen i projekt grøn kommune. Barrierer og potentialer for en borgerinvolvering i udviklingen af et bæredygtigt lokalsamfund* (Lyngby: Danmarks Tekniske Højskole).

Læssøe, J. (1993) *Folkeoplysningens mulighed i lokale, handleorienterede, grønne borgerprojekter. Et empirisk studie* (Lyngby: Danmarks Tekniske Højskole).

Læssøe, J. (2001) *Evaluering af grøn guide ordningen 1997–2001* (Copenhagen: Den Grønne Fond/ Miljøstyrelsen).

Martinez-Alier, J. (2002) *The Environmentalism of the Poor. A Study of Ecological Conflicts and Valuation* (Cheltenham: Edward Elgar).

Miljøministeriet (1992) *Rapport om projekt grøn kommune* (Copenhagen: Miljøministeriet).

Nelkin, D. (1975) 'The political impact of technical expertise', *Social Studies of Science* 5(2): 35–54.

Nielsen, E. (1989) 'Folkestyret og miljøet', feature article in the daily newspaper, *Berlingske tidende*, 11th of October 1989, Copenhagen, Denmark.

Ophuls, W. (1977) *Ecology and the Politics of Scarcity* (San Francisco, CA: W. H. Freeman).

Remmen, A. (1998) 'Innovative concepts and cleaner technologies: experiences from three Danish action plans', in A. Jamison (ed.), *Technology Policy Meets the Public*, Pesto Papers vol. 2, pp. 173–88 (Aalborg: Aalborg University Press).

Rootes, C. (2003) 'Conclusion: environmental protest transformed?', in C. Rootes (ed.), *Environmental Protest in Western Europe*, pp. 234–57 (Oxford: Oxford University Press).

Røpke, I. (2006) *Consumption and Environment – Ecological Economic Perspectives* (Lyngby: Technical University of Denmark).

Scott, W. & Gough, S. (2003) *Sustainable Development and Learning. Framing the Issues* (London: RoutledgeFalmer).

Smith, G. (2004) 'Liberal democracy and the shaping of environmentally enlightened citizens', in Y. Levy & M. Wissenburg (eds.), pp. 139–52.

Welsh, I. (2000) *Mobilising Modernity – The Nuclear Moment* (London: Routledge).

World Commission on Environment and Development (1987) *Our Common Future* (Oxford: Oxford University Press).

Wynne, B. (1996) 'May the sheep safely graze? A reflexive view of the expert–lay knowledge divide', in S. Lash, B. Szerszynski & B. Wynne (eds.), *Risk, Environment and Modernity*, pp. 44–83 (London: Sage).

Sustaining the Unsustainable: Symbolic Politics and the Politics of Simulation

INGOLFUR BLÜHDORN
Department of European Studies, University of Bath, UK

ABSTRACT *Stirred by the contradiction between the mainstreamed castigation of merely symbolic eco-politics and the firm resolve of advanced consumer democracies to defend the core principles of democratic consumer capitalism, this contribution undertakes a meta-critique of the paradigm of symbolic politics. A tentative typology of different varieties of symbolic politics maps the terrain for a detailed analysis of symbolic politics in the popular understanding. A comprehensive cultural shift conceptualised as the post-ecologist turn is held responsible not only for a fundamental transformation of the ways in which late-modern societies frame and process their environmental problems, but also for the exhaustion of authentic eco-politics which, by implication, renders the critique of merely symbolic politics questionable. The concept of simulative politics is suggested as a more appropriate conceptualisation of late-modern eco-politics. Practices of simulative politics are presented as a key strategy which help late-modern societies to sustain what is known to be unsustainable.*

Too Little, Too Late: Calls for Effective Action

Hurricane Katrina, environmental refugees, melting ice caps, the breath-taking resource consumption of the buzzing Chinese and Indian economies; issues like these have generated a new sense of eco-political urgency. The finiteness of resources, the limits to growth and the unsustainability of the western model of democratic consumer capitalism are becoming painfully evident. Repackaged into the discourse of *environmental security* (e.g. Dalby, 2002; Manwaring, 2002; Lacy, 2005) eco-political issues have become a key concern at the very centres of global politics. The firm institutionalisation of eco-political actors, the unprecedented accumulation of eco-political knowledge and the implementation of a wide range of environmental policy instruments have brought about significant improvements in many areas of eco-politics. Yet, whatever

68   *The Politics of Unsustainability*

has been undertaken and achieved so far has at best tackled symptoms but never addressed the root causes of environmental decline. Even in the richest and technologically most advanced countries, the strategies of ecological modernisation and environmental management have been unable to halt, let alone reverse, the trajectory of environmental consumption and destruction. Technological progress has not brought about sufficiently *intelligent* solutions. Environmental economics has an at best erratic record of quantifying and internalising the massive costs which traditional economics routinely externalises. Environmental policy measures perpetually appear as half-hearted. What they accomplish is invariably too little and too late.

But undoubtedly, sustainability and *future-fitness* (Blühdorn, 2004a, 2007a) have never figured more prominently in the discourse of policy makers from local city councils up to the World Trade Organization – and not just in the ecological sense. Throughout the industrialised world, there are serious concerns about the unsustainability of pensions systems, health care systems, transport systems, the system of representative democracy and so forth. Accordingly, welfare reform, democratic renewal, economic reform, etc. are as high on the agenda as ecological reform. In all of these policy areas there is a sense of acute crisis and much talk about 'radical shake-ups', 'tough decisions' and 'hard policy roads'. There is a striking consensus between political elites and general electorates that it is time to stop *talking* about things and take *decisive action*: Cut through the rhetoric! Get down to the issues! But how serious and effective is this declaratory commitment to decisive action? Lip-service, spin doctoring, political showbusiness are terms commonly used to express dissatisfaction with political and economic elites who are not genuinely committed to the values they are advertising, who always deliver less than they are promising, who are deceiving democratic electorates and credulous consumers. *Symbolic politics* is the term that captures both the criticism of insufficient policies and the criticism of those who make them.

The phenomenon of symbolic politics is as old as politics itself, yet in late-modern societies it has gained unprecedented significance,[1] and its quality and function have, I will argue, fundamentally changed. Its rise has been facilitated by a range of factors including, *inter alia*, the ever-growing complexity of political issues and interest constellations, the relocation of political discourse and competition into the realm of the mass media and the crisis of legitimacy in contemporary politics. But symbolic politics, it is widely believed, only reaches so far. The new sense of urgency, not only in the field of eco-politics, derives from fundamental 'doubts whether an autonomous politics of performance', i.e. 'the priority of presentation over content can be sustained in the long term' (Nullmeier, 2005: 201)[2]. Surely there must be limits to the capacity of glossy rhetoric and political marketing to compensate for the progressive degeneration of politics in terms of its substance and its moral quality. There must be a point when *the chickens come home to roost*, when 'the social crisis can no longer be concealed by symbolic activity' (Meyer, 1994: 143). In the eco-political literature this has often been described as the point when *nature strikes*

Symbolic Politics and the Politics of Simulation 69

back and *takes revenge*. And as this point is feared to be nigh, there is widespread demand, not only in eco-politics, for a more serious and effective politics that places less emphasis on rhetoric and presentation and more emphasis on the substantive issues and substantive policy making. But there are good reasons to believe that, in eco-politics and elsewhere, this new discourse of seriousness and effectiveness does not really *abandon* symbolic politics but merely adds an *additional layer* of performance: the 'performance of seriousness' (Nullmeier, 2005: 202).[3] Most importantly, this suspicion is nurtured by the unprecedented consensus of defence that protects the 'blessed way of life' (Fleischer, 2001) in advanced modern societies, that secures the continuation of the system of democratic consumer capitalism and that resolutely obstructs the exploration of any socio-economic alternatives.

Stirred by the contradiction between the mainstreamed castigation of *merely symbolic* politics and this consensus of defence, this contribution will suggest that the paradigm of *symbolic politics* is a rather one-dimensional explanation of eco-political insufficiency, and a very unsatisfactory conceptualisation of late-modern society's eco-politics. Indeed it will be argued that the paradigm of symbolic politics, which had once been launched as a critical weapon against the ideological superstructure that protects an exploitative and enslaving system, has itself become an ideological tool that helps to sustain what it apparently criticises. For this purpose, i.e. for the meta-critique of the paradigm of symbolic politics and the narratives it implies, this contribution develops the concept of *simulative politics* which challenges a series of assumptions that are implicit in the notion of symbolic politics. The main argument to be elaborated is that despite their vociferous critique of *merely symbolic politics* and their declaratory resolve to take effective action, late-modern societies have neither the will nor the ability to *get serious*. Their *performance of seriousness*, however, is an effective response to certain challenges which are particular to the late-modern condition, and the discourses of symbolic politics are an important part of that performance. They are an integral part of the *politics of simulation* by means of which late-modern society manages to sustain – at least for the time being – what is known to be unsustainable.[4]

This argument will be developed in four stages. In order to facilitate a differentiated understanding of the complex phenomena which tend to be conflated into the concept of symbolic politics, the next section distinguishes several different and interlocking dimensions of symbolic politics. The third section narrows the perspective to the understanding of symbolic politics that Murray Edelman (1964, 1971) once established and popularised, and explores the narrative of *authentic politics* which this concept always implies. Focusing on eco-politics, in particular, the fourth section then elaborates how the *post-ecologist turn* has undermined the foundations of both the popular critique of symbolic politics and its supposedly more authentic counterparts. On this basis the fifth section investigates the specifically late-modern quality and function of symbolic politics and reinterprets, drawing on Baudrillard's concept of simulation, the contemporary critique of symbolic politics as a form of *simulative*

70   The Politics of Unsustainability

politics. The concluding section raises some questions about the validity and applicability of the model of simulative politics.

Dimensions of Symbolic Politics

'There is no doubt about the necessity of the use of symbols in politics – and thus also in environmental politics' (Hansjürgens, 2000: 146). The term symbolic politics is used in a variety of different ways, and although in political practice the different phenomena to which it may refer are often closely interlinked, it is useful to try some analytical distinctions. In particular, a more differentiated approach can help to illustrate that any generalised condemnation of symbolic politics is inappropriate and that the common distinction between symbolic politics that is staged for the media and real politics that brokers hard interests behind closed doors is too simplistic. As the tentative typology set out in Figure 1 illustrates, there is, firstly, an important difference between symbolic politics understood simply as the use of symbols in political

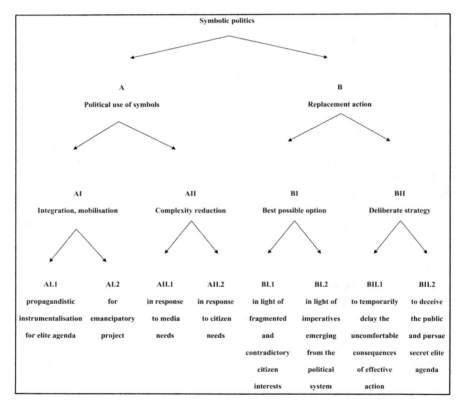

Figure 1. Understandings of symbolic politics

Symbolic Politics and the Politics of Simulation 71

communication (type A), and symbolic politics understood as ineffective replacement action for policies which would be genuinely effective in achieving their declared purpose (type B). Symbolic politics in the first sense, i.e. the use of symbols as tools employed by political actors when communicating – verbally or non-verbally – with each other or with the wider public is indispensable for political actors of any provenance. Symbols extend the significance of a statement or action beyond the directly articulated meaning or immediate purpose. They are 'vehicles for the imagination of objects' (Sarcinelli, 1989a: 295); they 'help the mind to see the potentialities in a situation' (Edelman, 2001: 13); they 'do not reflect but transcend the day-to-day reality' (Sarcinelli, 1989a: 295). Symbols refer to a body of social values, knowledge and practices which offer guidance for interpreting, processing and coping with specific issues or situations. Whilst allowing for a variety of interpretations, symbols mobilise pre-existing cognitive patterns and trigger ritualised forms of behaviour or action. As a tool of political integration and mobilisation (type AI), i.e. a tool for creating a sense of unity and community among a group of people and for providing them with a shared narrative about their current situation, their political goals and their collective political agency, 'political symbolism' (Sarcinelli) is therefore equally essential for anti-democratic authoritarians (type AI.1) aiming to control and instrumentalise credulous crowds, and for emancipative and democratic social movements (type AI.2) whose 'symbolic politics from below' (Nullmeier, 2005: 213, referring to Meyer, 1992) anticipates the liberated alternative to the *status quo*.[5]

Beyond its function as a tool for integration and mobilisation, the political use of symbols is, furthermore, also a strategy of complexity reduction (type AII). In highly differentiated societies where politics is rarely based on direct contact between decision makers and those who are affected by these decisions, where political discourse often centres on issues which are well beyond the citizens' world of personal experience or even imagination, and where the management of these issues by far outstretches anyone's intellectual and moral capabilities, this second function of symbolism in politics is particularly important. In this understanding, symbolic politics is the condensation or compression of complex and remote issues into readily understandable, preferably visual, symbols. Sarcinelli (1987; 1989a, b; 1998), Sartor (2000) and many others have explained the increasing significance of symbolic politics in this sense as a response firstly to the imperatives of the media industry (type AII.1), and secondly to the desire at the grass roots of society for simplicity, orientation and meaning (AII.2) (Dörner, 1996: 25). For political actors, this kind of symbolic politics is a strategy for reducing the risks which come with the ever-rising complexity of political issues and the increasing density of information and discourse in the media society. It is also a strategy of media management, whereby political acts are carefully choreographed in order to maximise the chance that journalists and media makers take them up, and minimise the transformation of the intended message in the *mediation* process. In so far as complexity reduction is always a matter of selectively highlighting

72   The Politics of Unsustainability

certain dimensions at the expense of eclipsing others, and in so far as the symbolic images arranged for the mass media, rather than 'speaking for themselves', release, first and foremost, the political messages which have been packaged into them, symbolic politics in this understanding always entails the strategic construction of realities and manipulation of mass audiences. Nevertheless, symbolic politics as a means of complexity reduction is neither intrinsically immoral nor necessarily a cause of ineffective policies. In advanced modern societies it is just as indispensable as symbolic politics in the sense discussed before. It has become a categorical imperative of political communication.

The political use of symbols as discussed so far (A types) needs to be clearly distinguished from symbolic politics in the sense of *substitute* or *placebo* politics (B types). Symbolic politics in this second sense implies political action that does not achieve its apparent purpose because the respective policies 'do not have teeth'. This does not mean to say that such political action is in every respect ineffective – they may be very effective politically – but from the perspective of the declared purpose it certainly is, and it may therefore be described as *replacement action* and *action replacement*. Once again two varieties of this surrogate politics need to be distinguished: it may either result from a political dilemma which does not leave any viable alternatives (type BI), or it may be a strategic choice that consciously avoids alternative forms of action (type BII). A political dilemma that does not leave any viable alternatives may, for example, arise if a polity, whilst agreeing in general terms on the urgency of a problem, fails to achieve consensus about the specific policy goals and appropriate means of accomplishing them (type BI.1). If agreement is then reached it is often a compromise that gives rise to soft, watered-down policy approaches which, whilst fulfilling the demand that *action ought to be taken immediately*, make only a marginal contribution to resolving the problem that was supposed to be addressed. A political dilemma of a slightly different nature may arise if imperatives of *political* effectiveness, i.e. to generate and stabilise power, are in conflict with imperatives of *other forms of* effectiveness (type BI.2). Whilst in the previous scenario the dilemma arises from the diversity of interests which the political system is supposed to take into account and represent, this slightly different dilemma can be traced back to incompatibilities between the priorities of the *political* system and those of *other* societal function systems.[6]

If surrogate politics is a matter of strategic choice rather than inescapable pressures, i.e. if it is the intentional avoidance of theoretically available, more effective alternatives (type BII), this may either simply be a matter of convenience, i.e. the attempt to avoid – or at least postpone – uncomfortable implications of a policy measure that is in principle accepted to be necessary and appropriate (type BII.1); or it may be a cunning and sinister strategic instrument used by power elites to deceive the public into believing that its concerns are being heard and addressed, whilst the elites are secretly pursuing their own interests which probably conflict with those of the public (type

Symbolic Politics and the Politics of Simulation 73

BII.2). An important difference of this variety of symbolic politics in comparison to the BI varieties is that in the latter the political class, rather than cunningly abusing their power for deceiving the masses, appear themselves as victims of unfavourable conditions which are beyond their control. The distinctive feature of symbolic politics in the present sense (type BII.2), however, is the malicious deception of the unsuspecting and vulnerable public. This type of symbolic politics is geared towards generating false impressions under the cover of which political elites may pursue their own agendas.

It is worth reiterating that in political practice the different forms of symbolic politics that are analytically distinguished in this tentative typology often cannot be neatly separated from each other. Political action has several interlocking layers and levels, and features of different analytical types of symbolic politics blend into each other. Nevertheless, this typology is useful because it illustrates that symbolic politics is a highly complex phenomenon that requires differentiated analytical approaches and sensitive criteria of assessment. The typology demonstrates that generalising assertions such as that 'symbolic politics is based on strategic action of political elites, who are interested in the in-transparency of the *true* and *underlying* processes of politics' (Nullmeier, 2005: 199; emphases in the original) are simplistic and unhelpful. It also sheds doubts on the popular idea of the 'duplication of the political' (Offe, 1976/2005: x) according to which 'politics breaks down into two realities: that of polished façades which is relayed to the citizens primarily through the media, and the politics of interests which is secretly conducted behind closed doors' (Nullmeier, 2005: 199).[7]

A Narrative of Deception, Repression and Authentic (Eco-)politics

As regards the insufficiency of environmental policy, much of this can be explained on the basis of symbolic politics types BI.1, BI.2, BII.1 or a combination of parameters which are analytically distinguished in these types. Yet, the common rhetoric of and complaint about *merely symbolic* environmental policies insinuates the prevalence of type BII.2. This is the meaning which Murray Edelman (1964, 1971) implied when he introduced the term symbolic politics, and today 'we are making implicit reference to the basic argument of his book, whenever we describe politics or a policy as symbolic' (Nullmeier, 2005: 199). For Edelman symbolic politics was clearly a matter of political elites making strategic use of symbols, myths and rituals in order to deceive and control the mass public and in order to maximise their own interests. Symbolic politics in this sense is subject to at least four kinds of criticism:

- it is mere performance, illusion, appearance;
- it is inadequate with regard to the concrete issues which politics is supposed to address;

74 *The Politics of Unsustainability*

- it is morally rotten because it aims to distort political realities, deceive righteous citizens and conceal hidden agendas;
- it is politically damaging in that it undermines public trust in political institutions, replaces free rational public deliberation with the dark power of psychological manipulation and emotional mobilisation and impairs the ability of citizens to make effective use of their democratic rights.

The first of these criticisms regards the inferior *ontological quality* of BII.2-type symbolic politics. The second criticism concerns its *effectiveness* or problem-solving capacity. The third concerns the *ethical predisposition* of political actors adopting strategies of symbolic politics. And the last aspect focuses on the *effect on the democratic culture.* Together, these four dimensions of insufficiency define the respects in which (eco-)politics supposedly 'can and ought to be different' (Hansjürgens & Lübbe-Wolff, 2000: 12). If *authentic politics* is an appropriate term for this supposedly better alternative, it may be described as politics that is genuinely committed to responding to the citizens' concerns and to effectively addressing the 'real issues'. Figure 2 summarises the expectations which are implied in the notion of authentic politics and contrasts them with the characteristics of symbolic politics.

In a more general sense, authentic politics is the form of politics that is committed to the emancipatory ideals of European Enlightenment and pursues the Habermasian *project of modernity.*[8] In so far as authentic politics is the ideal of politics which has never been realised but has always been a political

	Authentic politics	**Symbolic politics**
Ontological quality	True, original Being (*Sein*) Production of politics Substantive politics	False, forgery Appearance (*Schein*) Presentation of politics Virtual politics
Dimension of effectiveness	Socially effective: focused on concerns, needs and problem perceptions of the governed	Politically effective: focused on concerns, needs and problem perceptions of political elites
Ethical quality	Honest, genuine Straight, inclusive Transparent Trustworthy	Dishonest, deceptive Two-faced, exclusive Secretive, disguising Corrupt
Effect on political culture	Builds trust in democratic institutions, nurtures rational public deliberation, facilitates engagement and participation	Undermines trust in democratic institutions, suffocates rational deliberation, breeds disengagement and apathy

Figure 2. Authentic politics versus symbolic politics (type BII.2)

Symbolic Politics and the Politics of Simulation   75

vision for the mobilisation, integration and motivation of emancipatory movements; in so far as this ideal of authentic politics is expected to reconcile the deficient and alienated political reality of the present with the emancipative and empowering visions of the future, the notion of authentic politics is highly charged with symbolic value.[9] It may seem ironic that in popular language the term symbolic politics is used to describe the opposite of authentic politics, which at best *pretends* to be committed to the values and ideals of the Enlightenment tradition. Yet in the sense that symbolic politics always presents itself as, stands for and refers to its authentic counterpart it is indeed symbolic. And the popular discourse *about* symbolic politics always implies a story of deception and authenticity, of self-interested elites and disempowered masses, of domination and liberation and so forth. It evokes the image of committed, righteous, democratic citizens who, rather than being victimised by self-interested and malicious elites and their strategies of deception and manipulation, ought to be allowed to take political affairs into their own hands. This popular discourse of symbolic politics produces a societal self-description in which society portrays itself as being able and willing to do things differently – to genuinely ecologise.

In a number of respects, however, this very modernist story of symbolic politics and its counterpart provides a rather inadequate account of late-modern society and the ways in which it frames and manages its eco-political problems. For in the late-modern condition, the notion of authentic politics – be it in an ecological or any other sense – has, arguably, become *symbolically exhausted* and by implication its counterpart (symbolic politics) has become *symbolically empty*. In late-modern societies 'the other, to which' symbolic politics 'seems to refer ... exists exclusively as an appearance emerging in the perception of the symbolic act itself' (Meyer, 1994: 139ff.). Whilst the belief in authentic (eco-)politics has evaporated, symbolic politics is, Meyer suggests, 'more than anything ... an intuitively meaningful performance whereby the context of reference to which it seems to refer does not actually exist other than as a deceptive illusion' (Meyer, 1992: 54). 'A symbol, however', Meyer continues, 'which speaks only for itself is not a symbol', and what the popular discourse critically refers to as merely symbolic politics 'does not contain the very ingredient which is the defining criterion of its form'. In the second half of this piece the objective is, therefore, first to explore in more detail what the exhaustion of authentic (eco-)politics entails, and then to attempt a sociologically more adequate conceptualisation of what can no longer be described as symbolic politics because it is symbolically empty and no longer 'contains the very ingredient which is the defining criterion of its form'.

The *Post-ecologist Turn* and the Exhaustion of Authentic (Eco-)politics

In the preface to the 1990 edition of *Politik als Ritual*,[10] Edelman himself acknowledged that parts of the analysis which he had developed in the 1960s and early 1970s had become inappropriate. He noted that in contemporary

76 *The Politics of Unsustainability*

consumer democracies 'the disempowered are so well socialised' that genuine challenges to the established system have virtually disappeared, and citizens 'perceive the tactics of disobedience and disruption as illegal, immoral and risky' (Edelman, 2005: xiii).[11] Edelman recognised that contemporary citizens have positively embraced the constitutive principles of democratic consumer capitalism, yet he continued to refer to them as the 'disempowered'. Indeed, he described the virtual absence of radical challenges to the prevalence of symbolic politics as 'a shattering indicator of the degree of alienation suffered by the public, because it illustrates that a significant part of the citizenry no longer really *expects* their interests to be represented by the state' (Edelman, 2005: xviii; my emphasis). Being firmly committed to the tradition of critical theory, Edelman held fast to the categories of alienation and domination, yet he got caught up in a dilemma that he shared with critical theorists like Adorno or Baudrillard: once what Adorno called the *delusive context* of formally democratic consumer capitalism has become *universal*; once political reality 'is no longer anything but a gigantic simulacrum, never again exchanging for what is real, but exchanging in itself, in an uninterrupted circuit without reference or circumference' (Baudrillard, 2001: 173), it becomes increasingly difficult to imagine that things could also be different and to desire that they ought to be. Following the 'autonomisation of the symbolical' (Nullmeier, 2005: 201) and the adaptation of identity needs to what the established system provides, categories such as alienation, false consciousness or symbolic politics lose their meaning. The critical project, i.e. the emancipatory struggle for authentic politics and a reconciled and liberated society, then simply runs out of steam.

In the realm of eco-political thought, this exhaustion of the critical paradigm may be conceptualised as the *post-ecologist turn*. It is the result of major cultural shifts including what, making reference to Inglehart (1977), may be called the *silent counter-revolution* (Blühdorn, 2002), the transition from Beck's *risk society* (1992) to the contemporary *opportunity society*, and what I have elsewhere called the *post-democratic revolution* (Blühdorn 2004a, 2007b). In the same sense that what Inglehart described as the *silent revolution*, what Beck called the *risk society* and what the social movements celebrated as *grassroots democracy* became constitutive elements of ecologist thinking,[12] their counterparts are constitutive of the *post-ecologist* turn, a paradigm shift that may in general terms be associated with the period since the beginning of the 1990s.

The first of these expressions, i.e. the concept of the silent counter-revolution, aims to capture a revaluation of material interest preferences *vis-à-vis* Inglehart's post-material needs. Inglehart had noted that in the materially affluent industrial societies of the 1970s, the marginal utility of further material accumulation was declining and post-material interest preferences were gaining in relative significance. In late-modern consumer societies, however, this development has arguably reversed. As self-construction, self-expression and self-experience have, to an unprecedented extent, become a matter of product choices and acts of consumption; and as value pluralism, pressures for

Symbolic Politics and the Politics of Simulation   77

flexibility, ever accelerated innovation, reduced protection through public welfare systems and so forth have given rise to a new climate of both material as well as cultural insecurity, the marginal utility of libertarian post-materialism is declining again: in the present climate, neo-material and post-libertarian strategies seem more conducive for the achievement of autonomy and security. The 'political economy of uncertainty' (Bauman, 1999) and the permeation of identity by the market have triggered *post*-post-materialist security reflexes.

The notion of the *opportunity society*, secondly, aims to indicate that the unprecedented technological, environmental, economic and cultural uncertainties which Beck had conceptualised as the non-insurable and unmanageable threats that are characteristic of the *risk society* have successfully been re-conceptualised as unprecedented *opportunities* which are to be realised. The new opportunity society is no longer governed by Beck's imperatives of risk avoidance (1997) but instead by technological optimism, aggressive innovation and the pursuit of first mover advantages. Together, the silent counter-revolution and the optimistic outlook of the opportunity society lead to a positive identification with the established system of democratic consumer capitalism: this system offers optimal conditions for the realisation, expression and experience of the consumer-Self. As the consumer identity can be realised only within but not beyond the established system, potential experiences of exclusion and alienation can at best trigger demands for tighter inclusion into the system but not the desire to opt out of consumer capitalism and for abandoning it wholesale. Indeed, as alternative political and economic systems, to the extent that they can at all be imagined, represent a threat to the realisation of the consumer identity, the uncompromising defence of the esta-blished system becomes a categorical imperative.

The concept of the *post-democratic revolution*, finally, aims to indicate that the euphoric democratic optimism which had inspired the social movements' demand for civic empowerment and self-organisation has metamorphosed into democratic disillusionment and sclerosis. Contemporary debates about spreading political apathy, cynicism or even the *end of politics* (e.g. Bauman, 1999; Boggs, 2000; Gamble, 2000; Crouch, 2004; Dalton, 2004; Furedi, 2005) illustrate the decline of the social movements' democratic do-it-yourself enthusiasm. A supposedly more efficient *politics of delegation* (Thatcher & Stone Sweet, 2002; Flinders, 2004a, b) that empowers scientific experts, charismatic leaders, non-democratic regulatory bodies or market instruments is expected to deliver top-down what has not been achieved bottom-up. For the social movements of the 1970s and 1980s – and for ecologists and Green parties in particular – *anti-politics* had been the rebellion against established mainstream politics and the project of replacing this at best symbolic politics by the authentic politics that was supposedly being rehearsed in the societal margins. Yet, following *the third transformation of democracy* (Blühdorn, 2007b) anti-politics has fundamentally changed its meaning: it is frustration with politics and complete withdrawal into the private sphere (political apathy,

78 *The Politics of Unsustainability*

disengagement); it is *depoliticisation* (delegation) in the sense outlined above; and it is the obsessive pursuit of personal missions covering anything from fox hunting to paedophiles. Whilst the proliferation of itemised protest has become a defining characteristic of contemporary *protest societies* (Pross, 1992; Meyer & Tarrow, 1998), this political activism has little to do with the struggle for any societal alternatives.[13]

Together, the neo-materialist counter-revolution, the optimistic perspective of the opportunity society and the post-democratic revolution have fundamentally changed the way in which advanced European societies frame and manage their environmental problems; they have fundamentally changed the value system on the basis of which environmental problems are formulated and remedial strategies devised.[14] Indeed, in the era of post-ecologism, the new social movements' whole project of correcting the trajectory of modernity by tying the process of modernisation to a revised understanding of democracy, efficiency, futurity and identity has comprehensively failed (Blühdorn, 2004a, 2007a). Instead, late-modern societies are fully focused on reinforcing at all societal levels their technological and managerial systems of security, surveillance and control which are designed to protect exactly those structures and principles of the established order which are at the very core of the problem of unsustainability.[15] Within this context, the ecological virtues which the new social movements once sought to establish as the foundation of a radically different society have themselves turned into a problem. Commitment to minimal disturbance of eco-systems, to long term stability, the deceleration of change, a steady-state economy, risk avoidance, decentralisation, low-grade mobility, democratic deliberation, consensual decision making, social justice and redistribution, moderation of consumption and so forth: in the post-ecologist context these ecological virtues have become symbols of inefficiency and resistance to innovation. Figure 3 collates some features which are characteristic of the era of post-ecologism. It supplements what has been said so far with a number of additional points which cannot be further elaborated within present confines. It illustrates how the post-ecologist worldview is very different from the older eco-political narratives of alienation, domination, exploitation and so forth.

The notion of the post-ecologist turn does not imply any claims that radical ecologism has ever been a mainstream ideology, nor does it impose homogeneity onto the differentiated lifestyles and worldviews of late-modern societies. The point is rather to capture a late-modern *Zeitgeist* that is markedly different from the values and visions which had once inspired the new social movements. From a sociological point of view the post-ecologist turn cannot usefully be described in normative terms as cultural *decline* or accelerating *alienation*. Nor is it simply the victory of the neo-liberal ideology which has successfully been imposed by free market strategists. Instead, the post-ecologist turn is a complex cultural transformation in which much more inclusive understandings of eco-politics are superseded by technical and managerial approaches which are symbolically empty, i.e. which deal with

Symbolic Politics and the Politics of Simulation 79

- General and full acceptance of the *in principle* relevance of environmental issues.

- *Normalisation* of the environmental crisis and warning that, despite all undeniable seriousness, the crisis must not be overstated.

- Subordination of environmental issues under the priorities of economic competitiveness and growth, the security of Northern lifestyles and the preservation of established global power relations.

- Prominence of neo-materialist and consumption-oriented patterns of identity construction, self-expression and self-experience.

- Emancipation from restrictive notions of redistribution, equality, justice and solidarity, and confidence in the logic of competitiveness and individual success.

- Venturing and entrepreneurial outlook; readiness to experiment and take risks.

- Identification with democratic consumer capitalism and end of the vision of and desire for a *radically different* society in the ecologist sense.

- Institutionalisation of environmental concerns and delegation to 'experts' and 'professionals'.

- Inability to connect to ecocentric frames and narrowing of anthropocentric frames to issues such as consumer rights, health and safety questions and food standards.

- Reformulation of ecological problems as scientific, technological, economic or managerial issues.

- Prominence of the paradigms of *ecological modernisation* and *environmental economics* which see environmental protection as an opportunity for technological innovation and economic growth.

- Cultivation of narratives of technological efficiency revolutions, corporate responsibility, ethical consumption, fair trade, ethical investment, green consumerism, etc. which are consistent with the basic principles of productivism, consumerism, etc.

- Establishment of green consumerism and the wellness sector as major markets, whereby these formerly *alternative* business sectors now fully replicate the basic principles which ecologists once rejected and no longer understand themselves as the symbolic anticipation of a radically different lifestyle, human–nature relationship and society.

- Disillusionment with the practices and capabilities of grassroots democracy and increasing reliance on supposedly *more efficient* instruments for achieving the common good (experts, markets, political leaders, regulating bodies, etc.).

- Differentiation and fragmentation of ecological diagnoses and strategies and implicit mobilisation of environmentalism against itself.

Figure 3. Distinctive features of the post-ecologist condition[16]

80   The Politics of Unsustainability

> - Rise of the paradigm of *environmental security* which implicitly accepts the unsustainability of Northern lifestyles as well as the inevitability of resource conflicts and focuses on: (1) *securing* access for the 'free and civilised world' to natural resources; (2) *defending* the wealthy countries against environmental refugees; and (3) *managing* violent conflicts locally in order to minimise disruption of global markets.
> - Rejection of ecologist idealism and dogmatic insistence on *political realism* or *pragmatism* which asserts that there is no choice but to adapt to the non-negotiable imperatives of economic growth, technological progress, global competition, etc.
> - Robust defence against any alternative to the combination of liberal democracy and consumer capitalism including, for example, the stigmatisation of radical ecologists as (potential) eco-terrorists.

Figure 3. (Continued)

short term and narrowly defined problems, but are no longer inspired by any comprehensive ecological alternative to the established socio-economic system. Thus, the notion of authentic (eco-)politics has become symbolically exhausted, and its counterpart, the practice and critique of symbolic politics, has become symbolically empty: the Other that it claims to represent has neither empirical nor imagined reality. Whilst the hegemony of techno-managerial win–win–win[18] thinking has not exterminated narratives of alienation and radical change, the belief in authentic politics, i.e. the once popular suggestion that the fulfilment of the *authentic* Self and its *reconciliation* with a *liberated* nature can only lie beyond the confines of the established system of consumer democracy, is an idea which late-modern individuals can no longer relate to. By implication, the popular narrative of symbolic politics which had once been launched as a critical weapon against ideological deception has itself become ideological: it tells a dubious story of eco-political oppression and alienation and conceals the post-ecologist resolve to defend the ecologically exploitative and destructive system of democratic consumer capitalism.

The Performance of Seriousness

For Edelman the epitome of alienation had been the condition where citizens no longer *seriously expect* (anticipate) that politicians will really represent their interests and implement their demands. This *normalisation* of democratic deficits was the outer limit of what he could think within the critical paradigm. What his model of symbolic politics cannot capture is a condition where citizens articulate demands which they do not want to see seriously implemented. Put differently, Edelman's model is not suitable for a condition where citizens expect – in the sense of both *want* and *anticipate* – that the government *does not* seriously implement the demands which they, nevertheless, continue to

Symbolic Politics and the Politics of Simulation 81

articulate. This is a seemingly schizophrenic condition where citizens want politics to be no more than symbolic, but still complain about democratic deficits and 'merely symbolic' politics. This form of political communication can be aptly described with Nullmeier's expression 'performance of seriousness'. It is a political game that is, arguably, characteristic of late-modern society, and that is motivated by the characteristic dilemma caused by the post-ecologist turn and the exhaustion of authentic politics.

In their uncompromising commitment to defending the economic and political system that provides the best imaginable framework for the realisation of the late-modern consumer-Self, contemporary societies are confronted with three major challenges. Firstly, there are problems like resource shortages, climate change, species extinction, epidemics and so forth which constantly provide proof of the *ecological unsustainability* of the established system which no technological or managerial ingenuity has so far managed to fix. Secondly, late-modern society and its pattern of identity construction are firmly based on the *principle of exclusion* (Blühdorn, 2003) which breeds social conflicts, nationally and internationally, which in the long term no security and surveillance technology can keep under control. These conflicts are a persistent reminder of the *social unsustainability* of democratic consumer capitalism. And thirdly, late-modern societies are severely threatened by what may be described as a *crisis of self-referentiality* which provides evidence of the *normative* or *cultural unsustainability* of the established system. This crisis of self-referentiality surfaces, for example, as the individualised experience of spiritual disorientation and emptiness, but perhaps more seriously, it manifestly threatens the system of democratic politics which seems to centre ever more exclusively on its own reproduction. Furthermore, this crisis of self-referentiality also has the potential to destabilise the economic system: For its own reproduction, the system of the market depends on the existence of its counterpart, i.e. of something that can be marketed. Not only in material terms, but also in terms of extra-economic *values* that underpin the price of products and services, the economic system requires its non-economic Other which is, however, an increasingly scarce resource.[19]

Thus, the system of capitalist consumer democracy is threatened by a triple crisis of unsustainability, and late-modern societies are confronted with a severe problem: in order to address the crisis of unsustainability and ward off the threats of ecological, social and normative collapse, they need to radically change the established system, yet there is no vision of any viable alternatives, nor is there the political will or ability to deviate from the established path. It is the *late-modern dilemma* that following the post-ecologist turn and the exhaustion of authentic (eco-)politics the triple crisis of unsustainability *cannot* be resolved, but neither can it *not be* resolved. Against the background of this dilemma, the key question that guided Edelman's discussion of symbolic politics – How does the ruling class succeed in securing the support and cooperation of those who they aim to dominate, instrumentalise and exploit? – is superseded by the new question: How may the irresolvable problems of

82   *The Politics of Unsustainability*

ecological, social and normative unsustainability be *managed* and thus the unsustainable sustained? This is a genuinely post-ecologist problem which is categorically different from ecologist problem perceptions. For the analysis of this problem and of the ways in which it is handled the sociological tool-kit of critical theory and symbolic politics is no longer sufficient.

Meyer (1994) provides important pointers as to how late-modern societies manage this problem of sustaining the unsustainable. Focusing on one particular societal subsystem, the system of democratic politics, he highlights the widening discrepancy between rising popular pressures for better justification and legitimation of politics and the diminishing capability of the political system to generate this legitimacy. The depletion of this essential resource, legitimacy, combined with the persistent failure to find new sources of legitimacy, accounts for the sustainability crisis of contemporary consumer democracies. And in the management of this sustainability crisis, Meyer suggests, symbolic politics is playing a crucial role: the 'symbolic performance of politics' (1994: 141) 'offers its services as an effective and versatile gap filler' (1994: 140). 'Performed show politics', he argues, closes 'the delegitimising gap' (1994: 140). What this 'show politics' performs is that the political class are still offering alternative visions, that electorates are still making a choice between these visions and that political institutions are still capable of then implementing their decisions. The 'symbolic performance of politics' thus serves the *performative regeneration* of legitimacy, which is a resource on which the system of politics vitally depends but which it finds increasingly difficult to reproduce. Meyer does not make a very clear conceptual distinction between traditional-style *symbolic politics* and the contemporary *symbolic performance of politics*, yet he does point out that in the late-modern context, 'the function' of symbolic politics 'has changed in a fundamental way' (Meyer, 1994: 139). And his discussion of the performative regeneration of legitimacy clearly illustrates in what way it has supposedly changed: contemporary-style symbolic politics no longer primarily serves the deception, control or domination of the masses (Edelman), and also not primarily the function of complexity reduction (Sarcinelli), but it is a tool for the stabilisation of destabilised systems.

Thinking along similar lines Nullmeier, too, suggests that in a context where the rituals of democratic politics have 'no other purpose and no guiding interest' beyond the stabilisation and reproduction of the political system itself (2005: 201), symbolic politics might 'no longer serve the purpose of deception' (2005: 200). He suggests that contemporary 'calls for a more serious and more substantive rather than aesthetic politics' may have to be understood not so much as a 'turn away from symbolic politics' but instead as 'a change in the chosen *variety of symbolic politics*' (2005: 202; my emphasis). The expression 'performance of seriousness' is his provisional label for this *new variety* of symbolic politics, and what this expression aims to capture is exactly what Meyer calls the 'symbolic performance of politics'. The analysis of the post-ecologist turn and the exhaustion of authentic politics makes clearly visible

Symbolic Politics and the Politics of Simulation   83

how this new variety is very different from its traditional predecessor. Its primary function is no longer simply to conceal the true interests of political elites, but what the 'performance of seriousness' and the 'symbolic performance of politics' perform is something much larger: it is the vitality and viability of politics itself. It is the performance that the system of democratic politics is at all relevant. Ultimately, what is being performed is that in the context of a system-centred, depoliticised and efficiency-oriented global (late) modernity (Blühdorn, 2004a, 2007a), the traditional Habermasian *project of modernity*, i.e. the vision of authentic politics, is still alive. As an antidote to the triple crisis of unsustainability, i.e. as a tool for the *management* of the late-modern problem that cannot be *resolved*, this performative regeneration of authentic politics is indispensable. It stabilises the narrative of ecological (and other) sustainability, it pacifies the excluded, and it gives reassurance about the existence of the non-economic Other. And in this performance, the critical discourse which castigates the prevalence of *merely symbolic* politics is playing a lead role: whatever the perceived and declared intentions of those who are engaging in it, this critical discourse is a prime location for the performative regeneration of authentic politics, and thus a vital tool for sustaining the unsustainable.

Building on Baudrillard's concept of *simulation*, this new variety of symbolic politics can suitably be referred to as *simulative politics*. Reaching well beyond the narrow realm of eco-politics and the unsustainability of contemporary consumer democracies, Baudrillard conceptualises the loss of authenticity and the exclusive preoccupation with signs, symbols and performances as the central problem of late-modern societies. He describes the desperate attempts to regenerate the belief in the authentic as 'the characteristic hysteria of our time' (Baudrillard, 2001: 183). And the preferred strategy that late-modern societies are using for this purpose, Baudrillard suggests, is the strategy of *simulation*. Simulation on this account is the use of symbols, signs and images which do not *represent* or *refer to* anything that is authentic, but which themselves *produce* or *perform* a reality, and present themselves as evidence of its authenticity. Simulative politics then is, using Meyer's words, an exercise in which 'the fusion of presentation (*Darstellung*) and imagination (*Vorstellung*) of politics replaces its production (*Herstellung*)' (1994: 140). It is the 'artificial revitalisation' (Baudrillard, 2001: 184) of the authentic, the 'simulated generation of difference' (Baudrillard, 2001: 170) by means of which late-modern societies are trying 'to revive' the 'moribund principle' of authenticity (Baudrillard, 2001: 176), by which they 'rejuvenate...the fiction of the real' (Baudrillard, 2001: 172).

Simulative politics thus responds to the symbolic exhaustion of authentic politics and the symbolic emptiness of symbolic politics. As the performance of seriousness, the performance of authentic (eco-)politics, it is the form of political communication that – as was outlined above – articulates demands which are *not supposed* to be taken seriously and implemented, but which are nevertheless constantly rearticulated with politicians being criticised – as part

84   The Politics of Unsustainability

of the performance – for not implementing them. This seemingly nonsensical form of political communication is specifically geared towards the late-modern problem that the belief in, the desire for and the capability of authentic (eco-) politics are exhausted but still indispensable for the stabilisation of the ecologically, socially and normatively unsustainable system of democratic consumer capitalism. The performative regeneration of authentic politics is the key to the post-ecologist problem of sustaining the unsustainable.

Moving beyond the critical paradigm of symbolic politics, the notion of simulative politics thus questions the narrative of manipulation and domination. It challenges the distinction between the good (authentic) public and the bad (malicious) elites. It shifts the emphasis away from the power differential between so-called producers and so-called recipients of symbolic politics; it suggests something like a tacit strategic community between the public and its political elites; it supplements the idea of immoral deception of certain sections of society by other sections by the idea of a practice of *societal self-deception* (Blühdorn, 2007c); it shifts the emphasis from the activity of *symbolic representation* of the Other to the activity of *simulative regeneration* of the Other; and it counterbalances the focus on myth in the negative sense (superstition, lie, irrationality) by the notion of myth in the positive sense as a story that helps to generate meaning and sustain what would otherwise be unsustainable. These distinctive features of the paradigm of simulative politics are summarised in Figure 4 and contrasted with the paradigm of symbolic politics.

Where are the Data? What is the Point?

The objective of this contribution has been to critically investigate the popular description of contemporary eco-politics as *merely symbolic* politics. It has

	Post-ecologist practice of simulative politics	Ecologist critique of symbolic politics
Societal condition and social theory	Late modernity; post-critical, system-centred and geared towards efficiency in the economic sense	Traditional modernity; critical, subject-centred and geared towards efficiency in the social and ecological sense
Key objectives	To manage the crisis of unsustainability; to sustain the unsustainable	To resolve the crisis of unsustainability; to reinstate authentic politics
Main strategy	Regenerates dualism; recreates/replaces Other; performs authenticity	Highlights discrepancy; refers to/represents Other; claims and demands authenticity
Top/bottom relation	Common interest; strategic union; amoral	Opposite interests; power differential; corrupt versus sincere

Figure 4. The sociological paradigms of simulative versus symbolic politics; symbolic politics is here understood in the sense of the BII types specified in Figure 1[17]

Symbolic Politics and the Politics of Simulation   85

been argued that from a sociological point of view the paradigm of *symbolic politics* is an unsatisfactory conceptualisation of late-modern society's eco-politics and late-modern politics more generally. Indeed it has been suggested that this paradigm which had once been launched as a critical weapon against ideological deception has itself become ideological: it tells a dubious story of eco-political oppression and alienation; it conceals the post-ecologist resolve to defend the ecologically exploitative and destructive system of democratic consumer capitalism; and by performing the will and possibility of *authentic* eco-politics, it actually helps to sustain what it apparently criticises. Taking the perspective of eco-political and social theory, the analysis has endeavoured to capture the specific condition of late-modern society which gives rise to a form of political communication through which late-modern society distances itself from eco-political practices to which it at the same time fully subscribes. The diagnosis of the post-ecologist turn and of the exhaustion of authentic (eco-) politics has prepared the ground for the paradigm of *simulative politics*. This analytical paradigm suggests that the pervasive criticism of *merely symbolic* politics and the ostentatious declaratory commitment to effective action must not be read – in the ecologist sense – as evidence of the political will and ability to address and resolve the problems of unsustainability but instead – in the post-ecologist sense – as a societal strategy for sustaining the unsustainable.

The model of simulative politics is not restricted to the analysis of contemporary eco-politics. Its centrepiece is the performative regeneration of the exhausted dualisms of modernity in general, and it can therefore productively be applied wherever the problems inherent to the late-modern condition manifest themselves.[20] The suggested theory of simulative politics is to the critical discourse of symbolic politics what the latter is to the political practices which it criticises. In other words, the theory of simulative politics represents an extension of the critical paradigm. As the critical investigation of the societal self-description that is produced in the discourse of symbolic politics, it is the attempt to undertake a form of meta-critique – which is, however, itself disabled by the exhaustion of authentic politics. In conclusion one may ask: But where are the data? Where is the evidence? Can the thesis of the post-ecologist turn and the assertion that the critical discourse of symbolic politics including its more or less explicit demand for authentic politics is no more than the *performance of seriousness* be empirically verified?

With a mixture of admiration and critique commentators once noted that 'Edelman presents a style of political analysis that self-confidently forsakes the formalised and quantitative techniques of the present-style social sciences' (Offe, 1976/2005: ix). Edelman was praised for reasserting the 'critical enlightenment capabilities of political science' which the discipline has by and large lost in the process of its cooptation as a professionalised service provider to the established system (Offe, 1976/2005: ix). Yet he was criticised for presenting his analyses 'in a rather essayistic fashion' without 'the required empirical verification and verifiability' (Nullmeier, 2005: 214–15). Undoubt-edly, this criticism of Edelman's model of symbolic politics is applicable to the

86   *The Politics of Unsustainability*

model of simulative politics as well. Yet it is worth calling to mind that it is nonsensical to expect empirical proof for the models of social and political theory. It is the very nature and task of social and political theory to look beyond the restrictions of established worldviews. The empirical methods and standards of verifiability, however, which are expected of the *professional* social sciences, tie social theory into the system and into the role of a service provider. In other words, these methods and standards are applicable only to the extent that social science serves the purpose of stabilising and reproducing the established system. Speaking in Luhmannite terms one might say: communications must adhere to a system's code only if they want to contribute to that system's *autopoiesis*. But surely there is much more to sociological enquiry than addressing the problems which the established system wants to see resolved.

So the question for empirical evidence is misconceived because the whole point is to reach *beyond* established societal self-descriptions whilst anything that is acceptable as empirical evidence would invariably just *reproduce* these societal self-descriptions. Still, it is entirely legitimate to demand *empirical plausibility*. It therefore seems advisable to anticipate and respond to at least some probable counter-arguments to the approach that has been developed here. One of these might be a point that has briefly been touched upon above, namely that the theorem of the post-ecologist turn does not take account of the plurality of competing and conflicting views which are characteristic of contemporary consumer democracies; that it is plainly wrong to claim that ecologism has ever been more than a marginal social movement ideology; and that it is difficult to overlook that there are still plenty of radical movements and activists who, if interviewed, would most certainly reject any suggestions that they have turned post-ecologist. These points are valid and fully taken. But they are entirely consistent with the observation that late-modern societies are framing and processing their environmental problems primarily in ways (as sketched in Figure 3) which are radically different from those promoted by the progressive social movements. And if these late-modern practices are measured against the standards of ecologism, they can be described as post-ecologist irrespective of the question of to what extent ecologism ever represented something like a collective movement outlook and identity. And in the same sense it is also entirely plausible and legitimate to explain the evolution of this post-ecologist *Zeitgeist* by making reference to certain shifts in social values, self-perceptions, preferences and practices which can indeed be empirically verified, albeit not within the confines of this piece.

It may furthermore be argued that the claim of the exhaustion of authentic politics is evidently wrong because there is plenty of empirical evidence that people still demand it. The assertion that these demands are not genuine and that these people are merely engaging in a *performance of seriousness* seems rather arrogant, and one may also raise the question from what kind of cognitive position and with what kind of intellectual resources such a diagnosis may be made. It is important to note that the practices of simulation and the performance of seriousness which have been discussed here cannot be described as conscious strategies which are deliberately adopted by individual or collective actors. The point of the analysis cannot be to question and judge the committedness and integrity of any particular actor. Instead, the objective has been to use the perspective of social theory in order to formulate problems and identify responses which are visible and relevant at the *societal* level. As regards the cognitive position and intellectual tools which are available for this exercise, it is evident that these are not categorically different from those available to any other member of society. And in particular, it is evident that no intellectual tools are available for the meta-critical model of simulative politics which were (or are) not available for the critical model of symbolic politics. Speaking once again in Luhmannite terms, one might say that the sociological paradigm of simulative politics can at best offer a *different* description of society, but not a *more valid* one. It can deliver *different* insights, but not *better* insights.

Thirdly, it may be argued that the theory of simulative politics as a societal *strategy* for the management of the late-modern dilemma is not convincing because highly differentiated and complex late-modern societies have neither the capacity to develop an awareness of problems which affect them as a whole, nor the ability to devise and implement remedial strategies. It was the outstanding contribution of Luhmann's post-critical social theory that it captured these limitations and spelt out their implications not least for the field of eco-politics (Luhmann, 1989; Blühdorn, 2000). The conceptualisation of simulative politics as a societal strategy is indeed problematic, and it ought to be seen as a heuristic device. In order to avoid the term *strategy*, it might be preferable to describe simulative politics as something like an instinctive reflex that is triggered by a combination of the human desire for meaning and the imperatives for self-stabilisation and self-reproduction which are inherent to all systems and organisations.

Lastly then one might ask: Does it make a difference? Does it really matter whether we describe contemporary eco-politics as symbolic or as simulative politics? More precisely the question is: Is there any eco-political or other benefit in knowing that – if this could be shown to be true – late-modern societies are engaging in simulative politics, with the critical discourse of symbolic politics being no more than one of the phenotypes of this simulative politics? Critics of Edelman's work once suggested that his critical observation of *symbolic* politics would remain 'the politically irrelevant privilege of a critical social science intelligentsia' (Offe, 1976/2005: ix). It might be argued that this will be equally applicable to the critical observation of the *simulative* practices by means of which late-modern societies are trying to sustain the unsustainable. Yet this assessment is unduly pessimistic, and the broad politicisation which symbolic politics has experienced since Edelman first presented his theory has proved his critics wrong. There is certainly a lot of benefit in knowing *that* contrary to its own self-descriptions late-modern society is engaged much more in *reproducing* the principles of unsustainability

88 *The Politics of Unsustainability*

than in *overcoming* them. And there is also a lot of benefit in identifying *exactly how* it is doing this. Trying to *make sense* of the evident contradiction between late-modern society's acknowledgement that radical and effective change is urgent and inescapable and its adamant resolve to sustain what is known to be unsustainable is a hugely important and difficult task. And making visible how the late-modern condition and the post-ecologist *Zeitgeist* have historically evolved and are therefore essentially contingent creates space for considerable optimism. It is certainly true that the analysis of the post-ecologist constellation and late-modern society's politics of simulation does not easily translate into environmental policy recommendations. Yet the attempt to *understand* the architecture of this constellation and the logic of these practices is one essential precondition of developing the capacity to *transcend* it.

Notes

1. Throughout this contribution I am using the terms *late-modern society* and *late-modern condition* in a very specific sense, namely to capture the categorical difference between *traditional modernity* which was centred on the idea of the autonomous subject and geared towards its emancipation and a new phase of modernity that has overcome the dualism of the *subject* and the *system* and is centred on abstract notions of efficiency (for a detailed discussion see Blühdorn, 2007a).
2. Translation of German Language Sources here and below by the author.
3. Note the double meaning of *performance* which can denote both hollow entertaining façadism and substantive measurable output. I have discussed the late-modern relationship between the two and the 'performance of performance' in some detail elsewhere (Blühdorn, 2005: 38–41, 2007a).
4. This contribution ought to be seen as a further addition to the body of work on the *politics of simulation* that I have done over recent years (see Blühdorn, 2002; 2003; 2004b; 2005; 2006; 2007a, b, c).
5. In this context see Susan Baker's analysis (this volume) of the European Union's commitment to the goals of sustainability as an integral part of the union's strategy of identity construction.
6. See Jens Newig's discussion (this volume) of German environmental legislation as an example of BI-type symbolic politics.
7. Nullmeier's own analysis reaches well beyond these simplistic views.
8. Note that *reconciliation with nature* and the protection of its integrity is an integral part of this *project of modernity* (Blühdorn, 2000). In line with the post-Marxist tradition of Critical Theory, the new social movements (or at least their intellectuals) have always seen the realisation of the authentic Self and the liberation of nature as two sides of the same coin.
9. Compare the concept of *authentic art* which in his Aesthetic Theory Adorno presents as the present anticipation of the reconciled and liberated condition. On *authenticity as a political problem* see Noetzel (1999). For a good example of the popular discussion of 'authenticity', the critical rejection of 'brands, fakes and spin' and 'the lust for real life' see Boyle (2004).
10. This volume collates German translations of selected chapters from Edelman's *The Symbolic Uses of Politics* (1964) and *Politics as Symbolic Action, Mass Arousal and Quiescence* (1971). It was first published in 1976 (prefaced by Claus Offe); a second edition with a preface by Murray Edelman was released in 1990. The third edition of 2005 contains an epilogue by Frank Nullmeier.
11. At the time Edelman did not anticipate the waves of radical action and *autre-mondialisme* which were to emerge a few years later, yet these movements, arguably, did very little to alter the fact that today radical alternatives to the established system are more difficult to imagine and less in demand than at any time since the launch of the critical project (for a more

Symbolic Politics and the Politics of Simulation 89

detailed discussion see Blühdorn, 2006/2007c; for a contrasting assessment see Ian Welsh, this volume).

12. In this context, *ecologist* thinking is understood as a comprehensive political ideology as defined in Andrew Dobson's classic *Green Political Thought* (1990).

13. This also applies to the waves of radical action since the 1990s which many observers have celebrated with overwhelming neo-democratic optimism. Protests from the by now legendary Battle of Seattle to the campaign against the Iraq War remained one-off eruptions which did little to revive democratic cultures or inspire the imagination of socio-economic alternatives. For a contrasting assessment see Ian Welsh's contribution in this volume.

14. Bjørn Lomborg's best-selling *The Skeptical Environmentalist* (2001) is an exemplary articulation of the post-ecologist *Zeitgeist*. The enormous success of the book may be explained by Lomborg's intuitive sensitivity to the cultural shifts outlined above. Lomborg supplied a narrative that responded to an implicit public demand.

15. Compare Ian Welsh's analysis of the 'defence of civilisation' in this volume.

16. This is not meant to be an exhaustive description of post-ecologism. It ought to be read in conjunction with, or within the framework of, my earlier, more theoretical, characterisation of post-ecologism as a post-natural, post-subjective, post-moral and post-problematic *politics without identity* (Blühdorn, 2000: 151–9).

17. Symbolic politics is here understood in the sense of the BII types specified in Figure 1.

18. The belief that techno-managerial innovation equals economic growth, social development and environmental improvement.

19. It is no coincidence that the regeneration of what is tellingly referred to as *social capital* has become a prime concern of late-modern societies. Equally striking is the level of attention that is devoted to the reinvention and cultivation of regional identities which are a vital resource for whole industries. A further indicator for the seriousness of the crisis is that businesses have never been more anxious to emphasise that they are *serving the community*, that they are *investing in people* and that everything hinges on the customer's *autonomous choice*.

20. See for example my analyses of *simulative democracy* (Blühdorn, 2007b) and *simulative radical action* (Blühdorn, 2007c).

References

Baudrillard, J. (2001) *Selected Writings*, 2nd edn (Cambridge: Polity).

Bauman, Z. (1999) *In Search of Politics* (Cambridge: Polity).

Beck, U. (1992) *The Risk Society. Towards a New Modernity* (Cambridge: Polity).

Beck, U. (1997) *The Reinvention of Politics. Rethinking Modernity in the Global Social Order* (Cambridge: Polity).

Blühdorn, I. (2000) *Post-ecologist Politics. Social Theory and the Abdication of the Ecologist Paradigm* (London: Routledge).

Blühdorn, I. (2002) 'Unsustainability as a frame of mind – and how we disguise it. The silent counter revolution and the politics of simulation', *Trumpeter* 18(1): 59–69.

Blühdorn, I. (2003) 'Inclusionality – exclusionality. Environmental philosophy and simulative politics', in A. Winnett & A. Warhurst (eds.), *Towards an Environment Research Agenda*, volume II, pp. 21–45 (Basingstoke: Palgrave).

Blühdorn, I. (2004a) 'Future fitness and reform gridlock. Towards social inequality and post-democratic politics', *Debatte. Review of Contemporary German Affairs* 12(2): 114–36.

Blühdorn, I. (2004b) 'Post-ecologism and the politics of simulation', in M. Wissenburg & Y. Levy (eds.), *Liberal Democracy and the Environment. The End of Environmentalism?* pp. 35–47 (London: Routledge).

Blühdorn, I. (2005) 'Social movements and political performance. Niklas Luhmann, Jean Baudrillard and the politics of simulation', in B. Haas (ed.), *Macht – Performanz. Performativität, Polittheater*, pp. 19–40 (Würzburg: Königshausen & Neumann).

90   The Politics of Unsustainability

Blühdorn, I. (2006) 'Self-experience in the theme-park of radical action? Social movements and political articulation in the late-modern condition', *European Journal of Social Theory* 9(1): 23–42.

Blühdorn, I. (2007a) 'Democracy, efficiency, futurity: contested objectives of societal reform', in I. Blühdorn & U. Jun (eds.), *Economic Efficiency – Democratic Empowerment. Contested Modernisation in Britain and Germany*, pp. 69–98 (Lanham, MD: Rowman & Littlefield/ Lexington).

Blühdorn, I. (2007b) 'The third transformation of democracy: on the efficient management of late-modern complexity', in I. Blühdorn & U. Jun (eds.), *Economic Efficiency – Democratic Empowerment. Contested Modernisation in Britain and Germany*, pp. 299–331 (Lanham, MD: Rowman & Littlefield/Lexington).

Blühdorn, I. (2007c) 'Self-description, self-deception, simulation. A systems-theoretical perspective on contemporary discourses of radical change', *Social Movement Studies* 4(2) (in press).

Boggs, C. (2000) *The End of Politics* (New York: Guilford Press).

Boyle, D. (2004) *Authenticity. Brands, Fakes, Spin and the Lust for Real Life* (London: Harper Perennial).

Crouch, C. (2004) *Post-democracy* (Cambridge: Polity).

Dalby, S. (2002) *Environmental Security* (Minneapolis, MN: University of Minnesota Press).

Dalton, R. (2004) *Democratic Challenges – Democratic Choices. The Erosion of Political Support in Advanced Industrial Democracies* (Oxford: Oxford University Press).

Dobson, A. (1990) *Green Political Thought* (London: Unwin Hyman).

Dörner, A. (1996) *Politischer Mythos und symbolische Politik* (Reinbek: Rowohlt).

Edelman, M. (1964) *The Symbolic Uses of Politics* (Urbana, IL: University of Illinois Press).

Edelman, M. (1971) *Politics as Symbolic Action. Mass Arousal and Quiescence* (Chicago, IL: Markham).

Edelman, M. (2001) *The Politics of Misinformation* (Cambridge: Cambridge University Press).

Edelman, M. (2005) *Politik als Ritual. Die Symbolische Funktion staatlicher Institutionen und politischen Handelns*, 3rd edn (Frankfurt: Campus).

Fleischer, A. (2001) White House press briefing, 7 May. Available at: http://www. whitehouse.gov/ news/briefings/print/20010507.html (accessed 2 June 2006).

Flinders, M. (2004a) 'Distributed public governance in Britain', *Public Administration* 82(4): 883–909.

Flinders, M. (2004b) 'Distributed public governance in the European Union', *Journal of European Public Policy* 11(3): 520–44.

Furedi, F. (2005) *Politics of Fear: Beyond Left and Right* (London: Continuum).

Gamble, A. (2000) *Politics and Fate* (Cambridge: Polity).

Hansjürgens, B. (2000) 'Symbolische Umweltpolitik: eine Erklärung aus der Sicht der neuen politischen Ökonomie', in B. Hansjürgens & G. Lübbe-Wolff (eds.), *Symbolische Umweltpolitik*, pp. 144–82 (Frankfurt: Suhrkamp).

Hansjürgens, B. & Lübbe-Wolff, G. (eds.) (2000) *Symbolische Umweltpolitik* (Frankfurt: Suhrkamp).

Inglehart, R. (1977) *The Silent Revolution: Changing Values and Political Styles among Western Publics* (Princeton, NJ: Princeton University Press).

Lacy, M. (2005) *Security and Climate Change. International Relations and the Limits of Realism* (London: Routledge).

Lomborg, B. (2001) *The Skeptical Environmentalist. Measuring the Real State of the World* (Cambridge: Cambridge University Press).

Luhmann, N. (1989) *Ecological Communication* (Cambridge: Polity).

Manwaring, M. (ed.) (2002) *Environmental Security and Global Stability* (Lanham, MD: Rowman & Littlefield/Lexington).

Meyer, T. (1992) *Die Inszenierung des Scheins. Voraussetzungen und Folgen symbolischer Politik* (Frankfurt: Suhrkamp).

Meyer, T. (1994) *Die Transformation des Politischen* (Frankfurt: Suhrkamp).

Symbolic Politics and the Politics of Simulation   91

Meyer, D. & Tarrow, S. (1998) *The Social Movement Society. Contentious Politics for a New Century* (Lanham, MD: Rowman & Littlefield).

Noetzel, T. (1999) *Authentizität als politisches Problem. Ein Beitrag zur Theoriegeschichte der Legitimation politischer Herrschaft in der Moderne* (Berlin: Akademie Verlag).

Nullmeier, F. (2005) 'Nachwort', in M. Edelman (2005), *Politik als Ritual. Die Symbolische Funktion staatlicher Institutionen und politischen Handelns*, 3rd edn, pp. 199–219 (Frankfurt: Campus).

Offe, C. (1976/2005) 'Vorwort zur Erstausgabe', in M. Edelman (2005), *Politik als Ritual. Die Symbolische Funktion staatlicher Institutionen und politischen Handelns*, 3rd edn, pp. vii–x (Frankfurt: Campus).

Pross, H. (1992) *Protestgesellschaft. Von der Wirksamkeit des Widerspruchs* (Munich: Artemis & Winkler).

Sarcinelli, U. (1987) *Symbolische Politik. Zur Bedeutung symbolischen Handelns in der Wahlkampfkommunikation in der Bundesrepublik Deutschland* (Opladen: Westdeutscher Verlag).

Sarcinelli, U. (1989a) 'Symbolische Politik und politische Kultur: das Kommunikationsritual als politische Wirklichkeit', *Politische Vierteljahresschrift* 1989(2): 292–309.

Sarcinelli, U. (1989b) 'Überlegungen zur Kommunikationskultur: symbolische Politik und politische Kommunikation', in W. Mahle (ed.), *Medienangebot und Mediennutzung: Entwicklungstendenzen im entstehenden dualen Rundfunksystem*, pp. 129–44 (Berlin: Spiess Volker).

Sarcinelli, U. (1998) 'Politikvermittlung und Demokratie: zum Wandel der politischen Kommunikationskultur', in U. Sarcinelli, *Politikvermittlung und Demokratie in der Mediengesellschaft. Beiträge zur politischen Kommunikationskultur*, pp. 11–23 (Opladen: Verlag für Sozialwissenschaften).

Sartor, R. (2000) *Symbolische Politik. Eine Neubewertung aus prozess- und rezeptionsorientierter Perspektive* (Wiesbaden: DUV).

Thatcher, M. & Stone Sweet, A. (2002) 'Theory and practice of delegation to non-majoritarian institutions', *West European Politics* 25(1): 1–22.

Symbolic Environmental Legislation and Societal Self-Deception

JENS NEWIG

ABSTRACT *The primarily symbolic quality of many environmental laws is widely held responsible for the fact that despite all eco-political achievements many major environmental problems still remain unresolved. This contribution works towards a clear conceptual distinction between symbolic and non-symbolic environmental legislation; it investigates different levels of effectiveness of symbolic legislation, tries to establish a series of external factors which are conducive to the production of primarily symbolic laws, and argues that such legislation must not simply be understood as wilfully deceiving the citizenry, but can also be read as reflecting a certain readiness of citizens to let them be deceived. Thus, the incidence of symbolic legislation may point towards practices of societal self-deception. The German Summer Smog Act 1995 and the Ordinance on Large Combustion Plants 1983 are analysed and compared as paradigmatic examples of symbolic and non-symbolic environmental legislation and as empirical cases for the study of the questions that have just been outlined.*

Introduction

In recent decades the protection of the environment and the sustainable use of natural resources have become an established field of public policy and legislation in modern societies worldwide. While this has brought about an increased professionalisation of environmental policy making, modern societies have also seen a decline in public interest in and support for environmental matters.[1] This has led observers to proclaim the 'era of post-ecologism' (Blühdorn, 2000) or even the 'death of environmentalism' (Shellenberger & Nordhaus, 2004). Although considerable progress has been made in improving environmental quality, there are numerous problems which environmental policy has largely failed to resolve.[2] In this context symbolic

Symbolic Environmental Legislation and Societal Self-deception   93

environmental legislation plays an important role. The term refers to laws which despite their often ambitious officially declared objectives are designed to remain ecologically ineffective. Considered at the societal macro-level, such inconsistencies can be viewed as a societal self-deception and an instrument for *managing* rather than *resolving* environmental problems (Blühdorn, this volume). At the micro-level of societal actors, however, such symbolic legislation represents either a deception of the public by politicians, or a self-deception of individuals who are psychologically divided between supporting meaningful environmental policies and worrying about the costs which such policies might entail (Davidson, 1985; Lazar, 1999; Hansjürgens, 2000).

Symbolic legislation is predominantly perceived as *failing* legislation and as a problem to modern societies.[3] Accordingly, the literature labels it a 'pathology' (Dwyer, 1990), law that deceives the public (Campbell, 1993), legislation 'with little substance' (Burnett, 1998) as opposed to 'serious', 'functional' (Dwyer, 1990), 'substantive', 'strong' or 'significant' (Witteveen, 1999) legislation. Laws that tackle problems in a merely symbolic way, despite the legislative possibility of more effective measures, remain both legally and substantively ineffective and costly to the public purse, not least because of the parliamentary time they absorb. Beyond this, the futile attempts to implement such laws waste the resources of enforcement agencies. Such legislation infringes upon the rule of law in that it violates the principle of proportionality that demands statutes to be appropriate for their declared purpose (Lübbe-Wolff, 2000). Agencies which are unable to take the statute's wording literally are left with the choice of either delaying implementation or 'rewriting' the statute in a more suitable form (Dwyer, 1990). In the case of lawsuits, courts of justice are in the paradoxical situation of having to interpret laws which had never been intended to genuinely fulfil the purpose which they supposedly pursue. Furthermore, symbolic legislation, being untrustworthy, unreliable and deceitful, may contaminate the population's sense of justice (Kindermann, 1988) with long-term negative effects. Finally, such legislation may obstruct more effective policy: once a societal problem appears to have been tackled by symbolic legislation, the effort to deal with it in a substantive way will be considerably less intense, often leaving the problem at issue largely unresolved.

The phenomenon of symbolic legislation was described three decades ago and has never gone out of date.[4] However, research on the topic has remained limited, and a number of key questions have so far been left unanswered.

- In much of the existing literature the phenomenon of symbolic legislation has been either underemphasised or overemphasised. Whilst the classical policy-cycle model, assuming a 'rational' law-making process, has failed to recognise hidden agendas embedded in the strategic behaviour of politicians and symbolic actions, analyses in the critical tradition of the symbolic politics approach (e.g. Arnold, 1962) regard virtually all politics and legislation as primarily symbolic.[5] Both views fail to acknowledge that not all legislation is merely symbolic and that even in the prototypical field

94 The Politics of Unsustainability

of environmental policy important improvements have been achieved by means of substantively effective laws.

- While much of the literature criticises symbolic legislation for its ineffectiveness, some scholars (e.g. Voß, 1989) have highlighted that such legislation does indeed have certain effects. However, the relationship of symbolic legislation to the issue of effectiveness still needs to be clarified.
- The specific conditions, mechanisms and factors that are conducive to the passing of symbolic rather than non-symbolic legislation remain unclear.
- The existing literature has interpreted symbolic legislation primarily as the deception of citizens by the law makers. Yet the issue of societal self-deception has hardly been considered.

To address these deficits of the existing literature on symbolic legislation is the objective of this contribution. The analysis will proceed as follows. In the second section I propose a concept of symbolic in contrast to non-symbolic legislation. Although it may seem counter-intuitive, I will argue that all legislation is symbolic (to a certain extent), and that almost all symbolic laws are also effective (at least in a political sense). In the third section, I will argue that the symbolic or non-symbolic nature of a piece of legislation is to a significant extent determined by the context of its production. I will develop a hypothesis-based model that identifies key factors which constitute favourable conditions for the production of symbolic legislation. In this exercise, public choice theory serves as a conceptual point of departure. The fourth and fifth sections present empirical case studies taken from German environmental legislation. Two contrasting cases have been selected in order to exemplify different constellations of symbolic and non-symbolic legislation: the federal German *Ozongesetz* (Summer Smog Act) as a paradigmatic example of symbolic 'alibi' legislation, and the federal German *Großfeuerungsanlagen-Verordnung* (Ordinance on Large Combustion Plants) as a prototype of non-symbolic, 'successful' environmental legislation. The two cases serve to illustrate the effectiveness and ineffectiveness of (symbolic) legislation, the law maker's clear intentions, the relevant mechanisms involved and the issue of deception and self-deception. The sixth section is devoted to conclusions about the role of deception and (societal) self-deception in symbolic legislation.

Two Dimensions of (In-)effectiveness: The Concept of Symbolic Legislation

The study of symbolic legislation stands in the tradition of research on the impact, implementation, effectiveness and ineffectiveness of law (e.g. Friedman, 1975). The underlying assumption is that pieces of legislation are a means to guide, regulate and control society in a desired fashion (see Cotterrell, 1992). This applies to environmental law in particular, as many environmental statutes set out with an explication of their desired impact. Symbolic legislation deliberately fails to meet its declared objectives. Yet not every apparently 'ineffective' law may be described as symbolic legislation in the sense of this

Symbolic Environmental Legislation and Societal Self-deception 95

contribution (Cotterrell, 1992). Many laws that *ex post* turn out to be 'ineffective' were enacted with the best of intentions. Symbolic legislation, in contrast, is passed by the legislature against the better knowledge of its creators (Noll, 1981; Kindermann, 1988; Dwyer, 1990). This implies that the notion of symbolic legislation is one of an *ex ante perspective*, taking into account what the responsible actors knew, intended and could have known (Blankenburg, 1977; Voß, 1989).

On the other hand, symbolic legislation is in fact often 'effective', and deliberately so, in a different sense. Normally its initiators are 'by no means lacking any concrete intention to affect society – indeed in the case of symbolic legislation this intention is most often particularly pronounced' (Kindermann, 1988: 223ff.). Conversely, non-symbolic legislation commonly has 'symbolic' qualities. This apparent paradox can be resolved by separately considering an *issue-related substantive* and a *political-strategic* dimension of legislation.[6] The former refers to a manifest, explicit end which the legislative act serves as a means. This end is in the first place *legal effectiveness*, but ultimately to change certain real-world (e.g. ecological) conditions. The political-strategic dimension in contrast concerns different, less obvious, but nonetheless equally significant intentions that aim at purely political effects. For instance, the legislators may wish to effectively remove a topical but contentious issue from the public agenda or simply to boost their popularity. The act of passing a law may release the legislature from political pressure, demonstrate political resolve, meet the emotional needs of the population or serve various other goals without, however, producing any legal consequences and thus without improving societal conditions in the sense of the law's declared objectives.

By regarding the issue-related substantive and political-strategic dimensions of legislation separately, the phenomenon of symbolic legislation may be clearly distinguished from different types of non-symbolic legislation. Accordingly, any piece of legislation may, in terms of its symbolic content, be characterised as a two-dimensional phenomenon. Any statute may be attributed a certain degree of prospective issue-related substantive effectiveness as well as a degree of prospective political-strategic effectiveness. As is illustrated in Figure 1, one may distinguish four different prototypes of legislation.

(1) Some regulatory acts are expected to be legally and substantively effective but are not passed with any significant political-strategic intentions. Examples include the German atomic energy law or the specification of duties of plant operators in the law on environmental protection against noxious intrusions. Rules of this type are designed to serve a smooth coexistence: statutes that 'do the job'; the 'workhorses of the law'.

(2) A rather rare type of statute are those that are neither intended to have any major legal or substantive effect nor pursue political-strategic ends but which are, instead, enacted primarily for formal purposes. This is 'legislation for the files'. One example is the federal German Titanium Dioxide Ordinance that specifies certain threshold values which were

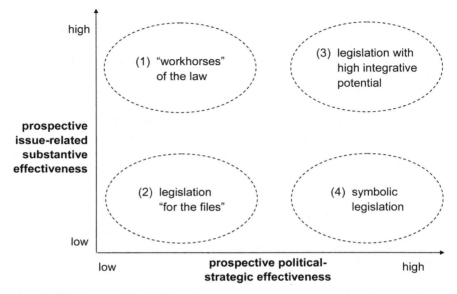

Figure 1. Prototypes of legislation

already being observed by industry and which only served the purpose of implementing European Union law in a legally valid way by replacing an existing administrative rule (Newig, 2003).

(3) In yet other cases, the legislature pursues both issue-related substantive and political-strategic goals. Such statutes are expected to effectively control societal matters of high public interest. In order to capture the diversity of their goals, we may call this type of law 'legislation with high integrative potential'. A paradigmatic example is the Ordinance on Large Combustion Plants, which is examined below-in some detail.

(4) Symbolic legislation, finally, encompasses those pieces of legislation which are not intended and expected to be legally and substantively effective but which are enacted with certain political-strategic intentions, as in the case of the *Ozongesetz* (federal German Summer Smog Act).

Symbolic legislation can thus be defined as a form of legislation with a low-prospective issue-related effectiveness and a high prospective political-strategic effectiveness. Both forms of effectiveness are graduated categories. Hence, symbolic legislation is also a graduated term, i.e. legislation may be more or less 'symbolic'. In order to measure the degree to which a piece of legislation is symbolic, indicators are required for both dimensions. Prospective *issue-related substantive effectiveness* is measured first and foremost in terms of:

- substantive suitability: the extent to which the substantive requirements specified by the law are suited to attain the objectives of the law;

Symbolic Environmental Legislation and Societal Self-deception 97

- enforceability: the legal provisions that entitle the implementing authorities to control compliance and to sanction non-compliance (Cotterrell, 1992; Lübbe-Wolff, 2000);
- recognition of framework parameters: factors regarding the broader context surrounding the law's implementation. These may include, for example, the availability of the resources required by the implementing administration (Lübbe-Wolff, 2000), or the structural ability and disposition of the addressees to comply with the law.

Criteria for the prospective *political-strategic effectiveness* measure whether and to what extent a law is suited to release the legislators from political pressure and to enhance their political acceptance. They include:

- severity of legal consequences in the case of non-compliance: apparently tough penalties demonstrate resolve to take effective action (Kindermann, 1988);
- position in the hierarchy of law: the 'significance' the legislature attributes to a legal rule by enacting it as a parliamentary statute (or even as an amendment to the constitution) rather than as an administrative regulation or ordinance;[7]
- timing: the passing of a law at a tactically 'right' point in time, e.g. shortly before elections or during the summer months when political actions tend to receive more public attention (see Newig (2004) on the relation of political action and public attention).

Alongside these 'objectively measurable' criteria, the 'subjective' criterion of *legislative intent* plays a key role in understanding the symbolic nature of statutes. This legislative intent can only be captured and assessed through personal interviews with the actors involved in the legislation process.

Explaining Symbolic Legislation: A Public Choice Approach

Public choice theory conveys a disenchanting view of politics and legislation.[8] It does away with any romantic or idealistic vision of law makers serving the public good. Quite the contrary: politicians, like all other rational, self-interested actors, are conceived of as pursuing their own private interests, which they seek to satisfy in practising their profession and which do not automatically coincide with the general interest (Buchanan & Tollison, 1984; Bernholz & Breyer, 1994). 'Parties formulate policies in order to win elections, rather than win elections in order to formulate policies' (Downs, 1957: 28). To this end, politicians (i.e. legislators and government officials) are primarily interested in maximising electoral gains and popularity ratings. Party ideology therefore plays a minor role; it is relevant only insofar as it is instrumental in attaining personal goals and objectives.

98   *The Politics of Unsustainability*

Public choice theory furthermore treats the members of the general public or electorate as broadly uniform and pursuing similar interests. Citizens are assumed to be interested primarily in maintaining or improving the quality of the environment which immediately surrounds them and which affects them substantively or emotionally, but they are keen to minimise their personal costs (Hansjürgens, 2000). In a representative democracy they seek to achieve their goals by voting for the political party which they believe best represents their personal interests. More specific interests are pursued by special interest groups, e.g. industrial or environmental organisations, or by citizens' initiatives, which engage in lobbying activities in order to influence legislation to promote their respective concerns (Tollison, 1997). Organised groups thus confront politicians as aggregated voter interests.

What can be deduced from these simple assumptions regarding symbolic legislation? Faced with a pressing issue on the political agenda – pursued by the media, by special interest groups or by competing political parties – politicians are expected to produce a political 'solution'. However, political and legislative acts normally entail costs which – once they have been recognised by large parts of the public – decrease the popularity of those politicians who are responsible. Therefore, effective legislative measures will only be enacted if their overall benefits are assumed to exceed their overall costs. If measures are demanded which are so costly that they are likely to negatively impact on the popularity of the respective politicians, the most logical choice would be to simply refrain from passing the piece of legislation. Yet this could put off the advocates of the political measures demanded, and legislators would therefore risk reducing their popularity and electoral support. In this dilemma, a merely symbolic 'solution' has, from the perspective of the politicians involved, the double advantage that it demonstrates that action is being taken whilst at the same time the costs any substantive solution would incur are avoided. These considerations lead to two hypotheses:

- *Hypothesis 1*: Symbolic legislation is more likely to occur in conditions of high political pressure (measured by the degree of public attention and the committedness of the actors involved). The higher the political pressure, the higher the likelihood of legislation displaying strong political-strategic features.
- *Hypothesis 2*: A socially relevant problem, for which at a given point of time there is either no appropriate solution or only one that entails short-term costs exceeding the short-term benefits, is likely to be dealt with through symbolic legislation. The greater the misfit between the costs and the benefits of a possible solution, the more likely the issue-related substantive qualities of a piece of legislature will be weakly developed.

The interest-group theory of government (Stigler, 1971; Peltzman, 1976; McCormick & Tollison, 1981; Becker, 1985), which is a particular strand of public choice theory, places much emphasis on the varying size and importance

Symbolic Environmental Legislation and Societal Self-deception 99

of societal interest groups (the general public with its interest in general public welfare being one of them) which are competing for the allocation of political goods. This strand, too, regards politicians as 'brokers' redistributing wealth in a society in such a manner that electoral gains are maximised. Yet, interest-group theorists point out that legislators will be inclined to ensure that larger and from their perspective more 'important' groups will gain more, while smaller and less important groups will lose transfers of political goods.

The general public in this view constitutes a large group that nonetheless has little specific importance to legislators. Given that the vote of each individual citizen will have virtually no measurable impact, citizens, as rational actors, are assumed to remain rather uninformed about political issues. To use Downs's expression (1957), they remain 'rationally ignorant'. Acquiring detailed knowledge about often complex and technical issues could lead to better informed voting decisions, but it would involve high information costs. Citizens are therefore faced with a typical principal–agent problem: by giving the law makers, i.e. their agents, the democratic mandate to act on their behalf, they not only delegate the need to be thoroughly informed and to make political decisions, but they also enable the political actors to act opportunistically, to misuse their information and possibly deceive voters to a certain extent (see Dwyer, 1990; Hansjürgens, 2000). Public choice theory therefore assumes that law makers tend to deliberately deceive citizens.

Further principal–agent interactions are assumed between the legislature and organised interest groups. Although politicians (government officials, in particular) accumulate considerable technical knowledge regarding the problems at issue, highly specialised industrial or environmental organisations are often even better informed about the particular matter that is supposed to be dealt with. Moreover, they can provide detailed knowledge of how their respective clientele would respond to certain pieces of projected legislation. This information can be of crucial importance to politicians. Therefore, politicians tend to collaborate with certain interest groups, introducing the danger of opportunistic behaviour on the part of the latter. Examples of this 'rent-seeking' behaviour (Tollison, 1997) include the supply of biased information, or collaboration solely in exchange for sufficient transfers such as, for example, less stringent emission standards.

This asymmetric distribution of information and unequal involvement of different actors opens the door to tactical measures by means of which politicians may seek to please a maximum number of voters whilst minimising the number who might be alienated by the projected policy. Given the asymmetric level of information, it may be rational for the legislature to enact purely symbolic laws whose foreseeable ineffectiveness in substantive terms will go largely unnoticed by the general public. In an ideal case scenario, the unorganised many do not realise that a substantially ineffective law is being passed, while the supposedly affected branches of industry will refrain from attacking government policy or even offer support. These considerations may be condensed into two further hypotheses:

100   *The Politics of Unsustainability*

- *Hypothesis 3*: The larger the societal conflict of interest among competing groups, the greater the probability of legislation of a symbolic nature.
- *Hypothesis 4*: In the case of conflicting interests, the legislature tends to satisfy the more 'important' interest groups in a substantive manner, whereas the less 'important' groups are satisfied merely symbolically.

Regarding information asymmetries as a driving factor for symbolic legislation implies that the problem to be addressed has to be so complex that the less informed social groups cannot fully grasp its implications and thus cannot detect any opportunistic behaviour on the part of the better informed. The distribution of information generally becomes more unequal as the complexity of the issue to be addressed increases. This is because the level of issue complexity determines the input that is required for comprehending and assessing the problem and its possible solutions. Thus, the more complex the problem at stake, the more special-interest groups can take advantage of their information surplus in the legislative process, and the more the general public – or other lesser informed groups – remain ignorant of legislation that addresses their respective interests in at best symbolic ways. If the media or the political opposition then discover and expose the deception, the politicians who have to take responsibility can still refer to the complexity of the issue, to unclear causal relations and similar factors which help them to deflect the blame (Newig, 2003). In summary:

- *Hypothesis 5*: The more complex and opaque a political issue is, the more likely is it to be addressed through symbolic legislation.

Symbolic Legislation in Practice: Two Case Studies from German Environmental Law

The empirical material on which the two case studies draw consists mainly of media reports, statements of interest groups and secondary literature. In order to explore the intentions of the law makers, guided interviews were conducted with those key politicians who were centrally involved in the deliberations preceding the legislative act. Between May 2000 and January 2001, 16 interviews were conducted lasting on average 80 minutes. Interviewees included members of parliament, the German Bundestag, as well as officials of the relevant ministries and of the German Environmental Agency (Umweltbundesamt; UBA).[9]

The Ozongesetz

The federal German *Ozongesetz* (Summer Smog Act) 1995 which was widely criticised in the media and in the legal literature as an 'alibi act', as 'symbolic politics' and as 'cobbled together' serves as a prime example of symbolic legislation. In the face of incidents of extreme summer smog in the late 1980s,[10]

Symbolic Environmental Legislation and Societal Self-deception   101

the health hazards of low-level ozone became a public issue in Germany. The debate was mainly forced by the oppositional Social Democratic Party (SPD) and the Greens (Die Grünen) as well as by some environmental groups, all of which favoured tough traffic restrictions as the most appropriate means to reduce ozone pollution. However, the federal government – a coalition of the Christian Conservative parties (CDU/CSU) and the Liberal Democrats (FDP) – first refused to recognise the ozone problem, and then clearly favoured technical long-term solutions over traffic restrictions. Moreover, the government counted on the delayed effects firstly of the *Großfeuerungsanlagen-Verordnung* 1983 which considerably reduced industrial NO_x emissions and, secondly, of the introduction of the catalytic converter for private motor cars in 1985. In 1993, when the ozone issue figured very prominently on the public agenda, some German *Länder* (federal states), governed by coalitions of the SPD and the Greens, started to enact state ordinances demanding temporary traffic restrictions in areas of high ozone concentrations. Given the questionable legal basis for these *Länder* specific rules, the respective states as well as the parliamentary opposition in the German Bundestag demanded a federal law in this matter. After public and political debate had become increasingly emotional, culminating in the confrontation of 'children's health' versus 'the liberty of motorists', the *Ozongesetz* was passed as a federal statute and entered into force in July 1995. It invalidated all existing state ordinances and was set to expire at the end of 1999.

The official legal purpose of the *Ozongesetz* was to 'prevent a further increase of peak levels of ozone by means of a ban on non-low-emission vehicles, and to lay the foundation for a further, enduring reduction in the basic load of ozone, which is primarily important' (*Bundestagsdrucksache* 13/ 1754: 4). Yet the ambitiousness of these objectives was not matched by the substantive measures specified by the statute. The law's main instrument, a general exercise ban on all non-low-emission cars, was considerably weakened firstly by the specified preconditions (ozone threshold value, spatial distribution of gauging stations, etc.) which would have to be fulfilled for the ban to kick in. These were restrictive to such an extent that they made the proclamation of a ban extremely improbable. Hence a 'further, enduring reduction' of ozone levels through the implementation of the *Ozongesetz* was logically impossible. Secondly, the law specified numerous exceptions from the ban (public transport, commuters, even tourists) which rendered it effectively impossible to even prevent a 'further increase' in ozone concentrations, let alone achieve a reduction. Hence, the law's substantive suitability was close to zero. Furthermore, it was well known that such a law would be most unlikely to be effective because previous experience with state summer smog ordinances had provided evidence that traffic restrictions were in fact massively violated. The interviews conducted with the politicians responsible reveal that they were well aware of this. They frankly admitted that they had not seen any substantive need for the law they had enacted. Indeed, the vast majority of the interviewees had not only been aware that

102 The Politics of Unsustainability

the law would most probably have no substantive effect, but they explicitly did not want it to be effective.

Instead, the prospective *political-strategic* effectiveness of the *Ozongesetz* was all the higher. Uncompromising political resolve was demonstrated by the seemingly 'radical' measure of banning individual automobility (while the numerous exceptions to the ban remained less clearly visible). Moreover, the *Ozongesetz* was enacted as a parliamentary statute (rather than as an ordinance, which is usual in Germany for such specific environmental regulations), and was thereby granted a high position in the hierarchy of law, which was justified by the 'eminent political character' of the summer smog issue (*Bundestagsdrucksache* 13/1524: 10). Finally, the timing of the law's enactment in mid-summer, when public attention towards the summer smog issue was at its highest, was politically well chosen. Accordingly, the interviewees regarded the *Ozongesetz* as a 'typical law made to pacify the public and not to do anything reasonable' (interview with a member of the coalition government, 17 January 2001).[11] Given the enormous 'emotional potential' of the issue and that politicians 'were incapable of dealing with the political pressure' (interview at the Ministry of Economics, 25 May 2000), the law was supposed to 'relieve the political pressure without changing the material situation' (interview at the Ministry of the Environment, 6 July 2000). Hence, the *Ozongesetz* was seen as a 'purely symbolic statute with a certain alibi function' (interview with a coalition member, 25 May 2000).

Not very surprisingly, the *Ozongesetz* in fact showed virtually no substantive effects. On one single day, a traffic ban was applied, causing no significant traffic reduction and hence no measurable reduction of ozone levels (BMU, 1999). However, the *Ozongesetz* showed effects in a political sense. As illustrated in Figure 2, public attention, which had increased steadily until 1995, dropped abruptly after the law's enactment. Evidently, the federal government succeeded in removing the summer smog issue from the public agenda by passing the *Ozongesetz*.[12] The problem of low-level ozone was thus effectively *managed* – but by no means *resolved*.

The Großfeuerungsanlagen-Verordnung

The Ordinance on Large Combustion Plants (*Großfeuerungsanlagen-Verordnung*) 1983 is often referred to as a highly effective and substantive environmental law (e.g. Mez, 1995). It is therefore a perfect example of non-symbolic legislation. By the late 1960s it had become internationally recognised that the policy of high chimney stacks, though it improved local air quality, led to long-distance transport of acid exhaust gases (mainly SO_2 and NO_x). These emissions caused damage to sensitive ecosystems, with Scandinavian lakes being the first visible victims of the 'acid rain' phenomenon. While advisors to the German government had highlighted this issue at an early stage (Rat von Sachverständigen für Umweltfragen (SRU), 1974), ministers persistently failed to react. It was only after the news media had taken up the issue with cover

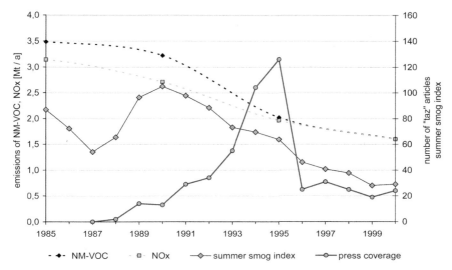

Figure 2. Summer smog and press coverage[13]

stories such as 'Acid rain in Germany: the forest dies' (*Der Spiegel*, 16 November 1981) that the issue leapt to the top of the public agenda and then remained there for a number of years. Forests being a particularly important 'national symbol' for Germans (Boehmer-Christiansen, 1998), the issue became a focal point of social movement activism. The federal government, at the time an SPD/FDP coalition, responded swiftly targeting the polluting emissions of large combustion plants. They could draw on earlier drafts of an ordinance that had been put on hold due to conflicts of opinion in the relevant ministries (Menke-Glückert, 1985). Despite heavy protests from the electricity industry, the *Großfeuerungsanlagen-Verordnung* was passed in February 1983, shortly before the early Bundestag elections which were held in March.[14]

The substantive goal of the *Großfeuerungsanlagen-Verordnung* was crystal-clear: as the then new chancellor Helmut Kohl stated:

> ... the German forest is in danger ... According to the estimation of experts, air pollution by SO_2 is the most significant threat. Large combustion plants are the main producers of air pollution by SO_2 ... This air pollution will decrease significantly as soon as the new ordinance on large combustion plants comes into effect. (Bundesregierung, 1983: 197)

The ordinance's officially declared objective was to 'drastically reduce these high total emissions of SO_2, NO_x ... by measures at the source' (*Bundestagsdrucksache* 95/83: 35–6).

In fact, the *Großfeuerungsanlagen-Verordnung* was in terms of its substantive elements well suited to achieve these ambitious goals. It stipulates stringent

104   *The Politics of Unsustainability*

threshold values for a number of air pollutants which were applicable to both new and existing power stations, implying that old stations had to be retrofitted with new exhaust gas filters within a tight time frame. The ordinance specified clear obligations for plant operators which could easily be monitored by the relevant authorities. Hence enforceability was outstanding, and further reinforced by the fact that non-compliance attracted serious fines. Furthermore, the total number of coal power stations, 90% of which were at the time owned by a handful of public utilities, was relatively small and easy to oversee by public authorities, which provided favourable framework conditions for the law to unfold substantive effectiveness. Interviews with politicians provided clear evidence of the expectation to 'achieve an immense breakthrough in the total air quality situation' (interview at the Ministry of the Interior, 22 December 2000).

Yet despite all this, the *Großfeuerungsanlagen-Verordnung* also had an important political-strategic dimension:

> No other instrument of air quality control has ever heated people's tempers so much, and has received such a degree of attention both in the media and from citizens as this piece of legislation has. This accounts for the high political importance of this ordinance as a means to combat air pollution and forest damage. (Kuhnt, 1983: 568)

Having realised its immense strategic potential, both the outgoing Social Democratic–Liberal government and its Conservative–Liberal successor used the ordinance as an instrument in the struggle for their respective political existence and particularly to capture votes from the newly emerged Green Party (Mez, 1995).

Overall the *Großfeuerungsanlagen-Verordnung* displayed a high level of both prospective substantive effectiveness and political-strategic effectiveness. It can therefore be classified as non-symbolic legislation with a high integrative potential. In fact, the emission reductions achieved by the ordinance exceeded all expectations. When in 1993 the public utilities had completed the retrofitting of their power plants, annual SO_2 emissions from West German public power stations were 90% below the level of 1982, and NO_x had been reduced by 75% (BMU, 1993) (see Figure 3). Moreover, the ordinance constituted a huge political success for the Conservative–Liberal government that even a decade later was still often highlighted.

Lessons from the Cases: Theory, Evidence (and Beyond)

On the basis of the two-dimensional scheme proposed above (in the second section) the two contrasting cases which have been analysed can be categorised as clearly distinct types of legislation. In Figure 1, the *Ozongesetz* qualifies as prototypical symbolic legislation in the lower right hand corner, while the *Großfeuerungsanlagen-Verordnung*, as a law that was highly effective in

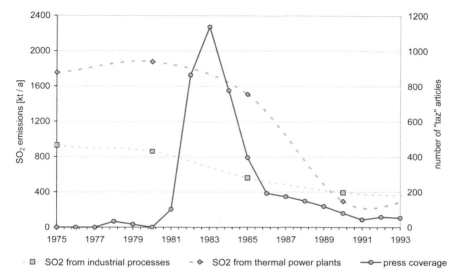

Figure 3. SO_2 emissions and press coverage of *Waldsterben*[15]

substantive terms and at the same time had significant 'integrative potential', would clearly have to be placed in the upper half of the diagram somewhere between the middle and the right hand side. Clearly both pieces of legislation display exceptional qualities and cannot be regarded as representative of standard law making. Indeed most other instances of environmental legislation will be positioned somewhere between these fairly clear-cut cases.[16] But for exactly this reason these two case studies are highly suitable to illustrate the way in which different external factors determine to what extent a piece of legislation is symbolic.

What then can be learnt about the factors that favour symbolic legislation? A comparative analysis shows that evidence from the cases confirms almost all the hypotheses formulated in the third section. *Political pressure* (hypothesis 1) was considerable in both cases. While in the *Ozongesetz* case it was mostly environmental interest groups and certain *Länder* governments which threatened to enact further state ordinances, the *Großfeuerungsanlagen-Verordnung* was backed by large public support whipped up by the *Waldsterben* issue. In both cases, legislation was enacted when public attention was highest (Figures 2 and 3). The subsequent decline of attention, which was particularly abrupt after the enactment of the *Ozongesetz*, provides evidence of the law's political-strategic effectiveness.

The relation of *costs and benefits* (hypothesis 2) clearly allows us to discriminate between symbolic and non-symbolic legislation: whereas the summer smog issue was a 'non-resolvable' problem that could at best be *managed* by means of a symbolic 'solution', it was comparatively easy to reduce

106 *The Politics of Unsustainability*

the industrial emissions which were held responsible for the damage to the forest. The ready availability of a technical fix allowed for a highly substantive regulation. A substantively effective *Ozongesetz*, in contrast, would have entailed massive traffic bans lasting for several weeks each summer (UBA, 1995), which would hardly have been accepted by the public. Moreover, the time-delayed effects of earlier policy measures were expected to soon cause a significant improvement in the summer smog situation (UBA, 2000). For the *Ozongesetz* the cost–benefit ratio was, therefore, highly unfavourable. For the *Großfeuerungsanlagen-Verordnung*, in contrast, it was not only much more straightforward to estimate the costs that would be incurred for retrofitting power plants with flue gas filters (approximately €1.5 billion per year), but these costs were also clearly below the estimated savings expected from an improved air quality (€1.5 billion–4 billion per year).

Measured by the two case studies above, the factor that is most revealing about the genesis of the different types of legislation is the difference in the respective *conflicts of interest* and *power constellations* (hypotheses 3 and 4). In the *Großfeuerungsanlagen-Verordnung* case, electricity suppliers were overtly against any strict measures. However, as they could pass the costs to their customers (who were largely unaware of the reasons for the considerable rise in their electricity bills), they changed their attitude after the ordinance had been passed and presented themselves as forerunners in environmental technology. Thus their opposition towards the ordinance was perhaps less fundamental than their initial rhetoric against the regulation had suggested. Moreover, the powerful coalition of *Großfeuerungsanlagen-Verordnung* proponents (forestry, environmental groups, the broad public, etc.) was supported by the manufacturers of flue gas filters, whereas the electricity industry, which has to guarantee the provision of electricity, could not realistically threaten to relocate their production sites (power plants), as is common practice in many other business sectors. Anyway, the summer smog conflict was not only about economic interests, but primarily about fundamental values: the health of children and the liberty of the motorist. This conflict materialised only partially as a conflict between different societal interest groups – environmentalists against the car industry and the motoring lobby – but also on the level of individual citizens.[17] Various surveys and polls indicated that about two-thirds of the public supported traffic restrictions in order to combat summer smog.[18] Yet very few people actually observed the occasional speed limits that were proclaimed in accordance with the *Länder* summer smog ordinances (Newig, 2003). This leads to an observation that points beyond both the frame of public choice theory and the scope of the original hypotheses: by symbolically integrating incompatible interests held by the same individual, the *Ozongesetz* successfully attended to a psychological division *within* rather than *between* individuals. It thus displays qualities of a tool of individual as well as societal self-deception.

The criterion of *issue complexity* (hypothesis 5) again constitutes a good measure accounting for the genesis of symbolic or non-symbolic legislation.

Symbolic Environmental Legislation and Societal Self-deception   107

Although scientists were keen to stress the complexity of the causes of acid rain and forest damage, the *Großfeuerungsanlagen-Verordnung* issue was publicly framed in a straightforward manner, with acid emissions from large coal power plants soon being widely regarded as the primary cause of *Waldsterben* and the obvious target for legislative regulation. In comparison to this, the summer smog issue appeared much more complex, firstly because local pollution levels were highly variable and unpredictable, secondly because several factors (e.g. weather conditions, precursor emission, non-linear effects) were poorly understood and made the effects of traffic restrictions very difficult to gauge, and thirdly because there was considerable scientific uncertainty about appropriate threshold values and the effects of low-level ozone on human health.

Symbolic Legislation, Deception and (Societal) Self-deception

The objective of this analysis has been to shed light on symbolic legislation as a means to *manage* rather than *resolve* environmental problems. It has been demonstrated that symbolic legislation may be very effective in achieving political-strategic goals such as removing 'hot' issues from the public agenda, whilst being very ineffective in terms of a substantive solution for the respective issues at stake. In order to take account of the fact that not all legislation is symbolic, I have employed a two-dimensional model of legislation on the basis of which symbolic legislation (such as the *Ozongesetz*) and non-symbolic legislation (such as the *Großfeuerungsanlagenverordnung*) could be clearly distinguished. In addition to conceptualising and illustrating the difference between the two, the main task of this contribution has been to investigate the *mechanisms* and *conditions* that favour the production of symbolic rather than non-symbolic legislation. On the basis of public choice theory, largely supported by the two contrasting empirical cases, it was identified that the following factors – a high level of public attention, high regulatory costs *vis-à-vis* low regulatory benefits, acute and value-laden conflict constellations, an asymmetrical distribution of information and a high level of issue complexity – all provide favourable conditions for symbolic legislation. The factor of issue complexity is particularly noteworthy, for an intricate maze of interdependent causal relationships seems symptomatic of many current environmental and sustainability problems (Voß *et al.*, 2007). It should, however, be pointed out that the analysis presented here only relates to the ways in which symbolic legislation *works*. There are no implicit assumptions or statements about the frequency or quantitative development of symbolic legislation. Such judgements are clearly beyond the scope of this contribution.

A central element in the concept of symbolic legislation is deception. Studies on symbolic politics and legislation have – critically – focused on the ways in which political and economic elites (mis)use their superiority to manipulate the general public or the electorate (see Blühdorn, this volume). Such concerns are also at the heart of public choice theory, which is therefore a particularly

108   *The Politics of Unsustainability*

suitable framework for describing and explaining the phenomenon of symbolic legislation. The interviews conducted for the *Ozongesetz* case study have indeed shown that law makers evidently intended to and were able to deceive the public in the face of a highly complex regulatory issue.

However, the *Ozongesetz* case has also revealed a different kind of deception. Clearly, the majority of citizens supported – or at least claimed to support – strict traffic restrictions in cases of severe summer smog for the sake of health protection. Yet, temporary speed limits were essentially not observed. This apparently irrational behaviour suggests that citizens are psychologically divided and manage this internal split by strategies of *self-deception* (Davidson, 1985; Ames & Dissanayake, 1996; Lazar, 1999; Hansjürgens, 2000). This 'paradox' occurs when an individual persuades herself that a certain fact is true while maintaining her original belief that the opposite is true (Pears, 1985). While some authors understand this as a genuine 'irrationality' (e.g. Lazar, 1999), others have interpreted self-deception as an intentional strategy (Davidson, 1985; Pears, 1985; also see Blühdorn, this volume), which is then basically compatible with the public choice approach.

Be it 'rational' or not – if a considerable part of society (or even its majority) is found in this state of self-deception, we may arguably speak of *societal self-deception*. As LaFleur (1996) has diagnosed in the case of Japan during World War II, whole societies can be in a 'state of self-deception' which is 'more than merely a top-down manipulation of the populace through deception and misinformation' but 'rather...something in the societal structure or in the national psychology...That is, the pattern of deception from above seemed to be complemented by a "national personality" given to collective self-deception' (LaFleur, 1996: 264). The 'pathology' of symbolic legislation (Dwyer, 1990) may thus be an expression of a societal state of 'schizophrenia' that develops under particular societal circumstances. While for Japan incomplete modernisation – a disparity between its technological development and the 'retarded condition of its social and political institutions' (LaFleur, 1996: 264) – was identified as the root cause of the problem, Blühdorn (this volume), drawing on Baudrillard, makes out a 'late-modern dilemma' that gives rise to seemingly schizophrenic forms of behaviour. Interpreted along these lines, the *Ozongesetz* could be said to reflect the divided interests of the public which could only be symbolically reconciled, with the phenomenon of societal self-deception being a key ingredient of the contemporary 'politics of unsustainability'.

Notes

1. In Germany, for example, the percentage of people naming 'environmental protection' as one of the most important national problems declined from 65% in 1988 to 18% in 2004 (Kuckartz & Rheingans-Heintze, 2004).
2. While the quality of air and inland waters has improved considerably since the early 1980s, there has been very limited success in areas such as noise reduction or energy policy (including global climate change) (Rat von Sachverständigen für Umweltfragen (SRU), 2004).

Symbolic Environmental Legislation and Societal Self-deception   109

3. Some authors have noted that there are varieties of symbolic legislation which are socially desirable, for example because of their integrative and stabilising effect on society, or because they contribute to meeting the population's emotional needs (Noll, 1981; Voß, 1989; Wenger, 2003). Symbolic legislation may also appeal to the population's morale (Henderson & Pearson, 1978) and cause changes in public attitudes (Friedman, 1975). However, such 'declaratory' (Noll, 1981) and 'aspirational' (Henderson & Pearson, 1978) legislation differs from the kind of laws which are the object of this study in that it *a priori* dispenses with legal obligations and does not purport to be effective in a substantive sense. It does not involve any form of deception or self-deception and will not be further discussed in this piece.

4. There is only a small number of conceptual analyses most of which can be found in the German and Swiss literature. Many of them draw, explicitly or at least implicitly, on the more general idea of symbolic politics as developed in the early publications by the American scholars Arnold (1962), Gusfield (1963) and Edelman (1962, 1971).

5. Edelman (1962) argues in a very similar spirit. Even the more recent conceptual contributions (Dwyer, 1990; Hansjürgens, 2000) imply a *general tendency* towards symbolic politics and legislation.

6. The pertinent literature refers to 'instrumental' and 'symbolic' dimensions of legislation (Gusfield, 1963; Carson, 1974; Kindermann, 1988; Dwyer, 1990). Although this distinction is crucial to the understanding of symbolic legislation, the terminology is somewhat misleading for, assuming strategic behaviour on the part of the legislator(s), 'symbolic' purposes are equally instrumental in achieving certain political goals (see Edelman, 1962, 1971). Since the term 'instrumental' thus does not serve to distinguish both dimensions, it should be avoided altogether.

7. Due to the country's federal system, the German legal hierarchy is somewhat complex. Generally, federal law is considered to be of higher standing than that of the federal states (*Länder*). Constitutional law is superior to statutes, ordinances and administrative rules (in that order). Complexity is further increased by European Union law, which shall not be addressed here.

8. Public choice theory is an application of rational choice theory to political decision-making processes. As such it resorts to the basic conjectures of methodological individualism (i.e. societal macro-phenomena are explained by the characteristics and interactions of individual actors) and the rational actor paradigm ('Homo oeconomicus') assuming that actors weigh the costs and benefits of alternative options and choose the one that best suits their own personal interests.

9. For further details of the interview process and analysis see Newig (2003).

10. Formed under high solar radiation with a time delay out of gaseous precursor substances – mainly non-methane volatile organic compounds (NM-VOCs) and nitrous oxides (NO_x) – ozone, the leading substances of 'summer smog', can cause lung damage, especially in sensitive persons such as children, and can also damage vegetation. Precursors are emitted mainly from the combustion of fossil fuels in industry and traffic, but also from organic solvents and varnish for NM-VOCs. Because of the particular physico-chemical properties of summer smog components, the seemingly paradoxical situation frequently occurs that the highest concentrations are measured in rural rather than in metropolitan areas.

11. All original citations are in German, translation by the author. For further details see Newig (2003).

12. The alternative hypothesis that in accordance with the logic of *issue attention cycles* public interest would soon have decreased even without the *Ozongesetz* seems implausible because public attention dropped very abruptly, whilst public attention dynamics in environmental issues normally show a much smoother decline (Newig, 2004).

13. To even out random fluctuations, a three-period moving average has been applied to the latter two time series. For sources and a detailed discussion of methodological issues see Newig (2003, 2004). The daily paper *die tageszeitung* was chosen for its early electronic full-text availability. Although this politically left-wing newspaper is not representative of German

110 The Politics of Unsustainability

public *opinion*, it is a reliable indicator of public *attention*. All other major German supraregional newspapers Frankfurter Allgemeine Zeitung (FAZ), Südddeutsche, Frankfurter Rundschace (FR) show the same pattern (Newig, 2003).

14. In the meantime the Social Democratic–Liberal coalition government had been replaced by a Conservative–Liberal coalition.
15. *Waldsterben/Großfeuerungsanlagenverordnung* – problem severity (total emissions of SO_2 from large combustion plants), and press coverage (numbers of articles in the German daily newspaper *Die Tageszeitung* regarding the issue of *Waldsterben/Großfeuerungsanlagenverordnung*). For sources and methodology see Newig (2003, 2004) with further references. For sources and a detailed discussion of methodological issues see Newig (2003, 2004).
16. The German Waste Avoidance, Recycling and Disposal Act (*Kreislaufwirtschafts- und Abfallgesetz*) 1994 is a third case that is analysed in Newig (2003). Whilst in substantive terms, this law was almost as ineffective as the *Ozongesetz*, it was still less 'symbolic' than the latter, not least because it had been enacted with good intentions and in the genuine belief that it would offer a substantive solution for the mounting waste problem.
17. The car industry was adamantly opposed to any temporary speed restrictions because it did not want to have a precedent for a general speed limit on German motorways.
18. According to an 'Emnid' poll, 72% of the population supported a general traffic ban in metropolitan areas once certain ozone limit values were reached; only 22% opposed this (*Der Spiegel*, 10 May 1993: 14). Another poll by the public TV channel ZDF revealed that 69% of all German citizens supported general speed limits; 86% supported speed limits in times of summer smog; 70% supported a traffic ban in this case (*Die Tageszeitung*, 6 August 1994).

References

Ames, R. T. & Dissanayake, W. (eds.) (1996) *Self and Deception: A Cross-cultural Philosophical Enquiry* (Albany, NY: State University of New York Press).

Arnold, T. W. (1962) *The Symbols of Government* (New Haven, CT: Yale University Press) (original edition 1935).

Becker, G. S. (1985) 'Public policies, pressure groups, and dead weight costs', *Journal of Public Economics* 28: 275–399.

Bernholz, P. & Breyer, F. (1994) *Grundlagen der politischen Ökonomie. Band 2: Ökonomische Theorie der Politik* (Tübingen: Mohr).

Blankenburg, E. (1977) 'Über die Unwirksamkeit von Gesetzen', *Archiv für Rechts- und Sozialphilosophie* 1977: 31–56.

Blühdorn, I. (2000) *Post-ecologist Politics. Social Theory and the Abdication of the Ecologist Paradigm* (London: Routledge).

BMU—Bundesministrium für Umwelt, Naturschutz und Reaktorsicherheit (1993) 'Zehn Jahre Großfeuerungsanlagen-Verordnung. Großer Erfolg für die Luftreinhaltung in Deutschland', *Umwelt (BMU)* 1993(9): 354–55.

BMU—Bundesministrium für Umwelt, Naturschutz und Reaktorsicherheit (1999) 'Ozonsituation 1998 und 1999. Ozonbericht der Bundesregierung 1998; Kurzinformation zum bodennahen Ozon im Sommer 1999', *Umwelt (BMU)* 1999(12): 594–601.

Boehmer-Christiansen, S. (1998) 'Environment-friendly deindustrialisation: impacts of unification on East Germany', in A. Tickle & I. Welsh (eds.) *Environment and Society in Eastern Europe*, pp. 67–96 (Harlow: Longman).

Buchanan, J. M. & Tollison, R. D. (eds.), (1984) *The Theory of Public Choice* (Ann Arbor, MI: University of Michigan Press).

Bundesregierung (1983) 'Maßnahmen der Bundesregierung zum Schutz der Umwelt und der Wälder', *Bulletin des Presse- und Informationsamtes der Bundesregierung* 22: 197–99.

Burnett, M. L. (1998) 'The Pollution Prevention Act of 1990: a policy whose time has come or symbolic legislation?', *Environmental Management* 22(2): 213–24.

Campbell, R. M. (1993) 'Symbolic regulation: the case of third-party regulation of Canada Post', *Canadian Public Policy – Analyse de Politiques* 19(3): 325–39.

Symbolic Environmental Legislation and Societal Self-deception 111

Carson, W. G. (1974) 'Symbolic and instrumental dimensions of early factory legislation: a case study in the social origins of criminal law', in R. Hood (ed.), *Crime, Criminology and Public Policy: Essays in Honour of Sir Leon Radzinowicz*, pp. 107–38 (London: Heinemann Educational).

Cotterrell, R. (1992) *The Sociology of Law: An Introduction*, 2nd edn (London: Butterworths) (original edition 1984).

Davidson, D. (1985) 'Deception and division', in J. Elster (ed.), *The Multiple Self*, pp. 79–92 (Cambridge: Cambridge University Press).

Downs, A. (1957) *An Economic Theory of Democracy* (New York: Harper & Row).

Dwyer, J. P. (1990) 'The pathology of symbolic legislation', *Ecology Law Quarterly* 17: 233–316.

Edelman, M. (1962) *The Symbolic Uses of Politics* (Urbana, IL: University of Illinois Press).

Edelman, M. (1971) *Politics as Symbolic Action, Mass Arousal and Quiescence* (Chicago, IL: Markham).

Friedman, L. M. (1975) *The Legal System: A Social Science Perspective* (New York: Russell Sage Foundation).

Gusfield, J. R. (1963) *Symbolic Crusade* (Urbana, IL: University of Illinois Press).

Hansjürgens, B. (2000) 'Symbolische Umweltpolitik – eine Erklärung aus Sicht der neuen politischen Ökonomie', in B. Hansjürgens & G. Lübbe-Wolff (eds.), *Symbolische Umweltpolitik*, pp. 144–82 (Frankfurt: Suhrkamp).

Henderson, J. A. & Pearson, R. N. (1978) 'Implementing federal environmental policies: the limits of aspirational commands', *Columbia Law Review* 78: 1429–70.

Kindermann, H. (1988) 'Symbolische Gesetzgebung', *Jahrbuch für Rechtssoziologie und Rechtstheorie* 13: 222–45.

Kuckartz, U. & Rheingans-Heintze, A. (2004) *Umweltbewusstsein in Deutschland 2004* (Berlin: Bundesministerium für Umwelt, Naturschutz und Reaktorsicherheit).

Kuhnt, D. (1983) 'Die Verordnung über Großfeuerungsanlagen (13. BImSchV), Verfahrensgeschichte, Inhalte, Auswirkungen, Problematik', *Energiewirtschaftliche Tagesfragen*: 567–84.

LaFleur, W. R. (1996) 'A half-dressed emperor. Societal self-deception and recent "Japanokritik" in America', in R. T. Ames & W. Dissanayake (eds.), *Self and Deception: A Cross-cultural Philosophical Enquiry*, pp. 263–85 (Albany, NY: State University of New York Press).

Lazar, A. (1999) 'Deceiving oneself or self-deceived? On the formation of beliefs "under the influence"', *Mind* 108(430): 265–90.

Lübbe-Wolff, G. (2000) 'Erscheinungsformen symbolischen Umweltrechts', in B. Hansjürgens & G. Lübbe-Wolff (eds.), *Symbolische Umweltpolitik*, pp. 25–62 (Frankfurt: Suhrkamp).

McCormick, R. E. & Tollison, R. D. (1981) *Politicians, Legislations, and the Economy* (Boston, MA: Nijhoff).

Menke-Glückert, P. (1985) *Kommentar Großfeuerungsanlagenverordnung: Instrumentarium der Luftreinhaltepolitik* (Düsseldorf: Werner).

Mez, L. (1995) 'Reduction of exhaust gases at large combustion plants in the Federal Republic of Germany', in M. Jänicke & H. Weidner (eds.), *Successful Environmental Policy: A Critical Evaluation of 24 Cases*, pp. 173–86 (Berlin: Sigma).

Newig, J. (2003) *Symbolische Umweltgesetzgebung. Rechtssoziologische Untersuchungen am Beispiel des Ozongesetzes, des Kreislaufwirtschaft- und Abfallgesetzes sowie der Großfeuerungsanlagenverordnung.* Vol. 84, *Schriften zur Rechtssoziologie und Rechtstatsachenforschung* (Berlin: Duncker & Humblot).

Newig, J. (2004) 'Public attention, political action: the example of environmental regulation', *Rationality and Society* 16(2): 149–90.

Noll, P. (1981) 'Symbolische Gesetzgebung', *Zeitschrift für Schweizerisches Recht* 1981: 347–64.

Pears, D. (1985) 'The goals and strategies on self-deception', in J. Elster (ed.), *The Multiple Self*, pp. 59–78 (Cambridge: Cambridge University Press).

Peltzman, S. (1976) 'Toward a more general theory of regulation', *Journal of Law and Economics* 19: 211–40.

112 *The Politics of Unsustainability*

Shellenberger, M. & Nordhaus, T. (2004) 'The death of environmentalism. Global warming politics in a post-environmental world'. Available at: http://www.thebreakthrough.org/images/Death_of_Environmentalism.pdf (accessed 12 February 2006).

SRU (1974) *Umweltgutachten, BT-Drs 7/2802: Rat von Sachverständigen für Umweltfragen* (Stuttgart: Kohlhammer).

SRU (2004) *Umweltgutachten 2004: Umweltpolitische Handlungsfähigkeit sichern, Bd 1* (Baden-Baden: Nomos).

Stigler, G. J. (1971) 'The theory of economic regulation', *Bell Journal of Economics and Management Science* 2: 3–21.

Tollison, R. D. (1997) 'Rent seeking', in D. C. Mueller (ed.), *Perspectives on Public Choice: A Handbook*, pp. 506–25 (Cambridge: Cambridge University Press).

UBA. (1995) *Hintergrundinformation: Sommersmog* (Berlin: UBA).

UBA. (2000) *Daten zur Umwelt 2000*, CD-ROM (Berlin: UBA).

Voß, M. (1989) *Symbolische Gesetzgebung: Fragen zur Rationalität von Strafgesetzgebungsakten* (Ebelsbach: Gremer).

Voß, J.-P., Newig, J., Kastens, B., Monstadt, J. & Nölting, B. (2007) 'Steering for sustainable development – a typology of empirical contexts and theories based on ambivalence, uncertainty and distributed power', in J. Monstadt, J. Newig & J.-P. Voß (eds.), 'Governance for sustainable development: steering in contexts of ambivalence, uncertainty and distributed control', *Journal of Environmental Policy and Planning* 9(3/4) (in press).

Wenger, D. R. (2003) 'Symbolische Gesetzgebung oder die Tendenz zur Verrechtlichung des Nichtrechtlichen', *Zeitschrift für Schweizerisches Recht* 122(1): 215–46.

Witteveen, W. J. (1999) 'Significant, symbolic and symphonic laws', in H. van Schooten (ed.), *Semiotics and Legislation. Jurisprudential, Institutional and Sociological Perspectives*, pp. 27–70 (Liverpool: Charles).

Sustainable Development as Symbolic Commitment: Declaratory Politics and the Seductive Appeal of Ecological Modernisation in the European Union

SUSAN BAKER
Department of Environmental Social Sciences, University of Cardiff, UK

ABSTRACT *The European Union (EU) has declared itself to be committed to the goal of sustainable development. Ecological modernisation provides the framework within which it marries economic and environmental objectives. Yet, when judged against the authoritative Brundtland formulation of sustainable development, the strategy of ecological modernisation could be viewed as 'merely symbolic' politics. This contribution elaborates on the distinction between sustainable development and ecological modernisation and investigates why the EU continues to make declaratory commitment to the former, when it could make a more straightforward statement of allegiance to the latter. The analysis suggests that if 'symbolism' is understood as representation, the discourse on sustainable development can be seen as representing the EU in a particular way and thereby contributing to the construction of EU identity. Furthermore, it is argued that the EU's symbolic commitment to sustainable development is not simply an act of ecological deception, but bears important transformative potentials.*

Introduction

This contribution explores the symbolic dimensions of the European Union's (EU's) commitment to sustainable development, a commitment it holds alongside a strong loyalty to the promotion of economic growth. Ecological modernisation provides the framework within which the EU marries economic growth to its environmental protection policies. In this respect, the EU is no exception, because ecological modernisation has become the major discourse and strategy by which (western) industrialised countries frame and tackle their ecological problems (Blühdorn, 2001: 182).

When judged against the authoritative Brundtland formulation of sustainable development (World Commission on Environment and Development

114 *The Politics of Unsustainability*

(WCED), 1987), the strategy of ecological modernisation is not compatible with the commitment to the promotion of sustainable development. The Brundtland formulation is used because it commands authoritative status, acting as a guiding principle of economic and social development policy, particularly within the United Nations (Lafferty & Meadowcroft, 2000). In addition, the EU has declared itself to be guided by both the Brundtland formulation and its related United Nations Conference on Environment and Development (UNCED) process.

The adoption of the strategy of ecological modernisation allows the EU's commitment to sustainable development to be viewed as 'merely symbolic'. Here the symbolic is understood as empty rhetoric, as opposed to the adoption of a genuine and consequential policy approach committed to an effective eco-politics (see Blühdorn's typology of symbolic politics in this volume). Why then does the EU continue to make declaratory commitment to sustainable development, when it could simply make a more straightforward statement of allegiance to ecological modernisation? Answering this question exposes a more positive view of symbolic politics. By exploring 'symbolism' as representation, the discourse on sustainable development can be seen as having symbolic purpose: it is used to represent the EU in a particular way. This representation serves an important purpose, acting as a building block in the construction of EU identity. Through this, the EU presents a particular image of itself, both to its own constituents and to outsiders. Drawing upon Lefort, a functional unity is seen between the two approaches of the EU, one embedded in the declaratory commitment to sustainable development and other in the adoption of the strategy of ecological modernisation.

The contribution moves discussion beyond the argument that symbolic politics merely creates a sense of unity and community (see Blühdorn's discussion on type A symbolic politics in this volume) to a more positive view, one that points to the *enabling* function of symbols in politics. The final section turns to an examination of the use of symbolic discourse as a tool for social change. This opens up discussion on the *transformation* potential of the EU's discourse on sustainable development. This potential counters the argument that the adoption of the strategy of ecological modernisation marks the end of the transformational potential of environmentalism (Giorgi & Redclift, 2000).

This contribution begins by looking at ecological modernisation, both as a theory of social change and as a strategic agenda of ecological reform. The declaratory commitment made by the EU to sustainable development is examined, leading to an investigation of its ecological modernisation strategy. The relationship between ecological modernisation and the rationale for, and key developments within, the European integration processes are discussed. The objective is not to probe whether, and to what extent, the EU's ecological modernisation strategy has been successfully implemented. As a structure of multi-level governance, policy implementation in the EU takes place at the member state level. With this in mind, this contribution focuses only on the policy discourse as it is formulated at the EU level.

The Seductive Appeal of Ecological Modernisation in the European Union

Ecological Modernisation

Ecological modernisation is a theory of social change, exploring attempts in late industrial society to respond to the negative environmental consequences of modernity. Early literature argued that developments in advanced European economies since the 1980s have shown economic and environmental goals can be integrated within a framework of industrial modernity (Simonis, 1989; Jänicke, 1992; Weale, 1992; Hajer, 1995, 1996).

The theory also argued that capitalist liberal democracy has the institutional capacity to undertake further development (modernisation) to improve ecological outcomes. Second-generation literature thus turned to the socio-political process through which further modernisation can lead to, or block, beneficial ecological outcomes (Buttel, 2000: 59; see Mol, 1995, 1996; Mol & Spaargaren, 2000; Spaargaren, 2000; Spaargaren *et al.*, 2000). As attention focused on what can be achieved through ecological modernisation, the boundaries blurred between ecological modernisation as a theory of social change and as a normative proposition. Increasingly, ecological modernisation became a strategy of ecological reform, promoting the 'win–win' advantages of institutional and technological changes in response to the environmental crisis.

There is now a substantial body of literature on ecological modernisation and, as is so often the case in the social sciences, this has led to a widening and loosening of the theory's core concept and to a disparate collection of empirical approaches. There are also disputes over the sociological significance of findings, particularly in relation to other theories of social change, including those put forward by Beck (1997).

Despite these differences, however, it is generally accepted that there are four main themes at the core of the theory (Gouldson & Murphy, 1996: 13). First, there can be synergy between environmental protection and economic growth. Policies to protect the environment can enhance efficiency and accelerate innovation, thereby providing an engine for further economic development. Here a major role is envisaged for government in the redirection of the economy, including in relation to industrial policy and the promotion of research and development (R&D). Second, ecological modernisation requires the integration of environmental policy into other areas of government activity. This process, known as 'environmental policy integration' (EPI), is a core feature of both ecological modernisation strategies and those directed at the promotion of sustainable development, as discussed below. Third, promoting ecological modernisation requires the development of new environmental policy instruments (NEPIs) (Jordan *et al.*, 2003). These include voluntary agreements, eco-audit and management systems and reform of fiscal measures along ecological lines. Fourth, ecological modernisation takes place through sector-specific activity, particularly in the industrial sector where it involves the invention, innovation and diffusion of new technologies and techniques of operating industrial processes (Murphy, 2000).

116 *The Politics of Unsustainability*

The claim that the environmental *problématique* can be, and indeed has been, addressed through the structures and processes of modernity has been heavily criticised (Luhmann, 1989; Blühdorn, 2000a). The empirical basis of the theory, that is, the extent to which European states or industrial sectors have undergone ecological modernisation, remains open. The theory also fails to clarify adequately the causal connections between ecological modernisation and the macro-economic structural changes that occurred in western Europe, as part of the shift from energy- and resource-intensive industries towards service- and knowledge-intensive industries.

Conceptually, the theory has been criticised for presenting over-simplified assumptions about the role of the state in inducing ecological transformation and for under-theorising the role that capitalist eco-efficiency and rationalisation can play in environmental reform. Conceptual confusion has also been caused by a tendency to use the term 'ecological modernisation' as if it was synonymous with the term 'sustainable development' (Langhelle, 2000), discussed below. It has also a predominantly western European focus, despite recent efforts to investigate non-European cases (Mol & Sonnenfeld, 2000).

The argument that, through ecological modernisation, industrial society has begun to address the environmental *problématique* is also seen as reductionist. It reduces the environmental *problématique* to concerns about resource inputs, waste and pollutant emissions. This neglects the 'emancipatory' aims that featured in the environmental debates of the 1970s and 1980s in Europe (Blühdorn, 2000b). Environmentalism points to the aesthetic and moral values that ground our relationship with nature, natural systems and environment and calls for an ecological transformation of society based on major value changes (Luhmann, 1989; Eder, 1996). Focusing on the industrial, not the capitalist, nature of modernity means that the wider dimensions of the ecological *problématique* are not addressed. In short, ecological modernisation theory remains silent on issues of social justice, on the distribution of wealth and on society–nature relations.

Despite disagreement about the merits of ecological modernisation as a sociological theory, ecological modernisation *as a strategy of reform* offers distinctive advantages to advanced industrial society. Its offers the hope that the environmental *problématique* can be remedied without having to redirect the course of societal development (Blühdorn, 2000b; Buttel, 2000: 64). As such, it has a 'seductive appeal', because belief in an efficiency response minimises the degree of social and cultural change that is necessary, especially in the high consumption societies of the West (Von Weizsäcker *et al.*, 1997). In this sense, it has been called 'a discourse of reassurance' (Dryzek, 1997; Blühdorn, 2001; Blühdorn & Welsh, this volume). It provides reassurance at several levels (Blühdorn, 2001). First, it supports the notion of rational progress and the continuity of our established patterns of social organisation and societal development. Second, it restores confidence in the power of the political, economic and administrative system to respond effectively and efficiently to the negative 'externalities' of its economic model. Finally, it

The Seductive Appeal of Ecological Modernisation in the European Union 117

promises the continuity of modernity, with its principles of growth, profit and consumerist views of human welfare (Blühdorn, 2001). Unlike the reforms envisaged in Brundtland, or required in the stronger models of sustainable development, the strategy of ecological modernisation attempts to pre-empt any fundamental ideological conflict over modernity.

Why Ecological Modernisation is Not a Route to Sustainable Development

There is a tendency in the literature to approach the classic Brundtland formulation of sustainable development as if it were an empty conceptual shell. This tendency to conceptual pragmatism has allowed the term ecological modernisation to be used as if it were synonymous with the term sustainable development. However, the strategy of ecological modernisation stands, we argue, in sharp contrast to the discourse on sustainable development, especially that proposed by the classic Brundtland formulation (Baker, 2006a). This claim is contentious and requires careful argument, not least because the study of sustainable development is fraught with difficulties.

First, the concept of 'sustainable development' is interpreted in different ways, with sustainable development now conceptualised as ranging along a continuum from weak to strong models (O'Riordan, 1985; Baker, 2006a, b), as discussed by Blühdorn and Welsh in the introduction to this volume. Strong and weak versions of ecological modernisation have also been identified (Barry, 2004; Blühdorn & Welsh, this volume). However, the present analysis is not concerned with a general exploration of the range of models of sustainable development and contrasting these with possible ecological modernisation scenarios. Rather, it is contrasting the Brundtland formulation of sustainable development with the EU pursuit of ecological modernisation. The reason this contrast forms the subject-matter of this research is that the EU has made a declaratory commitment to sustainable development and has stated that it is guided both by the Brundtland Report and by the related UNCED process (Baker, 2000). This makes any gaps between the declaratory commitment and the policy practice of the EU politically significant.

Second, the interpretation, application and political significance of the Brundtland formulation of sustainable development are subject to dispute. Some reject the idea of sustainable development *as formulated by Brundtland,* but have gone on to modify the Brundtland position by injecting it with more radical, socialist considerations (Pepper, 1993). However, there is also a more radical critique, which rejects the pursuit of sustainable development as a political project. This follows the argument that the pursuit of sustainable development is another condition imposed by western nations to dictate the economic policies of the Third World (Starke, 1990: 9). This focuses attention on *how* the environment should be managed, whereas the real question, it is argued, was not how, but *who* will manage the environment and in *whose* interest it is managed (*Ecologist*, 1993). As such, the attention has shifted from a critique of lifestyles and consumption patterns to a question of devising

118 *The Politics of Unsustainability*

better managerial strategies and more effective and efficient institutional control over the environment (Sachs, 1997). For radical greens, this approach tames the agenda of environmental politics and it has led some to reject the whole notion of sustainable development as flawed 'managerialism'.

We argue, however, that much of the critique is not addressed at the notion of sustainable development as such, but at the system of international environmental governance build up around the Brundtland report and in particular following the Rio Earth Summit. It is, we argue, possible to embrace the agenda of sustainable development, while remaining critical of its expression in and through international governance regimes. In addition, the fact that a neo-classical, free market perspective has often replaced the social democracy of Brundtland, as found for example in the highly influential environmental economics of Pearce, and subsequently in the sustainable development policy of many states, is not to find fault with the Brundtland formulation as such. Rather, it points to the influence of economic and political power on the ways in which key actors and agents engage with the pursuit of sustainable development.

Far from seeing the pursuit of sustainable development as flawed managerialism, we argue that the promotion of sustainable development is a wide-ranging and radical project of social change. Brundtland offers a strong model of sustainable development, premised on the belief that the industrialised world, viewing development primarily in terms of ever-increasing material consumption, consumes in excess of its basic needs. This excess threatens the planet's ecological resource base and bio-system health. The Brundtland report has forcefully argued that promoting sustainable development in an ecological system characterised by finite resources requires a reduction in growth in the high consumption societies in the North, in order to make way for 'ecologically legitimate' development in the South (Baker, 2006a).

'Sustainable global development requires that those who are more affluent adopt life-styles within the planet's ecological means' (WCED, 1987: 9).

We argue that, while the Brundtland understanding of sustainable development is open to different interpretations, at its core it challenges the industrialised world to keep consumption patterns within the bounds of the ecologically possible and set at levels to which all can reasonably aspire (Baker, 2006a). This requires a new development model, where the understanding of growth is reoriented in such a way that 'economies remain firmly attached to their ecological roots' (WCED, 1987: 40).

While technology and social organisation can be both managed and improved to make way for a new era of economic growth, limits are nonetheless imposed 'by the ability of the biosphere to absorb the effects of human activities' (WCED, 1987: 8) and by the need to 'adopt life-styles within the planet's ecological means' (WCED, 1987: 9):

> ...the concept of sustainable development does imply limits – not absolute limits but limitations imposed by the present state of technology

The Seductive Appeal of Ecological Modernisation in the European Union 119

and social organisation on environmental recourse and *by the ability of the biosphere to absorb the effect of human activities.* (WCED, 1987: 8; my emphasis)

There are thus ultimate limits to growth embedded in the Brundtland paradigm:

> Growth has no set limits in terms of population or resource use beyond which lies ecological disaster. Different limits hold for the use of energy, materials, waste, and land ... *But ultimate limits there are*, and sustainability requires that long before these are reached, the world must ensure equitable access to the constrained resource and reorient technological efforts to relieve the pressure. (WCED, 1987: 45; my emphasis)

Brundtland therefore, we argue, challenges the traditional growth paradigm. As such, it requires changes in the understanding of well-being and what is needed to live a good life. This change allows for necessary development in the South, in order to bring positive environmental, as well as social and economic, benefits (WCED, 1987: 51).

This is, we argue, in contrast to the ecological modernisation strategy. First, the North–South dimension of the sustainable development agenda is sidestepped in the ecological modernisation strategy. Indeed, it has been argued that ecological modernisation is not capable of having a global remit. This is because the pursuit of ecological modernisation, in both western Europe and Japan, has followed the exportation of highly polluting economic activity to less regulated countries. Similarly, while ecological modernisation has encouraged the preservation of natural resources in the industrialised world, this has been facilitated by the enhanced exploitation of natural resources in the Third World.

In addition, the wide-ranging tasks associated with the promotion of sustainable development, as detailed in Agenda 21, are reformulated under the ecological modernisation strategy as the technical, managerial task of 'decoupling' through eco-efficiency. Decoupling refers to breaking the link between economic growth and negative environmental impact. Ecological modernisation still frames nature as a 'standing reserve' of exploitable resources. This does not challenge the western economic development model either to limit growth or to change existing patterns of high consumption. This fails to address the basic ecological contradiction in traditional growth models, that it requires constant expansion of consumption in a world characterised by finite resources.

Furthermore, ecological modernisation places almost exclusive emphasis on technology and economic entrepreneurs as determinants of social change (Christoff, 1996). Social change, especially for Brundtland, is a process involving a wider set of actors, and the promotion of sustainable development involves engagement with a deeper set of principles. These include the normative principles of inter- and intra- generational equity (Baker, 2006a).

120   *The Politics of Unsustainability*

The social justice aspects of sustainable development are ignored by ecological modernisation (Langhelle, 2000). The result is that ethical considerations are sidelined by attention to efficiency procedures.

Thus, the promotion of sustainable development cannot be achieved by seeking to promote an ecologically modernised European economy. Ecological modernisation, rather than promoting sustainable development, seeks to encourage growth as a solution to the planet's ecological crisis. As such, the two discourses are incompatible. In short, while the Brundtland formulation shares a belief in the advantages of technological development with the ecological modernisation strategy, the former envisages a common future built on fundamental processes of change. Brundtland's formulation of sustainable development not only requires changes at the technological and institutional levels, but also demands more fundamental social, economic, cultural and lifestyle changes, particularly in the high consumption societies of the West, built upon acceptance of ultimate limits to growth.

The EU's Declaratory Commitment to Sustainable Development

The EU's declaratory commitment to the promotion of sustainable development is enshrined in its treaties. First mooted in the 1992 Maastricht Treaty, the Amsterdam Treaty (1997) subsequently called for 'balanced and sustainable development of economic activities', and adopted EPI as a key tool for policy delivery. The Amsterdam Treaty made sustainable development one of the *objectives* of the community, along with economic and social progress. This makes it applicable to the general activities of the EU, not just its activities in the sphere of the environment. Sustainable development has thus the status of a guiding principle of the European integration process. The Treaty of Nice (2000) confirmed this. The draft treaty establishing a constitution for Europe also views sustainable development as a principle having general application (European Communities, 2004). Because of these treaty modifications, there is probably no single government or other association of states with such a strong 'constitutional' commitment to sustainable development as the EU. Sustainable development is now a *norm* of EU politics, both domestically and internationally (Baker & McCormick, 2004).

Commitment to the principle of sustainable development is also found within strategic policy documents, in particular the medium-term Environmental Action Programmes (EAPs). Drawn up by the Commission of the European Communities (CEC), EAPs frame the context within which actions, secondary legislation, specific programmes and funding in the field of environmental policy are structured. The Fourth EAP (1987–92) (CEC, 1987) was the first to draw upon and promote ecological modernisation (Baker, 2000). The belief in economic growth as a tool for environmental reform found further expression in the Fifth EAP, *Towards Sustainability* (1992–2000) (CEC, 1992). The Fifth EAP remains the major policy document structuring the EU's commitment to sustainable development. It intertwines the twin imperatives of

The Seductive Appeal of Ecological Modernisation in the European Union 121

economic growth and environmental protection by declaring both compatible, mutually reinforcing aims of EU policy. In the Fifth EAP, sustainable development is strongly linked with the stimulation of economic growth because it leads to eco-efficiency, which offers both short-and long-term competitive advantages to European industry.

This quintessentially ecological modernisation argument was restated in the Sixth EAP, *Our Future, Our Choice* (CEC, 2001a). The CEC states that the programme '*makes the link* between environment and our European objectives for growth and competitiveness' (CEC, 2001a; my emphasis). The Sixth EAP also reaffirms that the promotion of sustainable development requires commitment to EPI. This is not least because environmental pressures, stemming for example from transport, energy or agriculture, often outweigh the benefits of new (environmental) regulations. EPI, as mentioned above, is also a component of the strategy of ecological modernisation, the difference being that in order to promote sustainable development, EPI requires a 'principled and consequential prioritisation of the environment' over and above sectoral interests (Lafferty & Hovden, 2003). Requiring a principled and consequential integration of environmental considerations into all sectoral activity, it involves a significant break with traditional models of economic development.

In addition to its strong focus on economic growth, the Sixth EAP encompasses a social dimension, by linking sustainable development to public health, especially food safety. Yet, it remains framed in an ecological modernisation discourse, by linking the enhancement of environmental standards, technological innovation and business opportunities:

> ...high environmental standards are an engine for innovation and business opportunities. Overall, society must work to de-couple environmental impacts and degradation from economic growth. Business must operate in a more eco-efficient way, in other words producing the same or more products with less input and less waste. (CEC, 2001a, executive summary: 1)

This favouring of 'clean, lean production' is an excellent example of the use of the ecological modernisation strategy of harnessing the forces of entrepreneurship for environmental gain (Gouldson & Murphy, 1996: 11).

Links were subsequently made between the promotion of sustainable development and ethical issues of justice, equity and democracy, especially in *A Sustainable Europe for a Better World: A European Union Strategy for Sustainable Development* (CEC, 2001b). This strategy was introduced in preparation for the UN World Summit on Sustainable Development, Johannesburg, 2002. However, while the understanding of sustainable development has been widened to encompass social and ethical issues, it nonetheless continues to be embedded in a sturdy dedication to economic growth. Less attention is given to implications of the Brundtland call for

122   *The Politics of Unsustainability*

necessary social and economic improvement in the Third World, that is, ecologically legitimate development, for European growth aspirations. Instead, environmental policy remains a tool for the stimulation of economic growth. Further, the discussion on the social aspects of sustainable development stresses issues of concern to western consumers, such as food safety and health, to the exclusion of global issues such as food security.

Attention now turns to an investigation of the EU's dedication to economic growth and to a closer look at why the strategy of ecological modernisation holds such a dominant place in the politics and policies of the EU.

Promoting Ecological Modernisation and Growth

At the 1993 European Council Summit in Copenhagen, the then European Commission President, Jacques Delors, argued for the adoption of a new model of development for Europe (Jones, 1999: 360). This would displace the Fordist paradigm of mass production, which centred on volumes of output and material notions of wealth and paid scant attention to environmental degradation and quality of life. The Delors model was based on three principles: (1) environmental protection creates jobs; (2) taxes on natural resources can replace taxes on labour; and (3) productivity growth must be used to improve the quality of life and create new jobs (Jones, 1999: 360). The promotion of a clean technology base would be critical to this new model of European competitiveness. These principles were subsequently to form the backbone of the highly influential White Paper *Growth, Competitiveness and Employment* (CEC, 1993).

The significance of the White Paper lies in its analysis of the structural links between environment and employment (Gouldson & Murphy, 1996: 16). It argued that industrialisation has substituted labour by capital, accompanied by continued increases in the use of energy and raw materials. The White Paper proposed a new model that encouraged labour-intensive, environmentally benign development, thereby reconciling economic and environmental objectives.

To support this new development path, the White Paper called for a reform of the tax system along ecological lines, reducing tax on labour and raising tax on the exploitation of environmental resources. It also called for the development of clean technology as a central means of decoupling (CEC, 1993: 147). Subsequently, this thinking was to be reflected in the initiatives funded under the EU Framework Programmes for the support of R&D (Giorgi & Redclift, 2000) and in subsequent science policy developments (Welsh, 2006). The White Paper also advocated localised job creation, thereby taking account of the quality of life effects of economic activity (Jones, 1999: 361). As the CEC later reiterated, 'the main message is that we need to change growth, not limit growth' (CEC, 2001a: 16).

The belief that environmental protection has the potential to enhance the competitiveness of the EU's economy, that is, its support of the 'double

The Seductive Appeal of Ecological Modernisation in the European Union 123

dividend' (employment and environment), is a key indicator of the imprint of ecological modernisation discourse on the White Paper (Andersen & Massa, 2000: 339). The White Paper sees no contradiction between sustainable development and economic growth objectives, and thus economic objectives do not have to change. While never adopted in its entirety, particularly at the member state level, the principles set out in the White Paper soon began to permeate other EU policy documents (Gouldson & Murphy, 1996: 17).

The CEC's (1994) *Economic Growth and the Environment: Some Implications for Policy Making* presented similar arguments. This held that technological development and changes in the sectoral composition of the economy had steadily reduced the environmental impact of economic growth. To ensure continuation of this ecological progress, the CEC reiterated its belief in the importance of clean technologies and stressed the supporting role of R&D in science and technology. The crucial role of technology in the promotion of sustainable development was restated in the CEC's (2002) report, *Environmental Technology for Sustainable Development*. This presents a typical ecological modernisation argument in that it enhances the role given to the economic sector in the promotion of ecological change and gives priority to technical solutions to the environmental *problématique*. The approach was to receive further institutional support when, in 1994, the European Parliament passed a resolution acknowledging the potential contribution that the environmental technology industry could make in generating new employment opportunities in Europe (Gouldson & Murphy, 1996: 17).

The White Paper's authority extended not just within the institutions of the EU, but influenced the development of the industrial and environmental policy of several western European countries (Binder *et al.*, 2001). In particular, it helped develop a strong social consensus around ecological modernisation in Denmark, Sweden and Germany (Lundqvist, 2000).

More recently, this thinking was reflected in the Lisbon Strategy (2000), which aims to make the EU the world's most dynamic and competitive economy by 2010 (CEC, 2005). The Lisbon Strategy believes that 'boosting growth and creating jobs are the keys for unlocking the resources needed to meet our economic and social ambitions and are important to reach our environmental objectives' (CEC, 2005: 981). The current Sixth EAP was designed to support the Lisbon Strategy which is further evidence of the dovetailing of the economic and environmental discourse of the CEC:

> If we can support and encourage the development of a greener market place, then business and citizens will respond with technological and management innovations that will spur growth, competitiveness, profitability, and job creation. A progressive environmental policy can thereby contribute to the objective of the Lisbon [Strategy]. (CEC, 2001a: 11)

However, the Lisbon Strategy has been strongly criticised on environmental grounds, including by the Executive Director of the EEA, Professor Jacqueline

124 *The Politics of Unsustainability*

McGlade. She argues that the Lisbon Strategy forms part of a concerted effort by particular sectors to force the direction of Europe into even more intense use of the world's natural capital. Arguing that the EU faces a choice between exploiting the rest of the planet or becoming dramatically more efficient in its use of resources, she cautioned:

> These demands on the natural capital have spilled out well beyond Europe's boundaries... to move forward on a trajectory designed to meet the Lisbon agenda, Europe will have no option other than to exploit the rest of the planet or fundamentally alter the way in which it does business by becoming dramatically more efficient in its use of land and other natural resources... The debate about Europe's future is not a sterile debate but one that will truly reflect what is possible today without exhausting our resources for future generations. (European Environmental Agency EEA, 2004)

From these examples, it can be seen that the EU only ever managed a limited and non-consequential integration of environmental considerations into its integration project. Nevertheless, belief in the importance of EPI continues at the declaratory level. Indeed, dismay over the slow rate of progress led the Swedish Prime Minister in 1997 to call for renewed efforts. This launched the so-called Cardiff Process, which aims to promote sustainable development through a focus on sector-specific integration strategies, identification of sustainability indicators and construction of monitoring mechanisms. This led to a call for the sector councils to develop specific EPI action plans.

Perhaps nowhere more clearly is the ecological modernisation discourse visible than in the action plans produced in response to this call. Most action plans adopt a positive environmental discourse, stressing the potential for constructive gains for the economy from environmentally sound policies. The Industry Council response provides a prime example, not surprisingly since 'Industry policy is... directly charged with those drivers – innovation and technology – at the heart of ecological modernisation' (Hertin & Berkhout, 2003: 48).

The founding Treaty of Rome (Article 130) calls for the development of an industrial policy which promotes competitiveness, enterprise, innovation and rapid structural adjustment. It also aims to improve the commercial exploitation of R&D. The decision to relaunch the EU integration project around the completion of the Single European Market (SEM) represents industrial policy 'par excellence' (Barrass *et al.*, 1997: 103). It is not surprising therefore that the Industrial Council's EPI strategy, while representing a shift towards a more positive attitude towards the environment (win–win), puts strong emphasis on those instruments and policy areas seen as most compatible with competitiveness. These include emphasis on NEPIs such as voluntary action, market-based instruments, eco-efficiency measures and the promotion of environmental management arrangements (Hertin & Berkhout, 2003: 49;

The Seductive Appeal of Ecological Modernisation in the European Union   125

Power, 1999). The CEC staff working paper on EPI in the industrial sector was particularly revealing when it argued that:

> ... environment and industrial policies are both important pillars for the achievement of sustainable development ... And it is clear that a highly competitive economy is better placed for pursuing a high level of environmental protection and promoting employment. (CEC, 1999)

This is a clear example of an 'eco-modernist discourse' (Hertin & Berkhout, 2003: 51). It is also an example of the EU's use of the discourse on sustainable development as symbolic rhetoric (see Blühdorn, this volume), as it is empty of effort to engage in fundamental ways with sectoral belief systems, as is required for the promotion of sustainable development through EPI.

The CEC's attempts to give a more central role to the industrial sector in ecological reform are also reflected in efforts to advocate the use of a range of NEPIs. Ecological modernisation is premised on the construction of a new relationship between the state or regulatory authority and industry. A hierarchical and legalistic style of policy making sits poorly with efforts to enhance the role of industry in ecological transformation (Lenschow, 2002: 20). The eco-management and audit system of voluntary agreements is a favoured tool of the CEC. It is based on the belief that successful organisational 'eco-change' can result from the adoption of an appropriate environmental technology and management system (Newton & Harte, 1997: 76). This image of a 'neatly ordered conversion to environmentalism' (Newton & Harte, 1997: 77) has been criticised for its bias in favour of only minor adjustments to existing economic and technological systems (Orsato & Clegg, 2005: 256). In addition, there is an explicit assumption that the decision to pursue a sustainable future will be undertaken voluntarily by business interests, an assumption that ignores several issues. First, the promotion of individualism and entrepreneurship appears at variance with the more collectively oriented objectives of sustainable development policy. Second, there is tension between the promotion of a deregulated SEM, endorsed through voluntary agreements, and the desire for a sustainable future. Many have argued that the 'greening' of business may require more, rather than less, state regulation and intervention (Newton & Harte, 1997: 84; Kenny & Meadowcroft, 1999).

In short, the EU approaches EPI as a 'light' new governance tool, forestalling more fundamental ecological action. As mandated by both UNCED and the EU's own commitment to sustainable development, EPI requires a clear emphasis on, and principled *bias* towards, environmental objectives (Lafferty & Hovden, 2003: 8). Instead of giving 'principled priority to the environment', evidence to date suggests that the EU has merely given what Lafferty and Hovden call more general, and *less consequential*, commitments to the employment of good policy-making strategies (good governance), applicable to any type of policy integration.

126   *The Politics of Unsustainability*

Explaining the EU Recourse to Ecological Modernisation

There is little or no agreement on how best to characterise the system of interest representation in the EU, having been variously described as pluralist (Schmitter, 2000), or even a mixture of elements of pluralism and corporatist elements (Hix, 1999). All acknowledge, however, the entrenched position of business interests in the complex and opaque policy-making system of the EU (Hunold, 2005: 330). Business and the EU, in particular the CEC, can be described as having a 'transaction relation' (Matten, 2003). This is characterised by the provision by the EU of a regulatory framework that is favourable to economic interests. This means, at a minimum, that EU environmental policy does not impose threats to the competitiveness of European business, either by rising production costs, restricting what is produced or altering market opportunities. In exchange, businesses not only provide member states with taxation revenues, but corporations assume practically the main responsibility for employment, which 'is probably even beyond taxation the most important function of business for government' (Matten, 2003: 220). The promotion of ecological modernisation allows the EU to maintain this transaction relation because, by framing the environmental *problématique* as a business opportunity, it allows the centrality of economic interests to be retained.

To understand this more fully, let us reset the study of the White Paper *Growth, Competitiveness and Employment* into a historical context. The White Paper was introduced at a time when the EU was facing a crisis of legitimacy following the troubled ratification of the Maastricht Treaty. It was, at least in part, an attempt to reassert the importance of social solidarity to the European integration project. It paid attention, for example, to quality of life aspects of economic development. The White Paper was *also* introduced at a time that saw a rapid rise in unemployment in the member states. It offered the prospect of a revitalisation of the European economy and a new way in which European competitiveness, particularly in the industrial sector, could be regained in the face of threats from Japanese and American economic domination. The combination of social dialogue and local employment emphasis in the White Paper suited all levels of labour organisation, while simultaneously offering the member states a seemingly practical solution to both their mounting crisis of unemployment and the rising environmental concerns among their citizens (Jones, 1999: 371). Ecological modernisation provides the EU with a strategy that provides much-needed reassurance about the future development of the integrated, European economy.

Symbolic Politics and European Integration

The close fit between the EU integration project and the discourse on ecological modernisation helps to explain why the EU embeds the strategy of ecological modernisation in its commitment to sustainable development. This,

The Seductive Appeal of Ecological Modernisation in the European Union 127

however, leaves unresolved the question as to why the EU continues to make declaratory commitment to sustainable development. Why not abandon this commitment altogether in favour of a more straightforward allegiance to ecological modernisation? Does the commitment to sustainable development represent sheer rhetoric – and little more? These questions turn attention to the exploration of the use of symbols as tools of politics. In particular, it requires consideration of the use of symbolism in the construction and the presentation of EU identity.

The continued declaratory commitment to sustainable development can be explained by reference to identity formation in the EU and the quest for shared goals and norms that can be used to drive and to legitimate the EU integration project. This need for identity and legitimacy stems from the fact that the EU is both an emerging and a hybrid entity, which is neither a state nor a nation, but a unique combination of supranational and international forms of governance. As a novel and somewhat risky political experiment, the EU is forced to pay a great deal of attention to the identification and articulation of shared values and legitimising principles that can help in the mobilisation of support for the integration project (Weiler, 1998: 60). Declaratory political statements are thus important in the EU integration project, as ideas and values act as a vehicle though which the EU, as a group, is defining its identity (Weiler, 1998; Manners, 2002). In the early days of the European Community, this mobilisation was elite-driven. However, in the post-Maastricht Europe, the need to mobilise a wider support base has taken on increasing importance.

The vision of sustainable development has many of the key elements needed for it to act as a legitimising, mobilising value for the EU integration process. At a general level, commitment to the Brundtland call for 'development that meets the needs of the present without compromising the ability of future generations to meet their own needs' presents a sentiment that is hard *not* to agree with. The title of the Brundtland report *Our Common Future* also has an inclusionary appeal. In addition, the formulation offered for the first time a way of reconciling what had hitherto appeared to be conflicting societal goals.

The three-pillar focus of sustainable development on the social, economic and ecological dimensions of development also conforms to deep-seated European social constructs. It is undeniable that the European integration project was founded on economic values, especially belief in the achievement of economic prosperity through the construction of a single, European, free market. However, it is also the case that the integration project has roots in a deep-seated belief in the ethos of collective societal responsibility for the welfare of the community as a whole (Weiler, 1998: 62). Despite differences within and between member states, there is nevertheless a general consensus in Europe that environmental protection cannot be left to market forces and that environmental protection is a legitimate goal of government, or 'the foundation of any society' (Krämer, 2002: 15). The European integration project has resulted in a gradual shift upwards of this task to the EU level. There is now consensus among member states that EU-level environmental

128   *The Politics of Unsustainability*

policy should continue to develop and that this development forms part of the building blocks of the European integration project. This has allowed Europeans to see environmental protection as part of the protection on the common good. As such, the commitment to the promotion of sustainable development allows the European integration project to be presented as part of the construction of a new European identity, based upon shared European values, grounded on the idea of social responsibility (Krämer, 2002). Here sustainable development offers distinctive advantages as a symbolic tool over and above the narrower, economic and overtly technological emphasis embedded in the ecological modernisation discourse. In addition, the principle of sustainable development coincides with other EU principles, especially its governance principles. Both are founded on a strong commitment to enhancing participation and sharing responsibility in environmental policy making.

Beyond the borders of the EU, the commitment to the promotion of sustainable development has also helped shape the EU's identity by marking it out as different from other actors. The fact that the Brundtland formulation has become the dominant concept in international discussions on environment and on development has enabled the EU to align itself with international best practice and to forge links, particularly with the Third World groupings in the United Nations. This is not to deny, of course, the existence of other tensions, including in relation to the size of the EU development aid budget. Nevertheless, the declaratory commitment to the promotion of sustainable development has acted as a constitutive factor determining the international identity of the EU. It has, for example, become essential in shaping the negotiating position and behaviour of the EU at the international level. This allows the EU to act as a normative power (as opposed to military power) in international politics (Manners, 2002). This marks a major difference with the USA, including in relation to climate change (Baker, 2006b).

Linking the EU's declaratory commitment to sustainable development with the normative underpinnings of the European integration project helps us to understand why the EU frames and processes its environmental problems in the way it does. This links the discussion in this contribution with one of the key concerns of this volume, namely to understand the specific conditions and constellations which determine the ways in which late-modern societies are framing and processing their environmental problems (Blühdorn & Welsh, this volume).

To deny the symbolic importance of the EU's commitment to sustainable development is to see the European integration project only in terms of its structural, procedural and material components. European integration is also a project based upon, but simultaneously rearticulating, shared European values. This allows us to see the commitment to sustainable development as the CEC's contribution to 'the flow of European intellectual history' (Weiler, 1998: 61). What is surprising is that the study of EU integration has been dominated by a rationalist approach that has concentrated on the institutional dimension, including how laws and policy-making processes have shaped integration,

The Seductive Appeal of Ecological Modernisation in the European Union   129

while simultaneously dismissing as 'merely symbolic' the discursive dimensions of integration (Baker, 2006b). Claude Lefort has rightly castigated political science for favouring a purely institutional analysis, particularly of power (*la politique*), to the neglect or even the denial of the fundamentally symbolic nature of power (*le politique*) (Lefort, 1988). It is in this symbolic nature that the unity or cohesion of a group or people is formed and it is this insight of Lefort that inspires this second interpretation of symbolic politics. This interpretation points to the positive, enabling function of the EU's symbolic commitment to sustainable development. It also makes us aware of the constructive dimension of the 'symbolic', as discussed by Blühdorn (this volume).

The sharp contrast between the constructivist function of the symbolic commitment to sustainable development and the political and economic interests that drive the promotion of ecological modernisation also points to the presence within the EU of simultaneous discourses composed of both 'radical change and uncompromising defence' (Blühdorn & Welsh, this volume). Both discourses are being held at the same time and there are identifiable interests that benefit from each.

Drawing again upon Lefort, a functional unity can be seen between the declaratory commitment to sustainable development and the adoption of the strategy of ecological modernisation. Sustainable development acts as the meta-narrative, framing and legitimising the integration project. In contrast, the promotion of ecological modernisation is the reflection of the reality of organised power and interest group politics in the EU. This distinction, between ideology and reality characteristics of EU environmental policy, is an example of the more general distinction between symbolic and real apposite of political power (Lindahl, 1998: 13).

Conclusion

The propensity for capitalist industrial society to co-opt the radical nature of the environmental critique of modernity is clearly seen in the way in which the EU makes a declaratory commitment to sustainable developments and then adopts a strategy of ecological modernisation. The strategy of ecological modernisation makes environmental management compatible with the *raison d'être* of the EU integration project. It is in keeping with its key tenet, namely the construction of a neo-liberal, free market economy in support of industrial competitiveness. With its substantial supranational authority over environment policy, the EU has played a role in promoting ecological modernisation, and in the diffusion of its principles, particularly to leader environmental states, and into the industrial sector. While the literature often confuses ecological modernisation with sustainable development, ecological modernisation is a more limiting concept. It does not address the underlying contradiction in capitalism: a logic of ever-increasing consumption in a world characterised by material resource limitations. The proposition that ecological

130 *The Politics of Unsustainability*

modernisation offers a viable solution to our ecological crisis is problematic for those that point to the expansionist character of capitalism as the main course of environmental degradation (Hajer, 1996).

However, we are not content to argue that the symbolic politics of sustainable development simply acts to 'sustain the unsustainable' of ecological modernisation. Rather, we also wish to give attention to the positive role that symbolic constructs can play in unmasking the politics of 'sustaining the unsustainable' (Blühdorn, this volume). Rather than seeing the EU's commitment to sustainable development as an act of ecological deception, we conclude this discussion by pointing to the potentials inherent within the symbolic politics of the EU. The decision to promote ecological modernisation and to embed this in the EU's understanding of sustainable development is a political act. Within this lies a set of choices about the future political and economic directions of the EU. At one level, then, the struggle between sustainable development and ecological modernisation is a struggle over the future direction of Europe. This points to another important function of symbols in politics – they act as stimulators of change. Despite the fact that the reality of democracy always falls short of the idea of a society of free and equal citizens, this idea is retained because it functions as the 'political absolute', that is, as society's 'truth measure' (Lindahl, 1998: 34). In the same way, the continuation of the symbolic discourse on sustainable development becomes critically important, because it functions as society's ecological truth measure. Within this concept are the seeds of radical social change. This change is increasingly called for as society confronts its own ecological irrationality. Rather than heralding the 'end of environmentalism', the symbolic commitment to sustainable development has transformational potential. Environmentalism is poised on the cusp of change. When a 'simple reinstatement of the historically older approaches of either ecological radicalism or eco-political denial is not an option' (Blühdorn & Welsh, this volume), recognition that symbols have transformational potential can anticipate 'the liberated alternative to the *status quo*' (Blühdorn, this volume). Here, the study of symbolic constructions reminds that we should never underestimate the power of ideas in politics.

References

Andersen, M. S. & Massa, I. (2000) 'Ecological modernisation – origins, dilemmas and future directions', *Journal of Environmental Policy and Planning* 2(4): 337–45.

Baker, S. (2000) 'The European Union: integration, competitions, growth and sustainability', in W. M. Lafferty & J. Meadowcroft (eds.), *Implementing Sustainable Development: Strategies and Initiative in High Consumption Societies*, pp. 303–421 (Oxford: Oxford University Press).

Baker, S. (2006a) *Sustainable Development* (London: Routledge).

Baker, S. (2006b) 'Environmental values and climate change policy: contrasting the European Union and the United States', in S. Lucarelli & I. Manners (eds.), *Values in EU Policy*, pp. 77–96 (London: Routledge).

Baker, S. & McCormick, J. (2004) 'Sustainable development: comparative understandings and responses', in N. J. Vig & M. G. Faure (eds.), *Green Giants: Environmental Policies of the United States and the European Union*, pp. 277–302 (Cambridge, MA: MIT Press).

The Seductive Appeal of Ecological Modernisation in the European Union 131

Barrass, R., Sprenger, R.-U. & Triebswetter, U. (1997) 'Cohesion and the environment: policy integration at European level', *European Environment* 7: 101–9.

Barry, J. (2003) 'Ecological modernisation', in J. Proops & E. Page (eds.), *Environmental Throught*, pp. 191–214 (Edward Elgar).

Beck, U. (1997) *The Reinvention of Politics: Rethinking Modernity in the Global Social Order* (Cambridge: Polity).

Binder, M., Jänicke, M. & Petscholow, U. (2001) *Green Industrial Restructuring: International Case Studies and Theoretical Interpretations* (Berlin: Springer).

Blühdorn, I. (2000a) *Post-ecologist Politics. Social Theory and the Abdication of the Ecologist Paradigm* (London: Routledge).

Blühdorn, I. (2000b) 'Ecological modernisation and post-ecologist politics', in G. Spaargaren, A. P. J. Mol & F. H. Buttel (eds.), *Environment and Global Modernity*, pp. 209–28 (London: Sage).

Blühdorn, I. (2001) 'Reflexivity and self-referentiality: on the normative foundations of ecological communication', *Critical Studies* 16: 181–201.

Buttel, F. H. (2000) 'Ecological modernisation as social theory', *Geoforum* 31: 57–65.

CEC (1987) Fourth Environmental Action Programme, *Official Journal* C328, 7 December 1987.

CEC (1992) *Towards Sustainability: A European Community Programme of Policy and Action in Relation to the Environment (1992–2000)* (Brussels: CEC, COM (92) 23, final).

CEC (1993) White paper *Growth, Competitiveness and Employment* (Brussels: CEC, COM (93) 7000, final).

CEC (1994) *Economic Growth and the Environment: Some Implications for Policy Making* (Brussels: CEC, COM (94) 465, final).

CEC (1999) *Commission Staff Working Paper on Sustainable Industrial Development* (Brussels: CEC, SEC (1999) 1729).

CEC (2001a) *The Sixth Environment Action Programme of the European Community 'Environment 2010: Our Future, Our Choice'* (Brussels: CEC, COM (2001) 0031, final).

CEC (2001b) *A Sustainable Europe for a Better World: A European Union Strategy for Sustainable Development* (Brussels: CEC, COM, final).

CEC (2002) *Commission Report on* Environmental Technology for Sustainable Development (Brussels: CEC, COM(2202) 122, final).

CEC (2005) *Communication from the Commission to the Council and the European Parliament: Common Actions for Growth and Employment: The Community Lisbon Programme* (Brussels: CEC, COM(2005) 330, final).

Christoff, P. (1996) 'Ecological modernisation, ecological modernities', *Environmental Politics* 5(3): 476–500.

Dryzek, J. S. (1997) *The Politics of the Earth: Environmental Discourses* (Oxford: Oxford University Press).

Ecologist (1993) *Whose Common Future? Reclaiming the Commons* (London: Earthscan).

Eder, K. (1996) 'The institutionalisation of environmentalism: ecological discourse and the second transformation of the public sphere', in S. Lash, B. Szerszynski & B. Wynne (eds.), *Risk, Environment and Modernity: Towards a New Ecology*, pp. 203–23 (London: Sage).

European Environment Agency (2004) 'Lisbon goal poses choice between efficiency leap or exploiting the planet', news release, Copenhagen, 24 November 2004.

European Communities (2004) 'Treaty establishing a constitution for Europe', *Official Journal* 47: C310, 16 December.

Giorgi, L. & Redclift, M. (2000) 'European environmental research in the social sciences: research into ecological modernisation as a "boundary object"', *European Environment* Vol. (10): 12–23.

Gouldson, A. & Murphy, J. (1996) 'Ecological modernisation and the European Union', *Geoforum* 27(1): 11–21.

Hajer, M. A. (1995) *The Politics of Environmental Discourse: Ecological Modernization and the Policy Process* (Oxford: Oxford University Press).

132　The Politics of Unsustainability

Hajer, M. A. (1996) 'Ecological modernisation as cultural politics', in S. Lash, B. Szerszynski & B. Wynne (eds.), *Risk, Environment and Modernity: Towards a New Ecology*, pp. 246–68 (London: Sage).

Hertin, J. & Berkhout, F. (2003) 'Analysing institutional strategies for environmental policy integration: the case of EU enterprise policy', *Journal of Environmental Policy and Planning* 5(1): 39–56.

Hix, S. (1999) *The Political System of the EU* (New York: St Martin's Press).

Hunold, C. (2005) 'Green political theory and the European Union: the case for non-integrated civil society', *Environmental Politics* 14(3): 324–43.

Jänicke, M. (1992) 'Conditions for environmental policy success: an international comparison', *Environmentalist*, 12(1): 47–58.

Jones, E. (1999) 'Competitive and sustainable growth: logic and inconsistency', *European Journal of Public Policy* 6(3): 359–75.

Jordan, A., Wurzel, R. K. W. & Zito, A. R. (eds.) (2003) *New Instruments of Environmental Governance? National Experiences and Prospects* (London: Frank Cass).

Kenny, M. & Meadowcroft, J. (eds.) (1999) *Planning Sustainability* (London: Routledge).

Krämer, L. (2002) 'Development of environmental policies in the United States and Europe: convergence of divergences?'. Paper presented at the 'Green giants? Environmental policy of the United States and the European Union' conference, EUI, Florence.

Lafferty, W. M. & Hovden, E. (2003) 'Environmental policy integration: towards an analytical framework', *Environmental Politics* 12(3): 1–22.

Lafferty, W. M. & Meadowcroft, J. (2000) 'Introduction', in W. M. Lafferty & J. Meadowcroft (eds.), *Implementing Sustainable Development: Strategies and Initiative in High Consumption Societies*, pp. 1–22 (Oxford: Oxford University Press).

Langhelle, O. (2000) 'Why ecological modernisation and sustainable development should not be conflated', *Journal of Environmental Policy and Planning* 2: 303–22.

Lefort, C. (1988) *Democracy and Political Theory*, trans. D. Macey (Cambridge: Polity).

Lenschow, A. (2002) 'New regulatory approaches in "greening" EU policies', *European Law Journal* 8(1): 19–37.

Lindahl, H. (1998) 'Democracy and the symbolic constitution of society', *Ratio Juris* 11(1): 12–37.

Luhmann, N. (1989) *Ecological Communication* (Chicago, IL: Chicago University Press).

Lundqvist, L. (2000) 'Capacity building or social construction? Explaining Sweden's shift towards ecological modernisation', *Geoforum* 31: 21–32.

Manners, I. (2002) 'Normative power Europe: a contradiction in terms?', *Journal of Common Market Studies* 40(2): 235–58.

Matten, D. (2003) 'Symbolic politics in environmental regulations: corporate strategic responses', *Business Strategy and the Environment* 12: 213–26.

Mol, A. (1995) *The Refinement of Production: Ecological Modernization Theory and the Chemical Industry* (Utrecht: van Arkel).

Mol, A. (1996) 'Ecological modernisation and institutional reflexivity: environmental reform in the late modern age', *Environmental Politics* 5(2): 302–23.

Mol, A. & Sonnenfeld, D. (eds.) (2000) *Ecological Modernisation around the World: Perspectives and Critical Debates* (London: Frank Cass).

Mol, A. & Spaargaren, G. (2000) 'Ecological modernisation theory in debate: a review', in A. Mol & G. Spaargaren (eds.), *Ecological Modernisation around the World: Perspectives and Critical Debates*, pp. 17–50 (London: Frank Cass).

Murphy, J. (2000) 'Ecological modernisation', *Geoforum* 31(1): 1–8.

Newton, T. & Harte, G. (1997) 'Green business: technicist kitch?', *Journal of Management Studies* 34(1): 75–98.

O'Riordan, T. (1985), 'What does sustainability really mean? Theory and development of concepts of sustainability', in *Sustainable Development in an Industrial Economy, Proceedings of a Conference Held at Queens' College, Cambridge, 23–25 June* (Cambridge: UK Centre for Economic and Environmental Development).

The Seductive Appeal of Ecological Modernisation in the European Union   133

Orsato, R. J & Clegg, S. R. (2005) 'Radical reformism: towards *critical* ecological modernisation', *Sustainable Development* 13: 253–67.

Pepper, D. (1993) *Eco-socialism: From Deep Ecology to Social Justice* (London: Routledge).

Power, M. (1999) *The Audit Society: Rituals of Verification* (Oxford: Oxford University Press).

Sachs, W. (1997) 'Sustainable development', in M. Redclift & G. Woodgate (eds.), *The International Handbook of Environmental Sociology*, pp. 71–82 (Cheltenham: Edward Elgar).

Schmitter, P. C. (2000) *How to Democratize the EU ... and Why Bother?* (Lanham, MD: Rowman & Littlefield).

Simonis, U. (1989) 'Ecological modernization of industrial society: three strategic elements', *International Social Science Journal* 121: 347–61.

Spaargaren, G. (2000) 'Ecological modernization theory and the changing discourse on environment and modernity', in G. Spaargaren, A. Mol & F. Buttel (eds.), *Environment and Global Modernity*, pp. 41–71 (London: Sage).

Spaargaren, G., Mol, A. P. J. & Buttel, F. H. (eds.) (2000) *Environment and Global Modernity* (London: Sage).

Starke, L. (1990) *Signs of Hope: Working towards our Common Future* (Oxford: Oxford University Press).

Weiler, J. (1998) 'Ideals and idolatry in the European construct', in B. McSweeney (ed.), *Moral Issues in International Affairs: Problems of European Integration*, pp. 55–88 (London: Macmillan).

Von Weizsäcker, E., Lovins, A., Hunter, B. & Lovins, L. (1997) *Factor Four: Doubling Wealth – Having Resource Use* (London: Earthscan).

Weale, A. (1992) *The New Politics of Pollution* (Manchester: Manchester University Press).

Welsh, I. (2006) 'Values, science and the European Union', in S. Lucarelli & I. Manners, pp. 59–76.

WCED (1987) *Our Common Future* (Oxford: Oxford University Press).

Dissolving the Nation: Self-deception and Symbolic Inversion in the GM Debate

EMMA HUGHES
School of Journalism, Media and Cultural Studies, University of Cardiff, UK

ABSTRACT *This contribution examines print media coverage of the cultivation and consumption of genetically modified (GM) crops in the UK press. It draws on arguments from Beck and Bauman to consider how the GM debate undertakes the discursive regeneration of security, purity, order and certainty through the invocation of the modernist categories of nation and boundary. A combination of in-depth textual analysis of national newspaper coverage and interviews with key media sources was used to explore how discourses of nation are promoted by different actors, and how the UK press then mediate these different viewpoints according to their own news values and reportage categories. In particular the contribution explores how the symbolic power invested in the concept of nation is an example of individual and societal self-deception; for in the globalised world we now inhabit, new technologies like genetic modification cannot be controlled by old frontiers like nation.*

Introduction

In 1999 UK press coverage of the growth and consumption of genetically modified (GM) crops exploded, as journalists identified GM crops as a contentious risk issue.[1] GM crops were identified as not just a risk to individuals but as a risk to the nation; they were not just a threat to the environment and people's health, rather they were a threat to *Britain's* environment and to *Britain's* health. This is evidenced in many of the headlines: 'GM ship set for Britain' (*Daily Mirror*, 28 February 2000), 'GM food is being foisted on Britain' (*Daily Mail*, 3 June 2003) and 'Ruling that could flood Britain with GM foods' (*Daily Mail*, 28 December 2005). The trend to discuss genetic modification in terms of nation cannot be ascribed to the media alone. Many different actors from every side of the genetic modification debate use nationhood as a framing device. The UK government, for example, links the

Self-deception and Symbolic Inversion in the GM Debate   135

two, as clearly signalled by the 'GM nation' debate. Within this debate the government appealed specifically to the concept of national citizenship; the public was appealed to as a nation of voters. Environmental organisations and environmental charities also utilise ideas of nationhood. Friends of the Earth England, for example, labelled their anti-genetic modification campaign 'Keep Britain GM free'. This primary framing established the integrity of island Britain as a key factor structuring a debate ostensibly addressed through categories of risk.

The continued prominence of the nation and the wider social significance attached to boundaries in the face of risks confounds elements of Ulrich Beck's (1992) *Risk Society* thesis. Risk was portrayed as abolishing both the 'foundations and categories', including national and continental distinctions, structuring thought *and* action (Beck, 1992: 22). The persistence of nation as a socially prioritised response to risk in an era of globalisation presents political and regulatory challenges in late modernity. Whilst media coverage plays a central role in this process, this analysis sets out to establish how multiple voices, media cultures and circuits of communication co-construct what is arguably a clear case of societal self-deception – namely the integrity of Britain as an island nation in the face of precisely the kind of synergistic, transboundary process postulated by Beck.

Genetic modification yields crops bearing pollen and seeds which can be transported considerable distances by both natural and human means. Whilst the English Channel represents a clear divide from continental Europe, there is evidence that gene flow is possible between the UK and France (Bond *et al.*, 2005). Such transboundary flows are subject to multiple levels of regulation with discrete nations being only one tier. In the UK case, Westminster legislates in the context of European Union (EU) directives; the Welsh Assembly and Scottish Parliament also have significant powers and local authorities can declare themselves GM-free. Beyond this lies a global regulatory tier: the World Trade Organization, which is intended to formalise and regulate access to world markets (Welsh, 2006). The existence of global supply chains means that if the rest of the world decided to grow GM crops it would be almost impossible for British citizens to avoid products containing GM ingredients. This multi-layered regulatory and commercial context enhances the potential for recourse to nation and nationalism in the face of risks perceived as foreign in origin. In what follows I argue that in the face of uncertainty, the GM debate demonstrates the tendency to recreate old boundaries as a means of restoring a sense of security.

Background

It is important to give some context to media coverage of GM in terms of the risks identified with the technology. Despite genetic modification being pursued by all advanced nations since the 1980s there remain some areas where scientific knowledge is incomplete (Welsh, 2006), although of course it is

136   *The Politics of Unsustainability*

important to note that scientific uncertainty is not always due to a lack of scientific knowledge but rather a lack of coherence among competing scientific understandings (Sarewitz, 2004). Established risks include the potential for environmental damage through reducing biodiversity via increased pesticide use, the creation of pesticide-resistant 'super weeds' through cross-pollination and the contamination of the 'primitive cultivars' from which staple crops were developed via selective breeding.

These risks to the environment sit alongside less clearly defined risks to human health from eating GM foods. Three linked news events brought these risks to public attention. In 1999 Dr Arpad Pusztai, a senior scientist from the Rowett Research Institute, claimed that a type of GM potato had resulted in slightly stunted growth and impaired immune systems in rats. Media attention intensified when Pusztai was suspended from the institute. In the same year the British Medical Association declared that there was not sufficient evidence that GM organisms were safe, and that they should not be released into the environment until there was greater scientific certainty. Finally, in 2003 Michael Meacher, the former Environment Minister, wrote a piece in the *Independent* declaring that he had been sacked because he was concerned about the potential health risks of GM foods.

Health and environmental risks are compounded by the threat posed to Britain's scientific and commercial bio-technology knowledge base. Fears of a 'brain drain' and 'capital flight' within the agricultural bio-tech sector are often cited as a potential risk caused by underinvestment in the technology. These fears combine with a perceived risk to development and aid agendas, underpinned by the promise that GM would constitute a second 'green revolution' and play a significant role in ending famine in regions like Africa. In order to address how ideas of nation are symbolically constructed it is important to outline the 'real' political and commercial context framing discussions on this issue. Significantly, the initial commercial application of agricultural GM was undertaken by US corporations and currently 90% of GM crops are grown in the USA, Canada and South America. They have also been planted in some parts of Africa, China and Europe. Commercial planting has not taken place in the UK though some residual cross-pollination could have arisen from over 100 GM field trials, despite the imposition of quarantine zones around these sites. The trials involved planting GM crops in the open air and monitoring them to assess the impact on biodiversity for a limited period, and in the process revealed negative impacts on biodiversity.

EU member states wanting to plant a licensed GM crop must place an application before the Agricultural Ministers' Council; if they cannot decide, the decision is passed to the European Commission. Within the UK there is another layer of decision making. If the EU approves a crop for commercial planting, it must be added to the National Seed List. All the devolved administrations must approve a seed before it can be grown anywhere in the UK. This means the Scottish Parliament and the Welsh Assembly are very important, as they have the power to stop GM crops being planted anywhere in the UK. Since June 1999, an EU-wide moratorium on GM products has been in place and no new GM corps have been licensed for use though food products containing GM continue to be imported. GM products not for human consumption and GM animal feed for livestock are also important. Whilst supermarkets stock products containing GM major UK chains' own-brand labels are sourced from non-GM suppliers. The EU's moratorium on further GM licensing resulted in an international trade dispute. The USA, backed by Canada and Argentina, lodged a complaint with the World Trade Organization claiming that the moratorium on GM crops was illegal. The World Trade Organization complaint was upheld in March 2006, weakening the EU's ability to bar the import of GM food. Irrespective of this, the principle of subsidiarity and the continuing commercial boycott of GM ingredients by supermarket chains effectively limit the potential of GM within EU member states. This demonstrates the many layers of policy making involved in the regulation of GM, layers which stretch from international bodies all the way down to centres of devolved government. Within this system 'nation' is just one of many layers of decision making in a process where it is impossible for a country to have total control over the flow of GM material across its borders.

Method

The core empirical data used for this contribution comprise a comprehensive archive of all UK national press coverage of genetically modified organisms between 1 January and 30 January 2004. Articles mentioning genetic modification in the headline, the first paragraph and/or the last paragraph were included in the sample. A total of 454 articles were identified. As well as analysing newspaper text, 18 interviews were conducted with sources quoted in the media texts. The interview sample included government figures, scientists, members of the bio-tech industry, campaigners, press officers and farmers. Verbal consent was agreed on tape with interviewees being asked to explicitly state the level of identification they wished to receive; this was then reviewed at the end of the interview. As all of the interviewees were happy to be identified by name I have included this information within the transcript to enable readers to identify an individual media source. The interviews provided a spectrum of viewpoints from those who were extremely pro-GM to those who were equally anti. Many people spoke from several standpoints; for example one Welsh Assembly Member was also a farmer, a farmer was also a campaigner and a campaigner was also a scientist. The fusion of multiple standpoints within a single individual illustrates the cross-cutting nature of debates concerning genetic techniques. Whilst this complicates the task of identifying where a particular discourse originates, it highlights the importance of following the circulation of discourses across different roles.

Combining newspaper text analysis with expert interviews allows one to track how ideas of nation are used across different circuits of communication

138   *The Politics of Unsustainability*

(Miller *et al.*, 1997). The discourses present within the press sample depend, in part, on what is said by media sources trying to promote their perspectives. These discourses are then 'mediated through news institutions, values and conventions involving editorial/journalists' choices such as which story to cover, whom to interview and how to edit and frame the debate' (Kitzinger *et al.*, 2007). By looking at both media texts and source interviews it is possible to analyse how discourses of nation are promoted by different actors and how the UK press then mediate these different viewpoints according to their own news values and reportage categories.

The Need for Certainty

The contemporary world is characterised by the uncertainties and insecurities faced by the individuals who inhabit it. The cause of these anxious times is the processes of globalisation which have the power to rip through and undermine categories and concepts which have traditionally dominated the way people think about themselves and the world around them; 'Nature, religion, the nation, the distinction between ourselves and "strangers"' (Beck, 1997: 66) are all called into question. Bauman (1999) writes about the anxiety produced by the loss of modernist categories, including nation, in what he calls the 'political economy of uncertainty'. A key feature of such uncertain politics lies in the prohibition of politically established and guaranteed rules and regulations, and the disarming of the defensive institutions and associations which stood in the way of capital and finances becoming truly *sans frontière* (Bauman, 1999: 173–4).

What Bauman refers to as the political economy of uncertainty, Beck calls the abolition of modernist categories and others refer to as the processes of globalisation. As the ever-increasing power of the global economy cuts across the borders of the world's political structures people feel powerless in the face of new international power structures over which they have no influence. As Bauman states, 'None of the most important levers and safeguards of their [contemporary men and women's] current situation comes under their jurisdiction, let alone control' (Bauman, 1999: 172). Pervasive conditions of uncertainty creates a society full of tension and anxiety which is simultaneously disempowering and corrosive of trust relations. As Blühdorn writes, 'The major challenge for late-modern society is to restore certainty, or at least to find effective strategies for the management of uncertainty, which is an unavoidable consequence of ongoing processes of globalization' (Blühdorn, 2002: 64). The search for certainty leads society to retreat back to the familiar modernist categories which so neatly structured life before the advent of globalisation. Paradoxically, then, nation is granted symbolic credence at exactly the same moment as the processes of globalisation are beginning to unravel nation as a coherent concept. The deconstructing of tradition goes hand in hand with its reconstruction; in fact the latter process supports and enables the former (Beck, 1997: 67).

Self-deception and Symbolic Inversion in the GM Debate 139

The reliance on the symbolic maintenance of categories, however, solves nothing. The processes which create uncertainty in the first place continue unabated. The recourse to the apparent certainty of nation represents an important part of the process of self-deception underpinning the politics of unsustainability (Blühdorn & Welsh, this volume). Meaningful lines cannot be drawn from the old frontiers no matter how dearly we cling to them; as Beck comments in a recent interview, 'Trying to solve these transnational problems on a national level by locking the national territory is like raising a garden fence to avoid the smog in town' (Wimmer & Quandt, 2006: 342).

As a transnational problem GM can no longer be contained along lines of nation; what this piece is concerned with exploring is how discussions around GM still focus on the nation as a meaningful category. This contribution, to quote Blühdorn & Welsh (this volume) is concerned with investigating one of the strategies by which late societies are trying to cope with the awareness and apparent inescapability of their unsustainability. Given the impossibility of regulating GM at the national level this focus provides a powerful example of societal need for certainty; the recourse to nation is a way of providing this certainty and the self-deception undertaken in order to achieve this certainty.

The GM-free Nation

Within the press coverage of GM crops Britain is regularly referred to as an entity that either is or could be made GM-free. Two national newspapers, the *Independent on Sunday* and the *Daily Mail*, ran campaigns based on defending Britain's status as a 'GM-free zone': 'Let's make Britain a GM-free zone now' (*Daily Mail*, 23 February 2006) and 'GM-free Britain may fall to Monsanto' (*Independent on Sunday*, 31 March 2002). In addition to this a plethora of other articles also describe Britain as GM-free; indeed just over one in three articles sampled described Britain as 'GM-free'. The depiction of Britain as a completely GM-free country is a clear case of self-deception given the presence of GM food products, animal feedstock and the possibility of contamination from GM field trials. In this sense Britain's GM barrier has long since been violated. Despite this the portrayal of Britain GM-free extends to campaigning groups. A prominent example is Friends of the Earth's (FoE's) current GM campaign, which runs under the tagline 'Keep Britain GM free'. Yet, when interviewed, campaigners acknowledged that Britain is not GM-free. Julian Rosser, Director of FoE Cymru, admits that when establishing the campaign in Wales the slogan 'GM-free Wales' was not their first choice:

> ... to be honest with you we didn't really brand the campaign when we started it in 1999, we called it 'The GM-free Welsh environment campaign' because we wanted to be, I suppose a bit more honest about this, we couldn't, we weren't stopping soya coming into the country ... almost everybody else would always call it the 'GM-free Wales' campaign anyway. (Julian Rosser, Director of FoE Cymru, 24 March 2005)

140   *The Politics of Unsustainability*

Indeed FoE's 'Keep Britain GM free' campaign is not actually about maintaining the barrier of nation at all but instead about encouraging local authorities to ban the planting of GM crops on their land. Clare Oxborrow, a GM campaigner for FoE Britain, describes the campaign as a specific way of bypassing national government:

> We felt it was pointless trying to direct a campaign at the UK government because they'd already made up their minds, weren't going to listen. So what we did was we deliberately took the campaign back to the local level. (Clare Oxborrow, GM campaigner, FoE Britain, 28 July 2005)

FoE's campaign is not targeted at the level of national government and they were aware that using the phrase 'GM free' is slightly misleading, but in order to create an effective campaign slogan FoE still found it had to rely on the symbolic power of both boundary and nation. It was Britain that had to be spoken about and for Britain's boundary to remain meaningful the nation had to be represented as GM-free.

Although physical risks may cross boundaries, society is still preoccupied with old divisions and frontiers. As a myth to live by, the nation as a symbolic boundary marker matters more now than ever precisely because physical boundaries are increasingly undermined. What the GM debate, and the plethora of other risk debates drawing on the discourse of nation, are undertaking is a discursive reconstruction of the mythic assumption that it was once possible for a nation to control what crossed its borders. There is in effect a symbolic evocation of unity and agency which is confronted by new challenges in the context of the complexity of global regulation and the cross-cutting nature of genetic techniques. Clare Oxborrow cites the ability to discursively construct a border as one of the key advantages of campaigning on GM:

> The other thing that is quite possibly unique about GM is that especially in the UK and Europe we're still at a point where we haven't got GM, well in any significant, well, obviously there are problems and it is coming in and out of our food and whatever but there is still an opportunity to kind of keep Britain GM free, still a sense of holding the line. (Clare Oxborrow, GM campaigner, FoE Britain, 28 July 2005)

Here Clare Oxborrow is describing how advantageous it is to create a sense of a tangible barrier. Even though GM material moves in and out of Britain, as she herself acknowledges, the absence of commercial GM crop planting sustains the sense of a line which can be held, a boundary which can be maintained. Oxborrow claims that 'what scares people is that loss of control, that feeling of not knowing where you're going to end up'. Therefore, by giving people a boundary you are installing a sense of agency or control; a discursive reconstruction of certainty is provided. The complexities of global flows and the multiple ways in which people could come into contact with GM

Self-deception and Symbolic Inversion in the GM Debate   141

are reduced down to a single line, a boundary which must be maintained at all costs.

Oxborrow compares GM with campaigns on climate change and recycling. These, she says, are much more difficult to communicate about because it is hard to see how to solve these problems. GM by comparison is much easier; the solution is in 'holding the line', creating the impression that a defensible barrier can be maintained around 'the nation'. Whilst climate change gases pass freely over the UK there are identifiable sources of GM contamination and viable alternatives to the product lines from these external sources.

This is evidenced in the GM debate by the power of the World Trade Organization to potentially break the European moratorium on GM produce. This anxiety about globalisation and the power of multinationals was a prominent response category in the interviews conducted with scientists, assembly members, farmers, government and activists. Virtually all respondents expressed concern about the power multinationals possessed and the specific uses that companies were choosing to make of GM technology. The only person interviewed who was not concerned about the power exercised by multinationals was a representative from the multinational company Monsanto. Activists were particularly concerned about globalisation; in fact they foregrounded this as one of their main anxieties about GM crops:

> Obviously it [the GM debate] was about these companies . . . the issue was to do with development issues, to do with control of multinational companies over third-world agriculture, and over western agriculture as well. (Ian Willmore, media co-ordinator, FoE, 28 July 2005)

When activists were interviewed, the issues they expressed most concern about were multinationals, globalisation and the industrialisation of agriculture. Yet despite the concern about globalisation voiced by campaigners in interview, hardly any newspaper articles in the sample discussed globalisation or the industrialisation of agriculture and no non-governmental organisation representative was quoted discussing these issues. The most likely explanation for this silence seems to be the reticence most campaigners expressed about trying to discuss complexities with the media; instead they spoke of the need to simplify, to provide soundbites or slogans:

> It is all about simplifying the message and trying to get across the one key point really, so I mean yeah on your average sort of media coverage you don't get the opportunity to go into a lot of issues. (Ben Ayliffe, GM campaigner, Greenpeace, 29 July 2005)

This approach, focusing on a simple core message, reflects journalists' reticence to discuss complexities, preferring instead to stick to established reportage categories and news values (Kitzinger *et al.*, 2007). The silence surrounding the global dimensions of the GM debate in UK press coverage

142 *The Politics of Unsustainability*

might then reflect campaigners' experience of dealing with the media, and their knowledge of what elements of a story are likely to make it into print. This reticence to discuss complicated issues with the media, and the media's reticence to report them unless they are 'the story', seems to mean that the global domain and associated interests are ignored. Instead of exploring the different forces that act to increase or stem the flow of GM produce around the world the argument focuses, almost exclusively, on Britain's borders and how we as a nation can defend them.

The Homogeneous Nation

Brookes's (1999) work on bovine spongiform encephalopathy (BSE) demonstrated how the dominant representations of nationhood deny complexity and contingency and despite the subsequent consolidation of globalisation the GM debate reveals that this process continues. In the GM case the representation of the nation, the natural political and cultural unit , also reduces subnational complexities. Wales and Scotland are only mentioned in 13 of the articles sampled, featuring in only three as the main focus. Subnational voluntary 'GM-free zones' are mentioned in only 12 articles, with four making this the main focus. The dominance of Britain's 'GM-free' status means that there is almost no recognition that the nation is made up of different countries with different levels of governance. In addition to this several county councils have also declared that they wish to remain free of GM crops.

National reporting also takes no account of regional and local implications. In East Anglia, for example, a large amount of wheat and barley is grown, with farmers producing more than a quarter of England's supply of these crops (www.nfu.co.uk). The established availability of GM versions of these crops would result in higher environmental levels of GM pollens in East Anglia compared to Wales where livestock farming dominates. Such differences illustrate the diversity of stakes and publics associated with the GM debate in stark contrast to the unitary depiction of nation. Britain is certainly presented as the natural unit within the GM debate. This is often achieved by referring to the British public as a homogenised whole and therefore creating a community of people whose views are defined by their nationality:

> The minutes of the Government's GM committee, agreed by the Cabinet last week, revealed a government determined to force GM crops on an unwilling British public. (*Independent on Sunday*, 7 March 2004)

Here, the opinions of the British public are represented as uniform and innovation-resistant in their opposition to GM. The homogenisation of the British public's view is not unusual in reportage; it is often used as a way of positing the nation as the natural unit through which to discuss an issue. Part of the reason the media naturally revert to the unit of nation is that the news

Self-deception and Symbolic Inversion in the GM Debate   143

value of stories which affect a particular community or social group is much smaller than the news value of stories which 'potentially affect the abstract community of nation' (Brookes, 1999: 261). This is because a risk to the nation is potentially relevant to every reader. Although newspaper readership varies according to age, gender ethnicity, social class and so on the default readership in the UK is the nation. The distribution of *national* newspapers therefore helps to reinforce the focus on nation that already exists within the GM debate. This is a particular circuit of communication which reduces complexity in terms of both issues and constituencies.

The Island Nation

A significant part of the symbolic importance of Britain's borders is derived from the nation's status as an island. As such Britain is isolated, set apart from other countries by the water that surrounds it. The nation's boundaries are indisputable, visibly marked and constitutive of iconic emblems such as the white cliffs of Dover. The symbolic status of Island Britain is evident within the coverage of GM in ways evocative of the sanctity of the coastal boundary. This was a prominent feature in coverage of a Greenpeace action that took place during the sample period. The action involved protestors using inflatable dinghies to stop a cargo of GM animal feed being delivered to Bristol docks. The story featured dramatic images of protestors framed by a stormy-looking sea sailing out to defend Britain from the cargo vessel of GM produce. This classic example of staged iconic praxis (Welsh, 2000) emphasised the nation's border; some pictures portrayed Britain's coastline in the background with the cargo vessel floating menacingly in front. In most of the articles the story ends with the ship being unable to dock in a British port, and the readers are left to assume that Greenpeace's aim of returning the ship to America was achieved. Only one article, in the *Independent* (22 June 2004), mentioned that the ship would be able to dock the following morning. By focussing on the temporary stoppage imposed by Greenpeace the impression of an inviolate boundary is implicitly maintained in the majority of articles. Within the coverage there are other embedded references evocative of Britain as an island nation as the following quote from Sarah North, a Greenpeace campaigner, demonstrates:

> Tony Blair has picked a fight with the British public. There are thousands of people ready to fight this decision in the fields, the streets, the courts and the supermarkets. (*Daily Mail*, 5 March 2004)

This quote constructs a single community of British people, all of whom are opposed to GM and united in an agenda of action within specified sites. This description of different spaces is evocative of Winston Churchill's famous 'we shall fight on the beaches' speech during the Second World War when the nation was under the threat of literal invasion by German forces. Within this speech Churchill makes specific reference to Britain's status as an island – 'we

144   *The Politics of Unsustainability*

shall defend our island' – and then goes on to list the different spaces that the island citizens will defend: 'we shall fight in the fields and in the streets' (www.winstonchurchill.org). By echoing this speech the quote from Sarah North draws on a historical discourse which posits Britain as a strong island nation which is used to fighting to defend its borders, be it on the beaches or in the supermarkets.

What is happening within the GM debate is very much a self-deception: Britain is not currently guaranteed to be GM-free and the nation's borders are not secure enough to stop more GM seeds or products entering the country. Beck has written about the threats that the world now faces, claiming that late-modern societies are either unable or unwilling to address their own destructive behaviour. Instead of removing unsustainability, society now works to discursively ignore it:

> Everything must take place in the context of a cosmetics of risk, packaging, reducing the symptoms of pollutants, installing filters while retaining the source of filth. Hence we have not a preventative but a symbolic industry. (Beck, 1992: 57)

As noted earlier, Blühdorn (2002) identifies the key political stakes following from such a position in terms of the restoration of certainty or effective strategies for its management. Within the GM debate the restoration of apparent certainty is a key element. Although campaigners who work on GM are practically concerned with working on many levels, encouraging local authorities to take action, challenging the rulings of the EU and considering how best to resist the power of the World Trade Organization (Purdue, 2000), at a discursive level they articulate very few of these complexities. As Clare Oxborrow says, GM has been such a successful campaign precisely because there is still a boundary which can be discursively constructed around the nation. In many ways, then, the GM campaign is about reinvesting the symbolic significance of the nation's border, creating a sense of an isolated community, one where the people of that nation have the power to control their own destiny.

The Pure Nation

The media coverage of genetic modification repeatedly defines the British nation as both important and unique. Articles consistently refer to the importance of Britain's genetic modification decisions at an international as well as a national level. For example, 'Britain's decision to back the commercial growing of a GM crop will have huge ramifications around the world' (*Daily Mail,* 10 March 2004). Britain's genetic modification status matters, the article implies, not just to British people but to the citizens of the world. These world stakes revolve around the 'green revolution' potential of GM crops, a potential blunted when many developing countries refused GM

Self-deception and Symbolic Inversion in the GM Debate   145

food aid following the EU's *de facto* ban. This fits with a long press tradition of Britain's technological achievements being portrayed by official sources in terms of renewed global importance for the nation. Welsh, for example, documents how the adoption of nuclear power was reported nationally as a 'message of hope to the people of the world' whilst expressions of public concern and opposition remained confined to local newspapers serving rural areas during the 1950s (2000: 51, chapter 3).

Within GM coverage the UK countryside is also represented as unique. One article stresses that 'Only a narrow range of existing GM crops were suited to British conditions' (*Independent,* 5 March 2004). This uniqueness is often associated with purity: 'Frankenstein crops spell ruin for a British agriculture that can only survive in the future by producing pure, high quality foods' (*Daily Mail,* 21 February 2004). The article suggests there is a special purity about the British countryside that makes it less suitable than other countries for GM crops. The symbolic importance of rural landscape in the construction of British identity has been noted by many scholars (Daniels, 1993; Taylor, 1995; Matless, 1998). By threatening the British countryside, then, GM crops threaten an important symbolic marker of nation as the distinctiveness of Britain's landscape helps to define the nation as a unique and coherent entity. Just over a quarter (27%) of articles within the sample used the words 'pure' or 'purity' when discussing Britain's food or landscape. Britain's uniqueness was something which most of the stakeholders interviewed made reference to. Campaigners spoke not just about how Britain's landscape was unique but also how people's relationship with it was unique:

> It's a risk to the environment and to societies' relationship with the environment reasonably acute here in the UK where there is a relationship with the land which simply doesn't exist in America. (Doug Parr, Chief Scientist for Greenpeace, 29 July 2005)

Britain's uniqueness was also discussed as a marketable quality: it was something that could be sold, and there were economic reasons for keeping GM out of Britain. Farmers and anti-GM government figures normally advanced this viewpoint. This is a quote from Gerald Miles, a farmer, talking about why he believes Britain should stay GM-free:

> British farmers are trying to market themselves as this great green country we live in and it's our selling point, we need to market it as such. It's only common sense, our natural assets are all around us, it makes us unique. (Gerald Miles, organic farmer and member of GM-free Cymru, 17 July 2005)

It is Britain's innate 'naturalness', Britain's image as a 'great green country', which Gerald Miles is positing as a marketable commodity. Marketable 'heritage countryside' is of particular importance to farmers urged to diversify

146   *The Politics of Unsustainability*

into tourism as a means of supplementing their incomes. This also reflects an EU-wide restructuring of agricultural subsidies to promote bio-diversity and sustainability whilst reducing the various produce 'mountains' resulting from previous subsidy regimes. The ability to sell Britain as a country with an abundance of natural assets is something which Gerald Miles claims GM crops would undermine. Scientists also describe Britain as unique, especially in relation to the farm-scale trials and when considering why GM has not become as popular in Britain as it has in America:

> You need to understand that we have been manipulating the British countryside since the Iron Age. Every square inch of what you look at is managed. So what we consider to be the natural environment isn't, and this balance here is extremely important for the UK. (Chris Pollock, Chair of the Advisory Committee on Releases into the Environment, 19 August 2005)

Professor Pollock is putting forward a very different view from Gerald Miles. Instead of connecting Britain's uniqueness with 'natural assets' it is the heavily managed aspect of the landscape, particularly when compared to the farmlands of North America, that mark it out. It is not the uniqueness of nature that needs to be protected, but the precarious balance of an already manipulated landscape. This contrasts markedly with views of industry figures who denied that there was anything at all unique about the British landscape:

> Well I don't buy that at all. I very often hear it's because America is a big open space, whereas here we are all mixed up together ... but no, there is a lot of very mixed farming ... so I don't think that's different. (Colin Merritt, Biotechnology Development Manager, Monsanto, 23 August 2005)

By stating that there is no difference between British and American landscapes Monsanto is able to counter claims that a careful approach has to be taken when introducing GM crops in Britain because of the distinct nature of the British countryside. If the landscapes are similar then there is no need for caution; the technology can be introduced in Britain in exactly the same way as it has been in America. Colin Merritt is demonstrating how economic interests are indifferent to difference as long as profit is realised. Politically this becomes increasingly problematic for politicians advancing globalisation, as their electorates want difference to be maintained and lines to be drawn (Chesters & Welsh, 2006). This difficulty was evidenced in the GM debate as the government came under increasing criticism for pushing what were perceived to be big business interests over the interests of British citizens. These underlying tensions suggest that framing the GM Nation exercise in terms of 'risk' missed one of the primary frames shaping public perceptions.

Despite most of the interviewees referring to Britain's uniqueness, none of them described Britain as pure. Sources only described Britain as a fragile or unique country: this was evidenced both in the interviews and in the attributed quotes contained in the articles. In contrast to this, articles regularly referred to Britain as a pure country, suggesting that this was a discourse that the UK press introduced, rather than any of the sources.

The Contaminated Crop

As well as describing Britain as pure many of the newspaper articles described GM crops as contaminated. The link between genetic modification and contamination is taken as self-evident and is rarely questioned by the UK press. This is particularly evident when cross-pollination is being discussed. On most occasions the word 'contamination' is used instead of 'cross-pollination'. This occurs even in articles which are not taking an explicitly anti-GM line. One article begins with the headline 'How GM crops pollute two-thirds of the landscape'. It goes on to discuss how 'scientists found that normal American crops are now "pervasively contaminated by GM varieties"' (*Daily Mail*, 8 March 2004). The use of the word 'pollute' suggests that non-GM crops have become dirty or corrupted by the GM material. The phrase 'pervasively contaminated' suggests an irreversible change which has totally altered the once 'normal American crop'. The word 'normal' is implicitly invested with a certain purity. It can be substituted for the word 'natural'. The 'everydayness' of normal US food, food that was provided by nature, has now been corrupted by the artificial genes inserted into it.

Hybridisation, serendipitously and through human intervention, is of course historically not novel. What seems to be of concern here, however, is mixing across species, such as frost-resistant lettuce utilising a fish gene, and the potential for such 'artificial' varieties to contaminate 'natural' ones. Here, genetic modification allows new borders to be crossed and boundaries breached in ways which threaten the 'natural order' by locating 'matter out of place' (Douglas, 1966). In effect when GM material cross-pollinates, it becomes 'matter out of place' threatening the purity of our food and environment. In this manner both the human recipient and the organic environment are put at risk in terms of their symbolic integrity, irrespective of underlying technical risk vectors. Public unease thus reflects both symbolic and substantive concerns, leaving risk communication strategies which emphasise technical risks unable to address public concerns in their totality.

The Double Threat: Foreign Food and Foreign People

The focus on national boundaries, coupled with the language of purity and contamination, has some very real consequences for the way in which the risk from GM is reported in the press. Haraway has written about the genetic modification of humans, animals and plants; she claims that the debates have

148   *The Politics of Unsustainability*

the potential to become inflected with 'the unintended tones of fear of the alien and suspicion of the mixed' (Haraway, 1997: 61). Such inflections are prominent factors within the GM debate. This is highlighted by the way many articles, in both tabloid and broadsheet coverage within the sample, alluded in both conscious and unconscious ways to the immigration debate. Asylum and immigration have been extremely contentious issues in the UK over the past few years, with the media playing a central role in framing the debate. Media coverage of asylum seekers has been 'overwhelmingly negative and hostile' (Buchanan *et al.*, 2003), with tabloid papers, in particular, continually reporting an asylum 'crisis'. Media portrayals of activist communities involved in contesting both GM and wider globalisation issues have also drawn links to immigration issues (Donson *et al.*, 2004).

A popular image in the discussion of GM crops is that of flooding. A headline from the *Independent on Sunday* reads: 'GM soya and maize were flooding unnoticed into the UK' (7 March 2004) and *The Times* writes about: 'The extraordinary move which will open the floodgates to GM crops' (19 January 2004). Overall, 21% of articles refer to flooding. As Welsh (this volume) argues the control of floodwaters is a defining feature of western civilisation and the metaphorical linkage between inundation by water and inundation by immigrants is a long-established means of framing this issue (Theweleit, 1987). Given the centrality of flows in constituting globalisation (Lash & Urry, 1994), flooding metaphors point to the ways in which flows of people challenge established dynamics within nations as they introduce different ideas, religions and literatures, all of which call national identity into question.

The flood is the ultimate threat to border, washing distinctions and divisions away. It is the ultimate 'matter out of place', as Douglas (1966) would phrase it. When discussing how GM crops traverse boundaries it is a very powerful symbol. The flooding metaphor discursively links the asylum and immigration debate with the GM debate by evoking registers made familiar in previous decades, mostly notably through Margaret Thatcher's use of swamping in 1978.

The use of this sort of imagery was particularly noticeable following the expansion of the EU which took place on 1 May 2004. One of the risks which the newspapers focused on was the entry of GM foods from accession countries. On 14 February 2004 a headline in the *Guardian* read: 'EU races to thwart influx of food from east' following attempts by the US administration to get 'new Europe' (Poland in particular) to accept GM crops. No direct comparisons are drawn between genetic modification and asylum debates, but the polysemic nature of the language used means it is easy to make the connection; the word 'food' could so easily be replaced with the word 'people' and appear as a headline in the *Daily Mail*.

Furthermore, the reigniting of the immigration debate at the time of EU expansion meant that these connections might have been prominent in readers' minds. Press coverage about EU expansion during the weeks preceding the 'food influx' article carried headlines such as: 'Britain faces influx of Europe's

Self-deception and Symbolic Inversion in the GM Debate   149

gypsies' (*Sunday Times*, 18 January 2004), 'Sweden acts to stop influx of EU workers' (*Guardian*, 31 January 2004) and 'We'll halt the EU influx' (*Daily Mirror*, 5 February 2004).

In my sample, 26% of articles used the terms 'unseen' or 'hidden'. Asylum seekers are often portrayed as an unseen threat, creeping into the UK in the dead of night, hiding in the back of lorries. Implicitly such portrayals mirror Beck's emphasis upon the invisible nature of contemporary risks. Similarly, several stories report problems with detecting GM. One story discusses how GM tomatoes were grown undetected at the Eden project, and the *Daily Mirror* coverage of the cargo delayed by Greenpeace protestors portrayed it as 'arriving unseen in the middle of the night'. Several stories also ascribe agency to GM crops: for example, the *Daily Mail* (20 May 2004) writes: 'Mr Bryne admitted that GM food is sneaking unseen into the food chain all over the world'. GM crops are sneaky and deceptive, creeping in whilst our backs are turned. This echoes, almost exactly, the more right-wing newspapers' descriptions of most asylum seekers.

Blühdorn (2002) writes about the way in which the need for certainty has shifted certain issues like:

> ... the defence of ethnic, national and cultural identities; internal and external security; border control and defence against migration ... The transition from modernity to late modernity can be seen as a movement from an inclusive to an exclusive society, that is from a society whose accent was on assimilation and incorporation to one that separates and excludes. (Blühdorn, 2002: 64)

One reason why the asylum and GM crop debate share a similar language is because they are both concerned with reasserting certainty. The linking of environmental risk and race through the evocation of asylum issues within the media coverage of GM amplifies the sense of uncertainty already present as the threats to the nation's boundary multiply. Both debates are concerned with the anxiety produced by the intrusion of foreign substances and counter this by positing the nation's boundary as strong and if not impenetrable then at least defensible. As such, both debates utilise the categories Blühdorn prioritises: the focus on borders, defence of national identities and defence against migration. In effect both debates are a response to the flows of globalisation, be it the flow of people, the flow of products or, pertinent to both, the flow of risks. The response to the anxieties produced by these flows is to discursively retreat to the imagined firm boundaries of the past, even if in reality these barriers were and are permeable.

Conclusion: The Self-deceiving Nation

Uncertainty is a fundamental characteristic of late-modern society: the erosion of traditional modernist categories leaves society grappling for new ways to

150　*The Politics of Unsustainability*

meaningfully reimagine itself. Beck's theory of individualisation suggests that people today must constantly undergo the process of inventive self-definition to create their own categories of meaning: 'Individualisation means the disintegration of the certainties of industrial society as well as the compulsion to find and invent new certainties for oneself and others without them' (Beck, 1997: 96). Yet this creative reinvention of certainty is not borne out in the case of GM; instead old categories are reinvented and fiercely clung to. Bauman comments that:

> Attacking insecurity at its source is a daunting task, calling for nothing less than rethinking and renegotiating some of the most fundamental assumptions of the type of society currently in existence. (Baumann, 1999: 6)

In the case of GM at least such renegotiation of categories is yet to be achieved and instead the old divisions of 'boundary' and 'nation' retain a position of prominence. These categories evoke a sense of security and order: as Clare Oxborrow from FoE put it, 'a feeling of control'. Of course not all sources referred to national boundaries when talking about GM crops. In general there appeared to be a continuum from those who were very pro-GM, in particular biotechnology companies, who did not refer to boundaries at all, to those who were very anti-GM, in particular activists, who placed a large amount of importance on boundaries.

A possible reason for this difference is that the invocation of boundaries is used in response to a threat; they are used to discursively reconstruct security, and therefore if biotechnology companies were going to reference boundaries they would have to acknowledge that a threat existed. For campaigners, however, boundaries provide a way of creating a sense of agency; they create the impression that there is something people can do in response to the threat from GM. Even if British citizens are unable to stop other countries growing GM, at least Britain can be kept 'GM-free'. Politically the evocation of nation within GM debates has been profoundly challenging to political leaderships promoting globalisation agendas. Whilst coverage of the GM debate provides a powerful example of societal self-deception in terms of the evocation of a symbolic boundary condition giving a false sense of security, the accompanying sense of agency continues to hinder what John Vidal dubbed 'America's masterplan to force GM food on the world' (*Guardian*, 13 February 2006: 32).

Yet the defence of Britain's or even Europe's GM boundary is ultimately futile if the rest of the world continues to cultivate GM crops. Globalisation offers individual nations little chance of determining their own policy on GM or any other internationally traded product. If activists really wish to stem the flow of GM crops engagement is needed with the many layers of governance GM crops are subject to, and action needs to be mobilised not just around national boundaries but around all the boundaries across which GM products can flow.

What is the alternative then to a political self defined and motivated by the defence of a nation's borders? What kind of new subjectivity would have to be envisaged to relocate the site of citizen concern from the neat lines of Britain's frontiers to the tangled web of global flows? Perhaps the first place to turn is to Beck whose concept of individualisation offers us a new notion of the subject, one which is not built on traditional forms of identity but instead finds its own way of giving meaning to self. Haraway talks about envisaging a new political subjectivity claiming that subjects do not exist as pre-given entities but rather they are produced through the actions they take and the network of alliances they form. She refers to a specific kind of imaginative politics needed to envisage this network (Calloni, 2003). It is this kind of imagining that can perhaps offer a new political subject: one who views themselves as part of a global chain of actors; one for whom geographical location is but one point of connection. Within such a subjectivity, the boundaries of nation would neither be fiercely clung to nor revered, for an individual's nationality would become but one fragment of their identity.

Yet the politics of unsustainability (Blühdorn & Welsh, this volume) clearly works against such a creative reimagining of self. Simulative politics have become the life-support machine for the narrative of modernity which cannot be allowed to die (Blühdorn, this volume). The mobilisation of symbolic stakes works to reinforce old solutions and traditional forms of identity. The case of GM crops shows just how powerful the strategies of self-deception can be: even amongst those who are trying to challenge the current system self-deception is necessary to create a sense of agency. If society continues to be preoccupied with discursively managing risks, rather than changing the unsustainable lifestyles which led to the creation of those risks, then the categories of 'nation' and 'boundary' will remain the 'indispensable ingredients of late-modern consciousness and identity' (Blühdorn, 2002: 65). They help provide a sense of security and order, or as Clare Oxborrow from FoE phrased it, 'a feeling of control'. 'Holding the line' is therefore not just a rhetorical device used by NGOs but a constitutive part of the late-modern society.

Acknowledgement

The data used for this article were compiled for Project Five of the Social Contexts and Responses to Risk network (Grant Number: RES-336-25-0001), which focuses on media courses and framing. I would like to thank the Economic and Social Research Council for funding this network.

Note

1. When the Lexis-Nexis electronic database was searched for articles containing the word 'GM' in the headline for the year 1998 only 45 articles were produced, yet when the database was searched for the year 1999 1125 articles were produced. This demonstrates the huge increase in coverage.

152 *The Politics of Unsustainability*

References

Bauman, Z. (1999) *In Search of Politics* (Cambridge: Polity).

Beck, U. (1992) *Risk Society: Towards a New Modernity* (London: Sage).

Beck, U. (1997) *The Reinvention of Politics: Rethinking Modernity in the Global Social Order* (Cambridge: Polity).

Blühdorn, I. (2002) 'Unsustainability as a frame of mind and how we disguise it: the silent counter-revolution and the politics of simulation', *Trumpeter* 18(1): 59–69.

Bond, J. M., Daniels, R. & Bioret, F. (2005) 'Genetic diversity in *crame maritime* along the English Channel: the role of ocean currents in determining population structure', *Ecography* 28: 374–84.

Brookes, R. (1999) 'Newspapers and national identity: the BSE/CJD crisis and the British press', *Media, Culture and Society* 21(2): 247–63.

Buchanan, S., Grillo, B. & Threadgold, T. (2003) *What's the Story? Results from Research into Media Coverage of Refugees and Asylum Seekers in the UK* (London: Article 19).

Calloni, M. (ed.) (2003) 'Interview: feminism, politics, theories and science', *European Journal of Women's Studies* 10(1): 87–103.

Chesters, G. & Welsh, I. (2006) *Complexity and Social Movements – Multitudes at the Edge of Chaos* (London: Routledge).

Daniels, S. (1993) *Fields of Vision: Landscape Imagery and National Identity in England and the United States* (Cambridge: Polity).

Donson, F., Chesters, G., Tickle, A. & Welsh, I. (2004) 'Rebels with a cause, folk devils without a panic: press jingoism, policing tactics and anti-capitalist protests in London and Prague', *Internet Journal of Criminology*. Available at: http://www.internetjournalofcriminology.com/ Donson%20et%20al%20-%20Folkdevils.pdf (accessed 2 December 2006).

Douglas, M. (1966) *Purity and Danger: An Analysis of Concepts of Pollution and Taboo* (London: Pelican Books).

Haraway, D. (1997) *Modest_Witness@Second_Millennium. FemaleMan© _meets_ OncoMouse™ Feminism and Technoscience* (New York: Routledge).

Kitzinger, J., Williams, C. & Henderson, L. (2007) 'Science, media and society: the framing of bioethical debates around risk and embryonic stem cell research between 2000 and 2005', in Glasner & Atkinson (eds.), *New Genetics, New Social Formations* (London: Routledge).

Lash, S. & Urry, J. (1994) *Economies of Signs and Space* (London: Sage).

Matless, D. (1998) *Landscape and Englishness* (London: Reaktion Books).

Miller, D., Kitzinger, J., Williams, K. & Beharrell, P. (1997) *Circuit of Mass Communication: Media Strategies, Representation and Audience Reception* (London: Sage).

Purdue, D. (2000) *Anti-genetix: The Emergence of the Anti-GM Movement* (Aldershot: Ashgate).

Sarewitz, D. (2004) 'How science makes environmental controversies worse', *Environmental Science and Policy* 7(5): 385–403.

Taylor, J. (1995) *A Dream of England: Landscape, Photography and the Tourist's Imagination* (Manchester: Manchester University Press).

Theweleit, K. (1987) *Male Fantasies Volume 1: Women, Floods, Bodies, History* (Minneapolis, MN: Minnesota University Press).

Wimmer, J. & Quandt, T. (eds.) (2006) 'Living in the risk society: an interview with Ulrich Beck', *Journalism Studies* 7(2): 335–48.

Welsh, I. (2000) *Mobilising Modernity: The Nuclear Moment* (London: Routledge).

Welsh, I. (2006) 'Values, science and the EU: bio-technology and transatlantic relations', in I. Manners & S. Lucarelli (eds.), *Values and Principles in EU Foreign Policy*, pp. 59–76 (London: Routledge).

The Post-ecologist Condition: Irony as Symptom and Cure

BRONISLAW SZERSZYNSKI
Centre for the Study of Environmental Change, Department of Sociology, University of Lancaster, UK

ABSTRACT *Resources for an authentic response to the 'post-ecologist condition' as described by Ingolfur Blühdorn can be found in a cultural modernism which emphasises the contradictory nature of the human condition and whose master trope is irony. The concept of irony can help us both diagnose and respond to the crisis in public meaning which helps sustain unsustainable behaviour. Forms of dispositional irony, in which private and public meaning are disconnected from each other, are symptomatic of the post-ecologist condition; in response, forms of communicative irony are used by environmental movements to expose such dispositions and strategies. However, such tactics can only serve as partial and limited responses to the problem of unsustainability, unless they are embedded within and shaped by a generalised ironic stance towards the world and oneself. The contribution concludes by sketching elements of an environmentalism informed by this ironic 'world relation'.*

Introduction

> I'm washing out Marmite pots and they're digging for oil in Alaska. (Sean Locke)

At the heart of contemporary western culture there seems to be a constitutive tension between ecological awareness and ecocidal behaviour. On the one hand, we are confronted by mounting evidence of a host of interconnected ecological problems, ranging from resource depletion, through climate change and biodiversity loss, to the growing effects that chemical pollution is having on basic life processes. On the other hand, advanced capitalist societies seem irreversibly locked into a societal form of life that involves not just a

154 *The Politics of Unsustainability*

continuation but an intensification of the very activities which are producing these problems in the first place. Thus, despite over three decades of policy attention and civil society action, global, international and national indicators show little evidence of any fundamental shift towards more 'sustainable' trajectories (United Nations Environment Programme, 2002; Sustainable Development Commission, 2004; European Commission, 2005). States and corporations increasingly adopt forms of environmental responsibility which seem to focus more on self-presentation than on impact reduction – British Petroleum's 1989 'greening' and its 2000 rebranding as 'beyond petroleum' being perhaps the most infamous example (Beder, 2002). Against such a background, any individual act of environmental responsibility can feel *ir*responsible, an act of complicity in a collective dance of self-delusion.

So what can be done? How can we properly diagnose this situation, and then move towards identifying a remedy? Ingolfur Blühdorn has argued elsewhere (e.g. Blühdorn, 2004 and this volume) that in the contemporary political context it is naïve to imagine that political responsibility consists in countering empty, symbolic politics with real, authentic politics. Such is the pervasiveness of the Baudriallardian hyperreality into which we have wandered, a forest of mirrors in which signs merely reflect other signs rather than anything real, that the contrast between symbolic and authentic politics can no longer confidently be made. Indeed, rather than 'symbolic politics', Blühdorn suggests, what is endemic is a 'simulative politics' in which contemporary culture and the meanings through which it is reproduced have become self-referential, detached from any obligation to material referents or effects. And rather than simulative politics being merely a particular strategy adopted by particular actors, it is a pervasive syndrome in which even social movement activity is trapped.

I agree with Blühdorn that a meaningful response to our situation is not to be found in the mere castigation of ecological vice in others and the ensuring of ecological virtue in oneself. The persistence of unsustainability is due not simply to the ignorance or duplicity of individuals, or even to the mere logic of the capitalist system, but also to a *crisis in political meaning* in which we are all implicated. I also agree that the solution to this crisis is not to be found in a simple restoration of political language's reference to a reality outside language, as if language is a flapping sail that can simply be re-secured to its mast. It was the cul-de-sac of modernity's 'correspondence' theory of truth – the idea that language and the world are separate, and that language can be judged by how it more or less accurately corresponds to the world – that led to the crisis of representation in the first place. Nevertheless, I do not share Blühdorn's pessimism about the impossibility of an authentic political response in these circumstances, one that that does not bind us further in illusion. In this paper I want to suggest where we might find the cultural and intellectual resources for such a response.

To date, environmentalist thought has been largely dominated by two epistemological strategies, each grounded in a different current of modern thought. The first is that, broadly speaking, of the 18th-century Enlightenment.

Irony as Symptom and Cure   155

According to this tradition of thought, with its guiding metaphors of illumination, uncovering and exposure, the light of reason can be used to banish the shadows from the world. Then, no longer under the thrall of ignorance, superstition or deception, human beings will be able to bring their destiny under their own collective control. While this cultural trope has been frequently castigated by environmentalists as underlying the domination of nature by industrial capitalism and techno-science, in subtler forms it has also been used to underpin environmentalism itself. The prominence of this trope in environmentalism can only partly be explained by reference to the latter's debt to ecological science. Environmental politics also draws on an Enlightenment meta-narrative, more widely culturally available, in order to present ecological destruction as the result of a rationality deficit: if only we had more knowledge about how nature works, the story goes, and if only we allowed our actions to be guided by it, then we would live in harmony with nature.

A second important epistemological strategy in environmental politics, intertwined with the first, has been the *rejection* of reason, a call to return to nature and tradition, with roots in the Romantic reaction against industrialism in the 19th century. According to this current of thought, the ills of the world cannot be banished by reason, since it is reason – and specifically a form of disembedded, instrumental reason which alienates people from nature – that is their ultimate cause. Rather than humanity saving nature through the operation of scientific reason, it is nature that can save humanity; if only human societies can reject the artificialities and strictures of modern life, can reconnect with both internal and external nature, then both their own spiritual impoverishment and the associated despoliation of nature would be reversed. While this cultural current often invokes and extols traditional societies, it is in many ways as modern as the Enlightenment current described above, in its valorisation of the autonomy and power of individual human subjectivity, and its faith in the idea that the human interaction with nature can in principle be cleansed of uncertainty, contingency and struggle.

But in this contribution I want to draw attention to a *third* cultural current of modernity, one equally as modern as either of the others, but with a very different tenor. This current, which I will refer to as 'cultural' modernism, has, I suggest, been an important source of the environmentalist *sensibility*, but has heretofore not been as influential on the way that environmentalism has been formally expressed. According to this current, the human condition is full of shadows, paradoxes and absurdities. Like techno-scientific modernism, this rather different modernist current constitutes itself through a break from tradition and organised religion, but rather than stressing the power of human reason is more likely to emphasise its limits. This strand of modernism can be seen in Nietzsche's notion of the death of God and of the universe as meaningless, and in Freud's insight that most of what shapes our thoughts and actions is opaque to human consciousness. It even colours the ideas of Charles Darwin and Karl Marx that the real motor of history lies outside human hands, in the operation of blind material forces, conflict, structures and

156   *The Politics of Unsustainability*

accident. It finds expression in the very *form* of the modern novel, with its exploration of the multiple, incommensurable points of view that constitute any human situation. And it found one of its most sophisticated articulations in the work of the Danish philosopher Søren Kierkegaard.

I want to suggest that, were we to ground environmental politics in *this* cultural current, we would be in a better position to diagnose the contemporary situation of unsustainability described above, and to find an authentic response. I want to develop this claim by exploring the relevance of the polyvalent concept of 'irony' to the contemporary condition of unsustainability. After introducing the concept of irony in the next section, I then discuss how it can help us in the task of understanding the character of cultural phenomena that are symptomatic of the post-ecologist condition, phenomena such as dissimulation and apolitical disengagement. However, I then go on to suggest that, if irony is a cultural *symptom* of our situation of systemic unsustainability, in other forms it can also serve as a *cure* for this syndrome. I point out that the modes of irony typically deployed by environmental groups take a 'corrective' form, in that they draw attention to the gap between appearance and reality, or between stated intentions and behaviour, in order to try to overcome it – for example, by forcing corporations to act in conformity with their stated pro-environmental objectives. While recognising the value of such tactics, I draw attention to the dangers involved in corrective forms of irony, in particular the way that they seek to establish a stable triangular relationship between appearance, reality and a privileged observer able to clearly perceive the relationship between the two. In another twist of irony, the apparently privileged observer in such corrective forms of irony can *themselves* be accused of self-deception and bad faith. I will argue that it is only by adopting a stance of generalised, philosophical irony, one which recognises the impossibility of the subject escaping the contradictions of finite existence, that an authentic response to our predicament might be found. In so doing I will be arguing that the most appropriate philosophical foundation for ecological politics is neither techno-scientific modernism, nor a counter-modern reaction to techno-science, but a cultural modernism of which a generalised irony is the master trope.

What is Irony?

> ...where wit enables a man to see 'occult resemblances in things apparently unlike', to use Johnson's words, a sense of irony enables a man to see occult incompatibilities within a total situation and to see a 'victim' confidently unaware of them. (Muecke, 1969: 94)

As D. C. Muecke's masterful study makes clear, irony is a complex concept, one whose changing meaning over the last two millennia reveals much about wider changes in European culture (Muecke, 1969). Most accounts of irony focus on two main classes of ironic phenomena, which we might call

Irony as Symptom and Cure 157

communicative irony and situational irony respectively. Firstly, instances of *communicative irony*, whether verbal, visual or musical, involve a communication in which the overt, surface meaning of the communication is in tension with the actual meaning intended to be communicated. One of the most famous extended examples of communicative irony is Jonathan Swift's *A Modest Proposal* (1729), which seemingly advocates as a solution to the Irish potato famine the idea that rich Anglo-Irish should buy and eat the children of poor Catholics; Swift's *real* intention, we would say, was that the tract be read as an indictment of the attitudes of the English and the Anglo-Irish to the Irish poor. Secondly, in *situational irony*, by contrast, it is not acts of communication but situations that might be seen as ironic, when the understanding of a situation possessed by one or more actors acting within that situation is in dramatic tension with the reality of it as perceived by an outside observer. For example, a character in a story might seek to evade a threat, not knowing that the very choices they have made in order to save themselves are leading them more firmly into its clutches – a device employed perhaps most famously in Sophocles' *Oedipus the King* (1994). Thirdly, however, for the purposes of my discussion, we must also consider examples of *dispositional* irony, in which it is a person – or more exactly their character, comportment or sensibility – that might be judged ironic. This class of irony will be relevant in the diagnostic portion of my paper; here it will help us to identify and characterise two of what we might, following MacIntyre (1985), call the typical 'character types' of the post-ecologist condition, characteristic ways of conducting oneself which at once are fostered by and help to reproduce the crisis of public meaning described in the introduction to this paper, and in Ingolfur Blühdorn's contribution to this collection. But it will also find a new kind of relevance at the end of the paper, in which a particular form of dispositional irony, one in which we might say that an ironic sensibility is followed through to its logical conclusion, is offered as a model for environmental politics.

But given such a wide range of cultural phenomena that can be classified as ironic, what do they all have in common? What makes them 'ironic'? From his survey of 'the compass of irony', Muecke identifies three main criteria for a communication or situation to be meaningfully labelled as ironic. Firstly, there must be at least two layers of meaning within the phenomenon. 'At the lower level is the situation either as it appears to the victim of irony (where there is a victim) or as it is deceptively presented by the ironist (where there is an ironist) . . . At the upper level is the situation as it appears to the observer or the ironist'. Secondly, there has to be some contradiction or incongruity between the two levels. 'What is said may be contradicted by what is meant . . .; what the victim thinks may be contradicted by what the observer knows'. Thirdly, most forms of irony also contain 'an element of "innocence": either a victim is confidently unaware of the very possibility of there being an upper level or point of view that invalidates his own, or an ironist pretends not to be aware of it' (1969: 19–20).

158   *The Politics of Unsustainability*

Muecke's criteria can be illustrated with the help of Swift's *A Modest Proposal*. Firstly, then, the pamphlet contains both a literal meaning (that the rich should eat the children of the poor) and a hidden, intended meaning (that the attitude of the (English) rich towards the (Irish) poor is morally reprehensible). Secondly, it achieves its effect through the dramatic tension between the literal meaning and the intended meaning. Thirdly, it is written with an exaggerated sincerity that gives the impression that the author is wholly unaware of the horrific nature of what he is advocating.

However, the *way* that any example of irony might meet these criteria will vary from case to case, so that it is not possible to specify hard and fast rules for what is ironic and why it is ironic. This is partly due to the organic way that the concept and practice of irony have evolved across history, leading to a fairly loose 'family' of cultural phenomena that have been gathered together under the term. But it is also because the phenomenon of irony has an irreducibly *subjective* component. As Muecke observes, even if a remark or event has the formal features identified above, we would not be likely to call it ironic if the author of a remark did not *intend* it as such, or if an observer of a situation did not *feel* it as such. Put in the terms above, communicative irony implies the existence of an ironist, and situational irony the existence of an observer of the irony. For example, we would not call *A Modest Proposal* irony if Swift had actually meant it literally. Similarly, the audience of a performance of *Oedipus the King* does not simply 'discover' the dramatic irony that lies in Oedipus fleeing Corinth in order to avoid the fate predicted for him, and by that very act helping to bring it about; the presence of situational irony *requires* there to be an observer which can see the partial vision of the innocent protagonist, the wider dramatic picture and the awful tension between them. This subjective aspect to irony brings it close to the aesthetic in its logic. On the one hand, what is ironic to one person might not be to another; on the other, we can nevertheless argue about whether something is ironic or not – and indeed we can use aesthetic criteria to judge whether it is *good* irony or not – whether it is laboured or mistimed, or by contrast artful or poetic (Muecke, 1969: 14–15).

How can we apply the concept of irony to the politics of unsustainability? In the sections that follow, I will deploy the concept of irony to capture a range of specific aspects of the contemporary politics of unsustainability. Irony, I will first argue, can be used to describe the disconnection between private belief and public behaviour that can occur in individuals, states, corporations and even environmental organisations, whether in the form of an apolitical retreat from collective language and endeavours, or in that of outright cynical dissimulation. Secondly, irony can also refer to the rhetorical tactics that are used by environmental protest movements in order to draw attention to that disconnection – when they highlight the gap between 'is' and 'ought', or between appearance and reality, in the behaviour of individuals and organisations. In the terms used by Muecke in the quotation at the beginning of this section, an ironic sensibility can help identify and draw attention to the

Irony as Symptom and Cure   159

'occult incompatibilities' in the contemporary world – tensions, inconsistencies and absurdities which are rendered invisible by the dominant symbolic codes through which contemporary society is reproduced (Melucci, 1996). But, thirdly, I suggest that such tactics are always themselves vulnerable to being ironised, and that it is only in a generalised, philosophical irony that a meaningful political response can be developed.

Irony as Comportment

Given that modern understandings of irony are dominated by the first two categories discussed above, communicative and situational irony, it may seem strange to start by discussing dispositional irony. However, Muecke points out that the term *eironeia* did not come to mean verbal irony until Aristotle (although there were examples of what we would now call irony or mockery in early writers like Homer), and that what I have called 'situational' irony was not called irony until the late 18th century. With its earliest appearances, *eironeia* was applied to phenomena which later writers would not call properly ironic at all – those involving the behaviour or disposition of an individual or group. For classical Greek thinkers such as Theophrastus, an *eiron* is simply a deceptive person, someone who is 'evasive and non-committal, concealing his enmities, pretending friendship, misrepresenting his acts, never giving a straight answer' (Muecke, 1970: 14). In this reading, then, 'ironic' is a predicate that can be applied not just to certain *messages*, or to certain *situations*, but to certain *persons*, by virtue of their whole mode of behaviour in the world.

Such an irony of comportment, a radical disjuncture between outward behaviour and inner intention, is a key symptom of the crisis of political meaning that Blühdorn describes in terms of simulative politics. The case studies presented in other papers in this volume provide many examples of states and corporations behaving with what we might call a Theophrastian irony of spin and manipulation.[1] But perhaps more characteristic of our era is a slightly different form of irony-as-comportment – one we might loosely call 'postmodern irony'.[2] The Theophrastian *eiron* instrumentally manipulates his or her appearance and communications in order to bring about certain effects in the world (in Trilling's (1972) terms, he or she is neither authentic nor sincere); the postmodern ironist is simply detached from the world. The postmodern 'liberal ironist' lauded by the political philosopher Richard Rorty (1989) accepts the contingency of all of his or her final vocabularies, and recognises the impossibility of reconciling the inner demands of ironic self-creation with the outer demands of human solidarity. As such, the postmodern ironist strongly resembles the pseudonymous author, 'A', of Part I of Kierkegaard's *Either/Or* (1992a). The very freedom of A's aestheticised existence, his self-absorbed pursuit of sheer experience, is predicated on his disdainful self-distancing from the ordinary, immediate, shared world of existence. As Alex Callinicos rather disdainfully puts it, postmodern irony is 'the knowing and detached appropriation of experiences by an elite that

160   *The Politics of Unsustainability*

regards itself as too sophisticated for simple pleasures and unqualified commitments' (Callinicos, 1995: 205).[3]

Using de Certeau's (1984) distinction between strategy and tactic, this is irony as *strategy*, as a ruse of power. Following Muecke's analysis, these cultural phenomena exhibit their ironic duality as a tension (Theophrastus) or simple disconnection (Rorty) between inner intention and outer behaviour. In the Theophrastian irony of dissimulation, the disconnection of outer behaviour from inner intention is a device to generate power. Words and gestures are no longer in debt to the demands of a shared hermeneutic project of common understanding; instead, they become mere *tools* of power, instruments to bring about desired effects in the world (Habermas, 1979). By contrast, Rorty's postmodern irony can be seen as an *effect* of power, a device to hoard power that has already been amassed by a given social group. The disconnection of the project of developing a vocabulary through which one understands oneself, from that of developing a common understanding of our obligations to others, represents a hoarding of power. Thus, in the contemporary politics of unsustainability we can see *both* of these ruses. For example, we see the *symbolic politics* of companies cynically exploiting the goodwill of customers by (dubiously) claiming ecological virtues for their products. But, in Blühdorn's terms, we also see a more widespread and culturally complex *simulative politics*, in which contemporary culture and the meanings through which it is reproduced become self-referential, detached from any obligation to material referents or effects. Political commentators indulge in whimsical 'comic nihilism' about the likely effects of global warming ('Oh, bugger it and open another bottle!' (Ereaut & Segnit, 2006: 15)). And states and corporations collude in the self-delusions of an ecologism that has been reformulated along neo-liberal lines, in which any meaningful aspiration to robust monitoring and regulation has been replaced by systems of self-regulation and environmental management that are frequently little more than forms of 'impression management' (Goffman, 1959).

But if this is irony as strategy, what of irony as *tactic*? Perhaps, in the communicative irony deployed by social movements can be found a counter-response to the *eironia* of dissimulation, to the illusioning of other and of self that the ironic comportment of the powerful seems to involve. Through such communicative irony, can the disjunctures in meaning that lie at the heart of this irony of comportment be made visible and called to account, and political language restored to some kind of integrity? In sum, in communicative irony can we find irony as *cure* for unsustainability?

Irony as Tactic

The dominant understanding of the history of irony since classical Greece has not been as a classification of persons, dispositions or behaviours. At least since its codification by Aristotle as a form of rhetoric, 'irony' as a term has been largely applied to forms of communication in which the surface meaning of the

Irony as Symptom and Cure   161

language used is in tension with the meaning intended by the speaker. For Cicero, irony could be just a transient rhetorical figure, 'saying the contrary of what one means'; by contrast, for Socrates it could be a general pattern of discourse (Muecke, 1970: 15–16). But for the last two millennia the term 'irony' has been largely applied to instances of communication that exploit with varying degrees of sophistication the recursive character of language – its ability to have nested meanings, one inside another.

Muecke (1969: 64–98) distinguishes a number of variants of this 'communicative' irony. For example, 'impersonal irony', like that practised by Swift in *A Modest Proposal*, is characterised by a dryness of tone, in which the ironist absents themselves, simply presenting their words, and not indicating overtly to the listener that the communication is meant as ironic or sarcastic. By contrast, in 'self-disparaging irony' such as that practised by Socrates, the ironist's personality and feelings are to the fore, but in a disguised form: he or she presents him or herself as ignorant or naïve, but intends the audience to penetrate the disguise so as to discern the intended meaning.

Of course, both of these forms of communicative irony have long been deployed in political argumentation and invective. But of more significance for environmental politics is a mode of communicative irony which Muecke calls 'dramatised irony' (1969: 92–8). Thus, a common device in environmental protests is the use of framing devices to draw out and thematise the ironic tensions within the situation being protested about – typically, between truth claims or normative ideals on the one hand, and actual states of affairs on the other. Here, the rhetorical, persuasive effect is grounded less in the *presentation* than in what is *presented* – less in the artfulness of the ironist in creating an ironic communication, and more in the contrasts and tensions being 'revealed' in the world, tensions that have provoked, and are being exposed by, the protest in question. As such, presentations of dramatised irony draw on the logic of another set of ironic phenomena, not communications but meaningful situations, that are the topic of *situational irony*.

As mentioned above, Muecke identifies four features that a situation must possess to be judged ironic: the existence of two or more interpretations of the situation; a tension or incompatibility between these; a victim who remains unaware that the situation might be other than he or she perceives it; and an observer with a sense of irony (Muecke, 1969: 99–100). Yet many examples of irony in environmental protest draw attention to that most minimal form of situational irony, the 'irony of simple incongruity' (Muecke, 1969: 100–2), in which the ironic observer simply recognises the jarring juxtaposition of contradictory elements, such as great wealth and great poverty – or the coexistence noted in the first sentence of this contribution of both ecological awareness and anti-ecological behaviour. Much of the framing activity of social movements can be seen as dramatising such incongruities (Snow & Benford, 1988; Benford & Hunt, 1992).

Sometimes this dramatisation is not overt, and the cultural labour performed by the ironist in presenting the ironies not particularly foregrounded. In such

162 *The Politics of Unsustainability*

cases, environmental movements typically just draw attention to or heighten the ironies – the 'occult incompatibilities' – latent within a given situation. Many protests achieve this by making visible the 'backstage' (Goffman, 1959; Meyrowitz, 1985) of industrial behaviour. For example, Friends of the Earth UK did this in their first direct action in May 1971, when they deposited 2000 non-returnable glass bottles on the doorsteps of Cadbury-Schweppes's London headquarters (Finch, 1992: 8). Greenpeace are even more famous for this kind of protest, carefully designing actions in order to produce dramatic, media-friendly images at sites of 'backstage' industrial operations, such as nuclear reprocessing plant outflow pipes or deep-sea oil platforms (Dale, 1996).

However, in other forms of political intervention this dramatisation is made overt, with situational ironies and aporias being taken out of their natural context and re-presented within 'fictional' cultural genres, such as satire or morality play. This kind of ethico-political practice has a long tradition, and itself draws on a simpler species of communicative irony – that of mocking quotation, where an idea, belief, way of speaking or behaving, style of music or dress is quoted in an exaggerated way in order to poke fun at it. A key opportunity for such mockery in early modern times was Carnival, a time of misrule when established mores and customs of behaviour were overturned in favour of licence, and figures of authority were subjected to mimicry and mockery (Bristol, 1985). Such carnivalesque visual rhetorics have enjoyed a revival in political practice in the last few decades, and have frequently been deployed during environmental and anti-capitalist protests. For example, in December 1999 the meeting of the World Trade Organization in Seattle provoked a Carnival against Capital, during which protesters in costumes and controlling giant puppets were used to dramatise issues and satirise authority figures (Leclair, 2003).

Some recent dramatised interventions by groups such as the Yes Men, the Critical Art Ensemble and PLATFORM have involved more complex forms of communicative irony. For example, in 2000, members of the Critical Art Ensemble sought to render visible the appropriation of messianic rhetoric by biotechnology corporations by inventing a fictitious scientific cult, the Cult of the New Eve, which proceeded to evangelise members of the public.[4] In another action carried out in April 2004, one of the group known as the Yes Men posed as 'Erastus Hamm', of the Dow Corporation, and addressed a London banking conference, describing several lucrative industrial crimes as 'golden skeletons'. In character he then proceeded to introduce the 'Acceptable Risk Calculator', which promised to determine how many deaths are acceptable when achieving large profits, and managed to get many bankers, unaware of the theatrical nature of the event, to sign up for licences for the calculator – and even to pose for photos with the Acceptable Risk mascot, 'Gilda, the golden skeleton in the closet'.[5]

The use of irony in these actions is more sophisticated in a number of ways. Compared with the carnivalesque mockery above, the irony in these actions is *concealed*, the theatricality less obvious; observers have to work harder to

Irony as Symptom and Cure   163

recognise that there is a hidden meaning beneath, and in stark tension with, the overt meaning, thus making the final rhetorical effect even more powerful. But the irony is also *layered* – a double irony, at least. Firstly, there is the ironic tension between the ideas and values being presented by the characters within the theatrical frame, and those that suddenly come to the fore when the audience recognises the existence of that frame, and that the intended meaning is quite different. Secondly, there is an ironic tension *within* the theatrical framing, what Muecke (1969: 107–12) calls an 'irony of self-betrayal', in which the fictional characters played by the activists, and even the genuine bankers drawn unknowingly into the Yes Men's theatre, are made unconsciously to expose their lack of moral reflexivity.

This, then, is irony being deployed as tactic against the ruses of Theophrastian or postmodern irony. In the previous section we saw above how such forms of ironic comportment were symptomatic of the culture of unsustainability. Strategies of dissimulation or denial rely on a deliberate or unconscious disconnecting of public language and conduct from private belief and intention. There I suggested that such forms of irony-as-comportment are largely deployed by the already powerful as strategies to hoard power and avoid responsibility. Then, in this section, we have seen how irony can be used as a tactic *against* such ruses and self-deceptions. Social movements use various forms of communicative irony to make visible such ruses of power, and in particular a dramatising irony which draws attention to the situational ironies inherent within unsustainable and unjust cultural practices. As such, these tactics can be seen as attempts to restore the referential and normative power of language, to resist the attempts by powerful elites to turn language into a mere tool to be deployed to further their own projects, rather than a shared 'house of Being' (Heidegger, 1977: 193), to which we are all responsible and which makes responsibility possible.

However, such tactics can only serve as partial and limited responses to the problem of unsustainability, unless they are embedded within and shaped by a wider ironic stance towards the world – what I would call, borrowing a term from phenomenology, an ironic 'world relation' (*Weltbezug*). In a sense, then, the limits of such tactical forms of irony lie in the fact that they are not ironic *enough*. Using Kierkegaard's terms, they only use a 'quantitative' irony, setting up ironic relations with finite, particular features of the world, rather than a 'qualitative' irony, a distinctive stance towards the totality of existence (Kierkegaard, 1989). In particular, the irony generally deployed in environmental and alternative globalisation protests is a 'corrective' irony, Firstly, it operates by setting up the tension between two levels of meaning, only in order to more resolutely effect a resolution onto one of them. Movements reveal situational ironies in order to shame their targets into repentance (Szerszynski, 2002: 56): Schweppes, Shell or British Nuclear Fuels, for example, present themselves as responsible corporate citizens, but are revealed to be otherwise. Secondly, it positions the ironist as an outside observer of the irony, on the moral high ground looking down, rather than implicated in it. Such a positing

164   *The Politics of Unsustainability*

of the ethical actor seems inadequate for an age in which the logic of politics is that of Baudrillardian simulation, and in which even social movements get caught up in this logic (Blühdorn, 2006).

It is significant that the dominant form of irony used by environmental groups is one that was characteristic of the pre-modern, or at least the early modern, period. Before the late 18th century, irony, when it was employed, was generally expected to be subordinate to other, morally instructive communicative goals: it was 'irony with a purpose'. But gradually, as part of a wider cultural development in which literature and other artistic endeavours became understood as autonomous activities, driven by their own internal logic rather than as servants of religious or state power, irony too came to be understood as containing its own intrinsic virtues (Muecke, 1969: 94). Irony became not just rhetorical *form* but philosophical *content*; not just an indirect way of conveying messages that could have been communicated directly, without irony, but an all-embracing sensibility, developed with greatest intensity in the arts, perhaps most famously in Laurence Sterne's *Tristram Shandy* (Sterne, 1983).[6]

It is to this wider ironic sensibility that I now want to turn. For it is here, if anywhere, that we will find a differently modern philosophical grounding for environmentalism, one that recognises the contingency of existence and the limits of human knowledge, and that thus avoids the hubris and lack of reflexivity inherent in the first two epistemological strategies outlined in the introduction, those of techno-scientific modernism and romanticist immediacy.

Irony as World Relation

The irony-as-world-relation that I describe and advocate in this section as an alternative epistemological strategy for environmentalism is one which took shape in the current of 'cultural modernism' referred to in the introduction. In 19th-century Europe, a sensitivity to situational irony was often elaborated into what Muecke calls 'general irony', a metaphysical position in which the human condition is understood as riven with fundamental contradictions, such as those between freedom and determinism, intention and outcome, the infinite universe and finite existence. Unlike verbal irony, here there are no separate groups of perpetrators and victims; unlike conventional situational irony, there is no distanced observer, aloof from the folly and blindness they perceive being played out in front of them. Here, irony embraces even the observer, the identifier of the irony, within its grasp (Muecke, 1969: 119–58).

As I also suggested in the introduction, this deeply ironic cultural current of modernity has been highly influential on the environmentalist sensibility. It lurks behind Hardin's Law, the idea that 'we can never do merely one thing' (Hardin, 1963), with its reminder of the way that increased understanding of ecological interconnectedness seems to diminish rather than exalt humanity's mastery over its destiny. It permeates James O'Connor's (1988) idea of the second contradiction of capitalism: that capitalism, through its operation, undermines the natural and societal conditions necessary for its own

Irony as Symptom and Cure 165

reproduction. It informs the growing awareness of the tendency for the side-effects of new technologies to crowd out their intended effects in a generalised irony of events (Szerszynski, 2006). Such insights in different ways all reflect a stance of what Muecke (1969: 137–47) calls 'general dramatic irony', in which serene, but only temporarily blissful, ignorance of the real state of affairs is seen as the general human condition.

It is not insignificant that in considering irony as world relation, as an overall stance towards the world, we are returning to that class of irony I termed *dispositional* irony, which involves the application of the term 'ironic', not to communications or to situations, but to persons and their comportment towards the world. For, from a Kierkegaardian perspective, the dispositional ironies, discussed above as symptomatic of the contemporary culture of unsustainability, do in fact contain a partial truth. For what the Theophrastian and postmodern ironists both recognise in their way is that freedom and autonomy require the negation of concrete existence. Kierkegaard formulated this insight in *The Concept of Irony* (1989) in his discussion of the life of Socrates. The life of 'immediacy', simply living within the moral horizon of one's own culture (or, indeed, one might say, subculture) is inconsistent with the genuinely ethical life. For Kierkegaard, Socrates' ironic self-distancing from the culture into which he had happened to be born, and indeed from the concrete details of his own life, was the awakening of subjectivity itself, without which there can be no genuine moral responsibility.

However, as Andrew Collins (1998: 148–9) points out, a simple negation of concrete existence, a severing of private meaning from the shared, public world, can by itself only offer a *negative* freedom, not a positive form of life. Kierkegaard himself recognised this; in *Either/Or* he carries out a caustically perceptive critique of the constantly ironic Romantic aesthete in his depiction of the character 'A' – egotistical, bored and incapable of engagement (Kierkegaard, 1992a). And the very inadequacy of A's existence is connected to the fact that, with this conception of irony-as-world-relation as the simple negation of immediacy, the ironic attitude is not fully carried through. Similarly, the problem with both Theophrastian and postmodern ironists lies not in their irony, but in the *weakness* of their irony. Theophrastian ironists, who use communication and self-presentation cynically as instruments to advance their goals, take an ironic stance towards the public world of shared meaning and their participation in it, but they fail to similarly ironise themselves and their projects. Postmodern ironists are more consistent, in that even their own projects and values are only ironically committed to – yet here, the ironic attitude itself is the one thing that is unironised. The postmodern ironist is thus not free but captured by their own alienation from the public world, by an ironic attitude that becomes a new immediacy, a new and equally constraining horizon of thought.

In a later work, Kierkegaard (1992b), writing under the pseudonym Climacus, suggests a way out of this trap. For Climacus's ironist, the ironic distancing from immediacy is only a transitional stage to the fully ethical life of

166 *The Politics of Unsustainability*

responsible choice. Climacus's ironist identifies *neither* with the finite, empirical self of his immediate, conditioned existence, *nor* with the infinite, unconditioned ironic self of pure choice, but with the contradiction between the two. From the vantage point of his unconditioned, ironic distance, he thus regards his conditioned, finite existence not as a set of constraints to be rejected, but as 'a home in which he chooses to dwell' (Collins, 1998: 150). The ironist does not abandon, but *returns* to his finite, worldly existence, and takes *responsibility* for it. As John Evan Seery rather similarly puts it, the spirit of irony requires one 'to return to the finite world of politics, to act in and for such a world, even in the face of knowledge that puts the world and that activity into perspective' (Seery, 1990: 139).

A thoroughgoingly ironic environmentalism would involve a reflexive awareness of the limited and provisional nature of human understanding, while at the same time not lapsing into cynicism or quietism. An ironic self-distancing from the shared world of public meanings – if it is followed by the return gesture of re-entering it with a new sense of reflexivity towards and responsibility for the propositional and normative claims which one uses – does not have to erode the power of that shared world of meaning. On the contrary, it is only through the ironic negation of received meanings that our common language can become a fit dwelling place for ethical responsibility.

Conclusion: For an Ironic Ecology

The main thrust of this contribution has been to argue that environmentalist practice should acknowledge the debt it owes to aesthetic modernism, and more wholeheartedly align itself with that cultural current. I am aware that this might seem a rather counter-intuitive argument. Environmentalism, a critic might argue, is if anything a *rejection* of the attitude of general irony characteristic of cultural modernism. If metaphysical, general irony was made possible by the retreat of religious certainties from European culture, it could be argued that environmentalism arose in the late 20th century as a cultural movement that offered a new, secular antidote to this cultural development. Instead of accepting the Gnostic vision of a humanity set adrift in a meaningless universe, environmentalism seemed to offer a way of reorienting human behaviour to an idea of cosmic order. By attending to natural processes and limits, environmentalists seemed to be saying, we can maybe leave behind mere species self-assertion as the model of human action, and once again know how we should live by locating ourselves within a meaningful cosmic horizon (Szerszynski, 1996). As refracted through the first two epistemological strategies described in the introduction, this has indeed been the dominant way that the environmentalist critique of modernity has been articulated.

Yet, as Bruno Latour has recently argued (Latour, 2004), it may well be that the environmentalist *theory* we have is not best suited for understanding and realising the civilisational potential of environmentalist *practice*. Certainly, an ironic environmentalism, one which rejected the hope of a harmonisation of human affairs through a harmonisation with nature, but instead understood the human condition as intrinsically paradoxical and aporetic, would likely be a rather different sort of environmentalism than that offered by most accounts of environmental politics. But, I want to argue, it is in the embrace of general irony, rather than in its rejection, that the most clear-sighted antidote to the condition of unsustainability will be found.

What would a thoroughgoing ironic environmentalism look like? As I argued above, the environmentalist sensibility is already partially informed by the cultural current of generalised irony; it follows that the task of imagining an ironic ecology does not mean starting from scratch, but instead will involve gathering together a range of existing elements in environmentalist practice, in both civil society and public policy, and rearticulating them in terms of a more fundamental ironic world relation.

Firstly, ironic ecology would involve the recognition of the inevitability of failure and error, and at the same time the need to act, with due care, in the very face of that recognition. As Bob Jessop argues, the political ironist:

> ... accepts incompleteness and failure as essential features of social life but continues to act as if completeness and success were possible ... The only possibility open for a political ironist ... [is] to stand apart from her political practice and at the same time incorporate this awareness of her ironic position into the practice itself. (Jessop, 2003)

This would be a politics which emphasised the limits of human understanding, the growing significance in human affairs of what Ulrich Beck (1992) calls 'non-knowledge' and the likelihood of being surprised by events, and which took a precautionary stance towards projects involving radical and irreversible environmental and technological change.

Secondly, however, an ironic ecology does not entail the withdrawal from engagement and creative experimentation with nature. Far from it: it would imply the celebration and exploration of the mutual implication of nature and culture, but in a way which would emphasise the everyday, the aesthetic and the creative. Both techno-scientific modernism and romanticism have tended to reify a sublime nature outside and preceding human meanings – the former as an object of knowledge and intervention, the latter as one of contemplative appreciation. An ironic ecology informed by what I have been calling cultural modernism, rather than either dominating or venerating nature, would instead be more likely to value and proliferate 'impure' and vernacular mixings of nature and culture, new shared meanings and practices, new ways of dwelling with non-humans, new 'naturecultures' (Haraway, 2003). Its defining legacy would be neither the nuclear power station, nor the nature reserve, but a living, evolving plurality of shared forms of life.

Thirdly, a thoroughly ironic stance would involve a greater reflexivity about the provisional character not just of propositional but also of normative claims. Environmental politics has arguably been dominated by a moral

168 *The Politics of Unsustainability*

earnestness that has gone hand in hand with its over-estimation of the epistemic power of science, and by a neglect of the way that meanings and values about nature are not just socially situated and partial but also shot through with ironies and aporias. A reflexive stance towards one's own beliefs and values which does not collapse into manipulative or quietistic cynicism requires a truly ironic world relation – an irony not just towards particular things but towards the world's totality, including oneself and one's irony. And such a stance would necessitate a less moralistic and self-satisfied political style, one which acknowledges that no one can know political truths perfectly or live blamelessly, especially under current circumstances. Thus, although it would doubtless employ many of the ironic tactics analysed above, it would do so in a way that was less crudely 'corrective', and which was honed by a more general ironic sensibility in order to produce more effective calls to genuine personal responsibility (see, for example, the tactics employed by the Clandestine Insurgent Rebel Clown Army (CIRCA).[7]

Fourthly, ironic ecology would imply forms of political intervention (for example slogans, maxims, eco-labels and protests) that were more 'knowing' in their representational practice. Kierkegaard himself used Socratic irony and pseudonymous voices in his writings. He felt that the knowledge 'possessed' by people can act as a barrier to the apprehension of more fundamental truths, and used such literary devices to undermine the assumptions of knowledge and understanding amongst his readers, in order to force them to take existential responsibility for their own readings. Ironic ecology would similarly favour what Roland Barthes (1975) calls 'writerly' texts, ones which do not impose fixed meanings on readers, but treat them as co-producers of meaning. In the case of eco-labels, for example, dominant forms of product labelling have generally involved 'simple' forms of transparency which depend on agreed framings and high levels of trust. An ironic environmentalism would encourage forms of labelling which involved more complex modes of transparency, ones which encourage critical reflection about the limits and assumptions of any given frame. The 'green electricity' label in Sweden has done this inadvertently, by provoking public debates which have made a much broader range of issues and options visible than the original frame of 'cleanliness' entailed; ironic ecology would involve the development of forms of communications and labels which deliberately provoked such reflexive forms of 'inter-frame transparency' (Klintman & Boström, 2007).

Late capitalist society faces a profound cultural challenge, one grounded in the material contradiction between a form of life and its self-undermining consequences, and in the rational contradiction between the knowledge of impending environmental disaster and the resistance to change. But any remedy to this predicament will only be as subtle and effective as the diagnosis. If we operate with a simple conception of irony, then the cure will seem simple too – to replace 'mere rhetoric' with 'truth'; to replace symbolic, token action with 'genuine' action; to imagine the dividedness of finite being against itself can be healed; to erase the political, always grounded in plurality and

Irony as Symptom and Cure 169

difference, through moving too quickly to a clear and simple truth. If instead we recognise that our predicament is *itself* ironic, maybe we can be more clear-sighted about our problem and its solution. If we see that irony is not just evasion and dissimulation, but identifies themes that lie at the heart of the human condition, we can see it not as an enemy but as an ally in the quest for a more honest and sustainable form of society.

Notes

1. And even environmental and development non-governmental organisations have been accused of what Jean-Paul Sartre (1958) calls 'bad faith', of being driven less by the realities of environmental problems than by their own organisational interests (for example, see Eyerman & Jamison, 1989).
2. I do not thereby mean to imply that *all* postmodern thought exhibits this kind of irony.
3. Of course, Rorty himself believes that private irony can and should co-exist with public solidarity, but he then proceeds to ground that solidarity in the power of individuals to forge an 'imaginative identification with the details of others' lives' (Rorty, 1989: 190). Rorty seems to assume that the rejection of the positivist understanding of truth as a correspondence between words and things requires a view of language as wholly private, and thus reduces even the moral demand of solidarity with the other to an aesthetic act of imagination in the subject.
4. http://www.critical-art.net/biotech/cone, accessed 2 December 2006.
5. http://www.theyesmen.org. For other protest actions in a broadly similar vein, see http://www.thevacuumcleaner.co.uk and http://www.banksy.co.uk, all accessed 2 December 2006.
6. *The Life and Opinions of Tristram Shandy, Gentleman*, first published in the 1760s, is presented as the autobiography of the fictional Shandy, but any pretence to realism is overwhelmed by a constant series of digressions, culs-de-sac and a playful undermining of storytelling conventions.
7. http://www.clownarmy.org, accessed 2 December 2006.

References

Barthes, R. (1975) *S-Z* (trans. R. Miller; London: Jonathan Cape).
Beck, U. (1992) *Risk Society: Towards a New Modernity* (trans. M. Ritter; London: Sage).
Beder, S. (2002) 'BP: Beyond Petroleum?' in Lubbers, Eveline (ed.), *Battling Big Business: Countering Greenwash, Infiltration and Other Forms of Corporate Bullying*, pp. 26–32 (Totnes: Green Books).
Benford, R. D. & Hunt, S. A. (1992) 'Dramaturgy and social movements: the social construction and communication of power', *Sociological Inquiry* 62(1): 36–55.
Blühdorn, I. (2004) 'Post-ecologism and the politics of simulation', in L. J. Wissenburg & Y. Levy (eds.), *Liberal Democracy and the Environment. The End of Environmentalism?* pp. 35–47 (London: Routledge).
Blühdorn, I. (2006) 'Self-experience in the theme park of radical action? Social movements and political articulation in the late-modern condition', *European Journal of Social Theory* 9(1): 23–42.
Bristol, M. D. (1985) *Carnival and Theatre: Plebeian Culture and the Structure of Authority in Renaissance England* (New York: Methuen).
Callinicos, A. (1995) *Theories and Narratives: Reflections on the Philosophy of History* (Cambridge: Polity).
Collins, A. (1998) 'The perils of reflexive irony', in A. Hannay & G. D. Marino (eds.), *The Cambridge Companion to Kierkegaard*, pp. 125–53 (Cambridge: Cambridge University Press).
Dale, S. (1996) *McLuhan's Children: The Greenpeace Message and the Media* (Toronto: Between the Lines).

170 The Politics of Unsustainability

de Certeau, M. (1984) *The Practice of Everyday Life* (Berkeley, CA: University of California Press).

Ereaut, G. & Segnit, N. (2006) *Warm Words: How Are We Telling the Climate Story and Can We Tell It Better?* (London: Institute for Public Policy Research).

European Commission (2005) *The 2005 Review of the EU Sustainable Development Strategy: Initial Stocktaking and Future Challenges* (Brussels: Commission of the European Community).

Eyerman, R. & Jamison, A. (1989) 'Environmental knowledge as an organisational weapon: the case of Greenpeace', *Social Science Information* 28(2): 99–119.

Finch, S. (1992) 'Friends of the Earth: 1971–1992', *Earth Matters* 14: 8–9.

Goffman, E. (1959) *The Presentation of Self in Everyday Life*, revised and expanded edition (London: Doubleday).

Habermas, J. (1979) *Communication and the Evolution of Society* (trans. T. McCarthy; Boston, MA: Beacon Press).

Haraway, D. J. (2003) *The Companion Species Manifesto: Dogs, People, and Significant Otherness* (Chicago, IL: Prickly Paradigm Press).

Hardin, G. (1963) 'A second sermon on the mount', *Perspectives in Biology and Medicine* 6(3): 366–71.

Heidegger, M. (1977) *Basic Writings: From 'Being and Time' (1927) to 'The Task of Thinking' (1964)* (New York: Harper & Row).

Jessop, B. (2003) 'Governance and meta-governance. On reflexivity, requisite variety, and requisite irony', in H. P. Bang (ed.), *Governance as Social and Political Communication*, pp. 101–16 (Manchester: Manchester University Press).

Kierkegaard, S. (1989) *The Concept of Irony, with Continual Reference to Socrates: Together with Notes of Schelling's Berlin Lectures* (trans. E. H. Hong & H. V. Hong; Princeton, NJ: Princeton University Press).

Kierkegaard, S. (1992a) *Either/Or: A Fragment of Life* (trans. A. Hannay; Harmondsworth: Penguin).

Kierkegaard, S. (1992b) *Concluding Unscientific Postscript to Philosophical Fragments* (trans. E. H. Hong & H. V. Hong; Princeton, NJ: Princeton University Press).

Klintman, M. & Boström, M. (2007) 'Transparency through labelling? Layers of visibility in environmental risk management', in C. Garsten & M. Lindh de Montoya (eds.), *Transparency in a New Global Order: Unveiling Organizational Visions* (Cheltenham: Edward Elgar) (in press).

Latour, B. (2004) *Politics of Nature: How to Bring the Sciences into Democracy* (trans. C. Porter; Cambridge, MA: Harvard University Press).

Leclair, L. (2003) 'Carnivals against capital: rooted in resistance', in A. Opel & D. Pompper (eds.), *Representing Resistance: Media, Civil Disobedience, and the Global Justice Movement*, pp. 3–15 (Westport, CT: Praeger).

MacIntyre, A. (1985) *After Virtue: A Study in Moral Theory*, 2nd edn (London: Duckworth).

Melucci, A. (1996) *Challenging Codes: Collective Action in the Information Age* (Cambridge: Cambridge University Press).

Meyrowitz, J. (1985) *No Sense of Place: The Impact of Electronic Media on Social Behavior* (New York: Oxford University Press).

Muecke, D. C. (1969) *The Compass of Irony* (London: Methuen).

Muecke, D. C. (1970) *Irony* (London: Methuen).

O'Connor, J. (1988) 'Capitalism, nature, socialism: a theoretical introduction', *Capitalism, Nature, Socialism* (1): 11–38.

Rorty, R. (1989) *Contingency, Irony, and Solidarity* (Cambridge: Cambridge University Press).

Sartre, J.-P. (1958) *Being and Nothingness: An Essay on Phenomenological Ontology* (trans. H. E. Barnes; London: Methuen).

Seery, J. E. (1990) *Political Returns: Irony in Politics and Theory from Plato to the Antinuclear Movement* (Boulder, CO: Westview Press).

Snow, D. A. & Benford, R. D. (1988) 'Ideology, frame resonance, and collective mobilization', in B. Klandermans, H. Kriesi & S. Tarrow (eds.), *From Structure to Action*, pp. 197–218 (Greenwich: JAI Press).

Sophocles (1994) *Antigone. Oedipus the King. Electra* (trans. H. D. F. Kitto; Oxford: Oxford University Press).

Sterne, L. (1983) *The Life and Opinions of Tristram Shandy, Gentleman* (Oxford: Oxford University Press).

Sustainable Development Commission (2004) *Shows Promise but Must Try Harder* (London: Sustainable Development Commission).

Swift, J. (1729) *A Modest Proposal for Preventing the Children of Poor People from Becoming a Burthen to Their Parents or Country, and for Making Them Beneficial to the Publick* (Dublin: S. Harding).

Szerszynski, B. (1996) 'On knowing what to do: environmentalism and the modern problematic', in S. Lash, B. Szerszynski & B. Wynne (eds.), *Risk, Environment and Modernity: Towards a New Ecology*, pp. 104–37 (London: Sage).

Szerszynski, B. (2002) 'Ecological rites: ritual action in environmental protest events', *Theory, Culture and Society* 19(3): 305–23.

Szerszynski, B. (2006) 'Techno-demonology: naming, understanding and redeeming the a/human agencies with which we share our world', *Ecotheology* 11(1): 57–75.

Trilling, L. (1972) *Sincerity and Authenticity* (Cambridge, MA: Harvard University Press).

United Nations Environment Programme (2002) *Global Environment Outlook 3* (London: Earthscan).

In Defence of Civilisation: Terrorism and Environmental Politics in the 21st Century

IAN WELSH
School of Social Science, University of Cardiff, UK

ABSTRACT *The use of the term* civilisation *has assumed renewed prominence within high profile speeches by political leaders in the opening decade of the 21st century. Initially articulated in relation to the 'war on terror' following September 11 in 2001, the discourse of terrorism was extended to elements of environmental and social justice movements. This extension of the discourse of terrorism within the public sphere followed a period in which state surveillance and security resources were targeted on environmental protestors. Primary legislation, such as the US Patriot Act, and successive Crime and Criminal Justice Acts in the UK, combined with global collaboration between national security services, increased the range of formal charges which can be brought against individuals. This contribution explores the symbolic stakes and processes associated with this discursive return to civilisation as a prominent political discourse that simultaneously defends unsustainable 'western' practices against external and internal enemies. It is argued that the evocation of civilisation as part of a 'war' implicitly and explicitly legitimates the introduction of extraordinary measures consistent with wartime contingencies. Such measures apply to both internal and external affairs of state and include those sections of environmental movements explicitly linking environmental degradation with critiques of contemporary neo-liberalism. It is argued that the attempt to define such movements as 'enemies within' is a tacit recognition of the symbolic potency of both global and national stakes raised through recourse to extra-parliamentary forms of protest and the founding of alternative deliberative forums at a global level. Such movements render visible elements of a prevailing neo-liberal civilisation inimical to environmental and societal integrity.*

Introduction

Since September 11 in 2001 there has been a marked increase in the use of the term *civilisation* by prominent politicians in the context of a 'war on terrorism', a term which has been extended to include sections of the environmental and social justice movement contesting neo-liberalism. The use of *civilisation* as a rhetorical resource within political discourse represents a highly abstract appeal to values and beliefs associated with progressive culture. Murphy (2006) notes the steady increase in academic treaties on *civilisation* throughout the 20th century, underlining the importance of situating the contemporary return to *civilisation* in terms of this genre. I argue here that the contemporary return to civilisation represents an appeal to progressive European Enlightenment values such as freedom in the context of a global neo-liberal economic order. *Civilisation* is articulated with key terms constitutive of political legitimacy such as freedom, democracy and liberty implying at least the potential for global inclusion. Such usage ignores significant differences in the origins and meaning of words like freedom, presenting civilisation as compatible with the wider ideological portrayal of neo-liberal globalisation as the end of history.

The impact of ascendant neo-liberalism upon all forms of environmental politics over the past 20 years is an inescapable context, yet has received little explicit engagement. The argument here is that neo-liberal globalisation attempts to constitute a global civilisation that melds key cultural practices consolidated within Europe with distinctly US interpretations of freedom and democracy through the continued belief in the global efficacy of western techno-science and economic growth. The melding of techno-scientific and economic measures of progress and efficiency within global and national domains constitutes a politics of unsustainability by over-extending these particular rationalities by subordinating social and cultural relations. Whilst nation states have been central in terms of civilising processes, I am emphasising the operation of global civilising processes through the nexus of global institutions constituted from, but sitting over, discrete nation states. The continuing debates between those emphasising the primacy of nations and international arenas (Doherty & Doyle, 2006) and those emphasising the importance of global domains and networks (Castells, 1996; Chesters & Welsh, 2006) make clarity important here.

There are dual processes operating, with states and the international arena remaining centrally important in terms of structuring internal and external relations respectively. However, national and international factors co-produce distinctly global processes in terms of economic and environmental regimes which exercise 'global regulatory reach' (Welsh, 2000) substantively outside the direct influence of electoral accountability. The impacts of these regimes are distributed globally and differentially creating winners and losers with diverse and fragmented experiences. The experience of citizens within discrete national civil societies reflects the application of global regulatory formulae which, despite differences in national contexts, result in common themes.[1]

In terms of cultural politics the increased ease of communication and mobility across national borders becomes a key factor constituting an emergent global civil society that recognises both national and planetary stakes arising from global agendas. Whereas nation states as spatially defined containers of societies approximate to closed systems, the increasingly open nature of

174 *The Politics of Unsustainability*

exchanges constitutes contemporary societies as increasingly open systems (Urry, 2003). The evident increase in complexity is particularly problematic for formal politics precisely because all systems of political interest representation are forms of complexity reduction. One key issue at stake here is whether states and the associated international forums built around complexity reduction and inter-state competition in the pursuit of national interests can engage with global domain issues requiring collaboration and co-operation.

The civilisations constituting the 'west' are arguably better at social reproduction than social change. And as science increasingly recognises the importance of tipping points precipitating rapid climate reconfiguration, the capacity for historically unprecedented rates of social change becomes a significant challenge. In fact, this is not merely a challenge to *national* societies, as Beck's notion of a *world* risk society (1997) implicitly raises issues of world civilisation in jeopardy as a consequence of techno-scientific and economic progress achieved through national competition. When the social forces contesting global neo-liberalism are represented as 'folk devils' (Donson *et al.*, 2004) by prominent political figureheads within the public sphere this suggests an attempt to limit and marginalise certain forms of symbolic politics. At the heart of this contribution lies the proposition that within the contestation of globalisation on grounds of economic and environmental justice there is a cultural politics raising symbolic stakes with the potential for a more rational world beyond the prevailing post-ecologist politics of environmental main-streaming and subordination to free market economics.

The analysis proceeds with a discussion of key themes from European and American treatments of civilisation outlining an anatomy of the civilisation at risk. Through the extension of Elias's (1939/1994) notion of the civilising process it is argued that 'western' techno-scientific civilisation constitutes world risk society in all its forms including the current neo-liberal incarnation. After identifying and elaborating the key features and modes of transmission of the values and practices of this civilisation, the focus shifts to the question of why the Alternative Globalisation Movement (AGM) is aligned with the war on terror.[2] The centrality of symbolic politics is elaborated utilising the work of Bourdieu, and the analysis concludes with a discussion of the implications of cultural politics within open systems for a post-ecologist politics within which environmentalists become internal enemies charged with threatening the market freedoms associated with this civilisation.

The Civilisation in Question

The majority of political speeches using civilisation in relation to terrorism do not use any of the common prefixes associated with the term such as 'industrial' or 'western'. In US usage there has been a fluctuating ambivalence toward engagement with 'western' civilisation coinciding with phases of isolationism and engagement (Murphy, 2006: 65). Murphy addresses this ambivalence by distinguishing between Greco-Roman, Eurocentric western and settler society civilisations. America, as the prime 'settler civilisation', distinguished its national civilisation from the UK and old Europe laying the foundations for an enduring US exceptionalism arising from an autopoietic system. Key elements of this self-ordering system for present purposes include freedom to profit as a God-given right, an emphasis on individual liberty, an expansionist frontier mentality and an initial openness to immigration.

The overall system minimises entropy by remaining open, permitting the 'import and export of social energies' across boundaries to a far higher degree than in old Europe where the weight of tradition embedded in structures 'squeezes life out of energy' (Murphy, 2006: 69). Arguing that US settler civilisation has much in common with Greco-Roman orientations towards external relations Murphy notes that US exceptionalism also exhibits itself as 'outward-looking interventionism' as evidenced by the neo-conservative projection of 'America as a force for the global spread of democracy' (Murphy, 2006: 66). Murphy's account adds to those emphasising the differences between US and European orientations in terms of both political and business cultures, particularly in relation to techno-scientific approaches to environmental issues (Hutton, 2002; Welsh, 2006).

For Bateson, civilisations rise through the development of 'new technology for the exploitation of nature or a new technique for the exploitation of other men. But each civilization, as it reaches the limits of what can be exploited in that particular way, must eventually fall' (Bateson, 1973: 471). Bateson considered that the habits of mind threatening 'our' civilisation included: us against the environment and other men; the primacy of sub-global actors (e.g. me, my firm, my nation, etc.); control over the environment; perpetual belief in the frontier mentality; and economic determinism (Bateson, 1973: 468). He seriously suggested that 'we should trust no policy decisions which emanate from persons' (Bateson, 1973: 468) who have not transcended such habits. Whilst US rejection of the biodiversity and Kyoto treaties are prominent examples of exceptionalism in the environmental arena, it is important to recognise the recourse to exceptionalism on a range of grounds by states in general.

It is also important to emphasise that exceptionalism is a generic feature of American culture taking particular forms according to the political composition of US administrations. The transition from neo-liberalism to neo-conservatism aligned with religious fundamentalism represents both a continuation and an extension of US discourses on civilisation and terrorism for example. The implications of this extension for environmental politics as a symbolic cultural intervention are discussed below, but before this can be done it is important to consider how neo-liberal economic administrative procedures or regimes constitute both national cultures and global civilisation.

A Global Neo-liberal Civilisation?

For Torgerson 'constitutive politics deals with constructing or changing a civilisation as a cultural artifice' (2000: 511). I am suggesting that it is vital to

176   *The Politics of Unsustainability*

recognise the simultaneous construction of a global neo-liberal civilisation *and* the competitive reorientation of national cultures. The central feature orchestrating this elite-driven reorientation is the near universal application of market principles. Saul (2005) explicitly regards economic globalisation as part of such an initiative.

The dominance of the 'Washington consensus' within the International Monetary Fund (IMF), World Bank and World Trade Organization (WTO) is widely acknowledged as central in structuring this process. The decision-making cultures within these organisations embody central precepts of the civilisation outlined above derived from an extraordinarily narrow range of national elites (Stiglitz, 2002). Stiglitz criticised the IMF for granting universal primacy to capital market liberalisation, privatisation programmes, cuts in public expenditure, promotion of western technology sectors and trade rounds advantaging developed nations over developing nations. This is a rare example of the axioms of capitalism being contested within the public sphere (e.g. Crooks, 2002) as opposed to being presented as natural and thus beyond grievance or question.[3]

Stiglitz regards the IMF as a political institution within which 'financial interests have dominated thinking', with 'commercial interests' having 'an equally dominant role at the WTO' (Stiglitz, 2002: 216). The Nobel Prize-winning ex-World Bank economist contrasts the IMF's willingness to 'bail out banks' whilst refusing to find 'paltry sums to provide food subsidies' for people unemployed 'as a result of IMF programs'. Those pursuing reforms consistent with sustainable development agendas are told by the WTO 'that such regulation would be an unwarranted intrusion on free trade. They discover that trade considerations trump all others, including the environment!'(Stiglitz, 2002: 216). This account continues by underlining the genuine belief of those involved that they are acting in the 'general interest' and that finance ministers and some political leaders 'believe this so strongly that they support forcing countries to accept these *reforms*, through whatever means they can' (Stiglitz, 2002: 216):

> The problem is that the institutions have come to reflect the mind-sets of those to whom they are accountable. The typical central bank governor begins his day worrying about inflation statistics, not poverty statistics; the trade minister worries about export numbers, not pollution indices. (Stiglitz, 2002: 216)

In Stiglitz's view, the persistence of these 'mind-sets', reminiscent of Bateson's habits of mind, is one of the major challenges to be confronted. This quote also underlines some other tensions between (inter)national and global approaches in the juxtaposition of local economic and environmental knowledges. The point here is that global knowledge sets are extraordinarily limited with economics and environmental science being two of the more developed. Whilst Stiglitz is quite clear that there are tensions here requiring interventions from within global civil society, environmental sociology and politics remain less decided upon this. Jamison for example includes 'the environmental activities of the World Bank' (Jamison, 2001: 127) as a sign of structural transformation, whilst seeing 'signs that the old crap from the 1960s is coming back in the name of anti-globalism' threatening the '*new wave* of environmental politics that has been on the rise for some years' (Jamison, 2001: 148). I am arguing that dismissing the anti-globalisation movement as a repeat of 1960s Marxist–Leninist anti-imperialism ignores its success in challenging the established agendas outlined by Stiglitz through the mobilisation of symbolic resources.

It is only by considering the global civilising effects of the IMF/WTO/World Bank nexus that the importance of the declaration of symbolic stakes begins to become clear. A key point here is that national political figures strive to secure public acceptance of their global alignment inside and outside their bounded nations. The credibility of politicians' claims is seen as fundamental to the symbolic legitimacy of states (Loveman, 2005), and such claims become buttressed through pedagogical, corrective and ideological means. The 'routine exercise of symbolic power' is centrally underpinned by 'administration' (Loveman, 2005: 1657). This raises the question of how a global equivalent of this process might be identified.

Elias (1939/1994) focused upon the transmission of civilised norms from centres such as royal courts arguing that the transition to the state represented the civilising process. I would argue that the IMF/WTO/World Bank nexus represents a global equivalent to the court, administratively disseminating normative standards and behaviours deemed appropriate within neo-liberal civilisation. This is a dual process of national conformity within nation states brokering globalisation and global transmission through administrative agencies. Ilcan (2006) demonstrates how the United Nations' (UN's) humanitarian and technical programmes inculcate key precepts of neo-liberalism in terms of individual characteristics (e.g. entrepreneurial self-reliance), preferred technical practices (e.g. biotechnology) and an appropriate market orientation. Ilcan makes it clear that this is an ongoing programme based on the 'values, principles and objectives' set by world leaders at the UN Millennium Development Summit (http://www.developmentgoals.org) and equated with 'mainstreaming the *needs* of LDCs [less developed countries]' (Ilcan, 2006: 863 emph. added) within the current Unesco programme. The administrative programmes of the UN thus promote personal attributes of neo-liberal civilisation alongside technical programmes such as biotechnology. In Bauman's (2004) terms, these are part of an ordering process that transforms established customs, epistemologies and practices, as well as their human bearers, into 'waste'. The incorporation of such features of neo-liberal civilisation within governance initiatives places them within a category which, according to Latham (1999), has not been recognised as a contested site of power relations within political and social science. However, amongst those looking from what might be called a 'Southern' perspective (Sen *et al.*, 2004), and within the AGM, which has always been more diverse and pursued a far

178   *The Politics of Unsustainability*

greater 'Southern reach' than 1960s radicalism, such practices of incorporation are very prominent concerns (Notes from Nowhere, 2003; Chesters & Welsh, 2006).

Global Neo-liberalism and Environmental Politics at 'Home'

In the opening contribution to this collection, the question of a grassroots reinvigoration of eco-politics was left deliberately open in full recognition of the limitations associated with changed societal dynamics linked to consumerism, pathological individualism and the death of collective identity. It is time now to address the political extension of 'civilisation' and 'terrorism' to environmental activism and the AGM. This is approached as part of a symbolic struggle for legitimacy between states and movements within the public sphere within which critical civil society actors are actively marginalised as folk devils (Donson *et al.*, 2004). Space constraints impose limits on what can be achieved here but the central arguments advanced can be summarised as follows.

The increased targeting of state security resources and inter-state intelligence agency activities upon certain categories of activists is an implicit recognition of the potential for movements to articulate symbolic registers corrosive of the neo-liberal axiomatic within the public sphere.[4] The post-ecologist era is marked by some significant shifts in the resources available for the symbolic contestation and negotiation of symbolic stakes with trans-border computer-mediated communication (CMC) techniques being particularly important. In the face of extensive governance initiatives which originate within global forums and increase the costs of participatory inclusions for all social movement actors, remaining 'outside' and targeting power structures, civil society and the economy as sites for political action can be a viable strategy (Dryzek *et al.*, 2003: 4–6).

Contesting Global Neo-liberalism

To many commentators, the action against the 1999 Seattle WTO round marked the emergence of the AGM within the public sphere, something that contributed to the 'fast framing' of this as an 'anti'-movement. Amongst the factors missed in such accounts are more than three years of networked negotiations by diverse movement actors formalising a set of strategies consistent with the position advanced by Dryzek *et al.* (2003) in terms of 'global dynamics'. Their proposals explicitly focused upon neo-liberal institutions, extending and consolidating North–South linkages, combining Northern environmental and social justice organisations whilst challenging paternalistic attitudes and practices, and providing a means of co-ordinating protests and educational efforts. Political parties and groups were explicitly excluded on the basis of previous experiences of instrumentalism. It was deemed crucial to overcome the 'charitative, eco-imperialist' movement

In Defence of Civilisation   179

attitudes seen as representing a 'real barrier for the co-operation between people's movements in the South and solidarity/environmental organisations in the North' (Chesters & Welsh, 2006: 28–33). The World Social Forum and its constituent geo-regional and city social forums remain the most significant arena within which the wider proactive agenda outlined continues to be pursued (Fischer & Ponniah, 2003; Sen *et al.*, 2004).

Seattle, however, became the first of several high profile 'summit sieges' in which 'the signs' associated with global neo-liberalism were contested utilising embodied forms of the irony and self-parody called for by Szerszynski (this volume). The use of carnival in the midst of street protests marked by increasingly confrontational policing tactics emerged as a significant feature on the streets of Prague in 2000. Here, self-parodying women dressed as pink fairies juxtaposed themselves with Kevlar-clad riot police amidst textual slogans denouncing the environmental and social consequences of world trade (Chesters & Welsh, 2004). Whilst much of the literature on symbolic politics focuses upon language (Bourdieu, 1992/2005; Edelman, 1997), enactments introduce a wider range of symbolic registers in terms of human performance and interaction which circulate through mainstream and CMC media.

In Seattle, Prague, Genoa and numerous other sites, activists realised their 1996 aim of transforming representations of world summits from business as usual to contested events within the public sphere, raising issues of symbolic legitimacy for political and administrative elites. Solomon's (2000) study of US mainstream print media responses to Seattle underlines these points and has marked similarities with media coverage of subsequent events in other countries. The coverage emphasised the marginality of protestors, drew parallels with anarchist organisations and represented the protestors' view of the WTO as 'a handmaiden of corporate interests' representing 'the tyrannical symbol of a global economy that has shoved social priorities aside in a relentless quest for profits' (Solomon, 2000: 14). Public support for protestors by Seattle residents (as expressed in chants of 'Let them go!' as police pursued activists), Bill Clinton's public statements supporting the cause of many of the peaceful protestors and the view that a 'small knot' of 'more militant elements' had used police behaviour as 'a cue to go on a rampage' received widespread coverage (Solomon, 2000: 15). Solomon emphasises the way in which key market precepts like 'free trade' and 'liberalisation' were not elaborated or questioned within media commentary. They were simply accepted as facts of life 'like gravity' despite activist arguments that they represented 'a continuation of colonialism and imperialism' (Solomon, 2000: 15). The *Los Angeles Times* reported that 'economists regard free trade as just about as controversial as motherhood' (Solomon, 2000: 17).

By 2001 the alignment of such protestors with the wider 'war on terrorism' became discernible within public statements from politicians. Italian Prime Minister Silvio Berlusconi's post-September 11 comments, delivered whist

180   *The Politics of Unsustainability*

standing next to Chancellor Gerhard Schröder during a visit to Germany, declared that he and his host considered that:

> ...the attacks on New York and Washington are attacks not only on the United States but on our civilization, of which we are proud bearers, conscious of the supremacy of our civilization, of its discoveries and inventions, which have brought us democratic institutions, respect for the human, civil, religious and political rights of our citizens, openness to diversity and tolerance of everything. (*Guardian*, 27 September 2001, http://www.guardian.co.uk/waronterror/story/0,1361,558866,00html, accessed 20 August 2005)

The same speech was widely reported as arguing that there was a 'strange unanimity' between the anti-globalisation movement and Islamist terrorism (*Guardian*, 27 September 2001). American and European civilisation are elided here, and the term civilisation is used in a self-evident manner as a universal phenomenon comfortable in the face of difference. The association of the anti-globalisation movement with Islamic terrorism extends this discourse and positions both as enemies against which civilisation must be defended.[5]

Whilst Berlusconi's comments were rapidly condemned, like those of G. W. Bush when he used the term 'crusade' in relation to the Iraq war, such usages reflect the wider and more systemic tensions between 'civilisation', 'freedom', 'terror', 'war' and 'liberty' which have been addressed (Jackson, 2006). Jackson traces US political discourse on war and terror arguing that the contemporary discourse incorporates and develops themes established during Ronald Reagan's presidency. He distinguishes four variants: the *terrorism as war* narrative; the *terrorist as threat* narrative; the *good American – evil terrorist* narrative; and the *'good' war on terrorism* narrative (Jackson, 2006: 156).

Several important points are established in this analysis: the extension of the terrorist threat to all civilised peoples, the equivalence (via the invocation of weapons of mass destruction) of the terrorist threat to that posed by Soviet Communism, the status of the fight against terrorism as a war, the wartime necessity of special measures, the equivalence of terrorists on home soil with a contagious cancer threatening the body politic and the suppression of dissent. In terms of US external image, Jackson notes that the idea of defending civilisation immediately evokes notions of American exceptionalism in foreign relations as defender of democracy against the barbarian. Jackson's detailed analysis contains direct citations from major political speeches by a range of figures in a variety of contexts to a number of different audiences. I add two quotes from speeches by George W. Bush here, one from within the time period of Jackson's study and another drawn from more recent examples. In his address to the American people at the start of the war President Bush stated:

> We come to Iraq with respect for its citizens, for their great civilization and for the religious faiths they practice. (Guardian Newspapers,

In Defence of Civilisation 181

19 March 2003, www.//buzzle.com/editorials/text3-19-2003-37646.asp, accessed 20 August 2005)

Following the London bombings on 7 July 2005, G. W. Bush's presidential radio broadcast to the American people concluded with the words:

> The free world did not seek this conflict, yet we will win it. Here at home, federal, state and local officials are doing everything possible to protect us from another terrorist attack in America. The terrorists cannot shake our will. America and its allies will act decisively, because we know that the future of civilization is at stake in this struggle, and we know that the cause of freedom will prevail.[6] (*Independent* online edition, 11 July 2005, http://comment.independent.co.uk/podium/article298219.ece, accessed 20 August 2005)

The first quotation repeats the notions of tolerance of difference and recognition of another civilisation. In the second, the inclusionary civilisation of America and all its allies continues to be equated with the pursuit of an abstract freedom. The defence of freedom includes the defence of neo-liberal market freedom which constitutes an unsustainable economic order that is environmentally and socially corrosive. In terms of internal US relations, Jackson notes how quickly the accompanying range of internal special measures adopted in the defence of civilisation have become 'embedded in the cultural and political landscape [such] that most people remain unaware of its significance and may not even notice its presence at a conscious level' (Jackson, 2006: 186–7).

The process of embedding raised here refers to a wide range of administrative practices including depictions within entertainment broadcasts and measures such as the 2001 Patriot Act. Paye (2006) traces how key 'temporary' measures within the Act have become permanent in the subsequent Patriot Act Improvement and Reauthorization Act of March 2006. In sensitive states like New York, these Acts have made street mobilisations almost impossible to organise. They have heightened sensitivities to surveillance, intensified activist anxieties and produced a climate of fear.[7]

US inter-agency collaboration had extended far beyond the 'homeland' prior to the Act, for example with the deputy director of the Federal Bureau of Investigation and members of the Washington police 'briefing' Czech security forces in Prague (Welsh, 2004). Canada's Security and Intelligence Service also took an active interest in the AGM from the same period, identifying the wide range of environmental, animal rights, social justice, labour organisation and anarchist groups present within the networks. The report also identified key North American and UK 'hubs' including London, Reclaim The Streets (RTS), and key communication, mobilisation and street-organising techniques (Canadian Security Intelligence Service, 2000). The report is interesting in that it clearly displays a differentiated view of the diverse social composition of the

182   *The Politics of Unsustainability*

movement and the ability to identify the key actors within it likely to use violence. Despite this, subsequent policing operations in a number of countries have tended to adopt inclusionary approaches towards all participants (Chesters & Welsh, 2006). Part of this process has been the steady exclusion of protestors from places imbued with significant symbolic meaning (e.g. Whitehall in the UK) and the concrete sites of intervention selected by campaigns (e.g. specific companies). The maintenance of the right to protest combined with the enforcement of spatial separation raises key issues in terms of a symbolic politics of intervention.

In the UK, spatial considerations in terms of 'outsiders' creating breaches of the peace or criminal trespass became a prominent feature of anti-nuclear protests at reactor sites during the 1980s requiring clarification and a ruling by Lord Denning (Welsh, 2000). The proliferation of direct action and do-it-yourself groups through into the 1990s resulted in the 1994 Criminal Justice and Public Order Act (CJA). This consolidated a range of rulings redefining trespassory assembly and identifying specific lifestyle attributes as public order issues. Successive CJAs throughout the 1990s continued to specify increasingly narrowly defined acts as illegal. The Prevention of Terrorism Act 2000 represented a further consolidation of state powers making a wide range of activities previously undertaken by environmental groups such as Greenpeace open to legal sanctions. The BBC 2 programme *True Spies* revealed that throughout this period a range of police and security services infiltrated direct action groups delaying road developments and leading to the seizure of the last major occupied tunnel at Twyford Down. Following Twyford, attention turned to infiltrating the animal rights movement with 'sleepers'. Irrespective of these measures, chief constables continued to lobby for more powers, something confirmed by Amanda Webster, deputy sheriff of Lancashire, in her comments on her experience of running training sessions at the Metropolitan Police Academy at Hendon. In her view, amongst the police 'the will to stamp out extreme protest has intensified', producing an 'effective lobby... to curb the Movement'. The incorporation of animal rights and similar protests within the Terrorism Act 2000 was part of a 'backlash against extreme protest', to which she added 'similar draconian legislation will not be far behind' (Webster, 2002). A number of factors combined to add to pressures for further legislation from within the police.

Relatively small May Day protests in London during 2000 and 2001 proved embarrassing to police and politicians, producing high profile media images of disorder perpetrated at the spatial heart of British democracy by protestors who, despite the dominant media images, raised substantive questions about power and neo-liberal globalisation (Donson *et al.*, 2004). The sustained and increasingly extreme protests by animal rights activists, which extended to firms associated with the emergent bio-economy, resonated with Cabinet concerns over capital flight from the bio-economy in the aftermath of campaigns against genetically modified crops (Hughes, this volume). Whitehall was also well aware of forthcoming legislative agendas, including replacing

In Defence of Civilisation 183

Trident and streamlining planning law to permit the fast-tracking of 'strategic' applications such as nuclear power stations and airport expansion schemes. Given successive jury trials dismissing criminal damage cases against Trident Ploughshares activists, legislative reform in favour of the state and developers was an unavoidable preoccupation. The most important point for present purposes, however, is that the notion of economic terrorism entered the lexicon of UK political discourse. The spatial separation of protestors from specified sites on a temporary and sometimes a permanent basis became an area where further measures were deemed necessary.

In the UK, the Serious Organised Crime and Police Act of 2005 introduced provisions to prevent unlicensed protests within one kilometre of the House of Commons to secure, amongst other things, the visual enjoyment of Parliament Square. News coverage of the Act featured Nicholas Soames MP describing a four year peace vigil opposite the House of Commons as an 'offensive encampment...defacing a focal area of tourism' (*Today*, BBC Radio 4, 28 January 2005). Such legislation requires police enforcement, and the continued presence of Brian Haw's peace vigil was subsequently raised in the House of Lords. Here, Lord Preston asked whether the government had wanted 'to see that dirty *mess* in Parliament Square cleared up as soon as possible' when it passed the legislation. He continued that:

> A very long time has gone by and the *mess* is still there. I, for one, know of no place in the democratic world where anything like that would be regarded as a fundamental privilege for the sake of freedom of speech. Quite the contrary: in most of our friends' Parliaments, armed police would busily remove the bloke within a minute. (House of Lords Debates, 18 May 2006, emphasis in original, http://www.publications.parliament. uk/cgi-bin/newhtml-hl?DB=semukparl&STEMM, accessed 24 May 2006)

Towards the end of the year, Brian Haw was in effect declared an aesthetic terrorist – for spoiling the 'tourist gaze' ('A casualty of free speech', *Independent*, 10 December 2005, p. 1) – whilst others noted that the collection of banners, posters and other images on display was estimated to be worth thousands of pounds. The legislation has subsequently been used to arrest individuals for a range of offences. These include reading out the names of British war dead in Iraq at the Cenotaph and the arrest of a lone protestor carrying a placard and copies of 'subversive literature'. The placard bore a quote from George Orwell – 'In a time of universal deceit, telling the truth is a revolutionary act' – whilst the subversive literature comprised copies of an article from *Vanity Fair* entitled 'Blair's Big Brother legacy'. Such cases raise significant issues of free speech within contemporary democracy. Following its decision to reprint the *Vanity Fair* article, the *Independent* on 29 June 2006 ran with the headline 'WARNING: if you read this newspaper, you may be arrested under the Government's anti-terror laws'. These examples have to be placed in the context of the significance of, and struggle over, free speech

184 *The Politics of Unsustainability*

within the public sphere, where issues of public trust have historically found expression (Roberts, 2003). As such they underline the importance attached to the freedom to undertake direct action as the 'litmus test' of democracy by Habermas (1985).

State actors central to the global neo-liberal project have clearly used legislative means to target sections of the environmental and anti-war movements which overlap extensively within the AGM. By limiting freedom of manoeuvre and apparently exhausting and constraining opportunities to stage symbolic protest events, this contributes to the sense that the movement has gone into decline with no significant impact. Empirically the continued vibrancy of the World Social Forum demonstrates a contrary position which cannot be developed here. Within the UK, certain movement sectors have been legislatively targeted, their activities becoming defined as public order issues subject to 'special' policing measures analogous to striking miners in the 1980s. In the context of 'war on terror' – in defence of civilisation – opposition in the public sphere becomes the barbarian in Jackson's (2006) civilisation/barbarian opposition. This defence of civilisation raises some important questions in terms of the 'habits of mind' within which techno-scientific neo-liberalism, whilst struggling to sustain the unsustainable, appears to be sleepwalking towards ever deepening environmental (and social) instability.

Declaring Symbolic Stakes: Another Civilisation is Possible?

Given the tendency for states to limit the freedom of manoeuvre of the AGM it would be easy to regard it as a spent force but this would be to misunderstand the dynamics of how culture works (Schudson, 1989) and the symbolic underpinnings of legitimacy in the context of a globally mobilising, networked critical civil society actor. Bourdieu is amongst those arguing that the social movements can create the symbolic resources necessary to challenge neo-liberal ascendancy (Bourdieu, 1992/2005, 1998/2004; Costa, 2006). Bourdieu's prioritisation of language reflects a lifelong academic engagement with how language constructs what is possible through 'legitimate' and 'authorised' speech (Bourdieu, 1992/2005). For Bourdieu, the credible ritual performance of such language within symbolically significant institutional contexts constitutes 'new myths' structuring identity (Bourdieu, 1998/2004). Many of the key institutions within which these languages are rehearsed and from which they are enunciated appear as centres of substantive, technocratic rationality such as those discussed by Ilcan above. Bourdieu, like Thompson (1995), considers that behind such apparatuses lie both symbolic power and symbolic vulnerability as the same rituals also structure resistance in a global era. Within this, critical intellectual effort is given a position of prominence and, in this sense, the AGM contributes significantly by constituting a space within which such exchanges can and do take place.

This is one element of a diverse range of strategies implicit within the initial formalisation of the calls bringing the AGM into existence. Such 'intellectual'

In Defence of Civilisation 185

work tends to take place within Social Forum events in an environment containing a diverse range of participants. Given the size of Social Forum events and their multi-layered structures featuring official, convergence and informal network sessions, these are difficult fields within which to work as an academic. Researching within such environments presents major methodological challenges particularly in the absence of network engagement and wider credibility. Within these sessions, the diversity of participants noted in the Canadian intelligence report enter a space of complexity creation which maximises the potential to realise what Granovetter (1973) termed the strength of weak ties. In this sense, movement process is at least as important as, if not more important than, movement street presence. The formalisation of demands and issues generated within the AGM impacts even inside the global institutions of neo-liberalism (Jawara & Kwa, 2004). The need to engage with the AGM or risk losing a generation who have been convinced that capitalism is a negative force is also recognised in sections of the financial press (Norberg, 2003).

Linguistic and intellectual innovation aside, culture works by utilising available symbolic resources, and the practices and images generated by the AGM constitute and multiply symbolic registers of resistance through embodiment. Restricting the AGM's freedom of movement on the streets temporarily curtails street practices which authority finds difficult to deal with, or symbolically challenging. Yet, the capacity for reinvention and hybridisation within these networks is considerable, and the overlapping nature of the networks introduces a high tolerance of redundancy. For example, the Clandestine Insurgent Rebel Clown Army which Szerszynski (this volume) uses to illustrate the use of transformative irony was being actively discussed during the 2003 Paris European Social Forum.[8] Outside of heavily regulated national public spheres, like that around Parliament in London, such performative repertoires continue largely unnoticed by national media.

This leads into a third feature of the AGM as a form of media in its own right (Melucci, 1996) creating an interactive web-mounted means of portraying and linking the multiple locales unnoticed by national media. This is one example of the way in which publics fragment, becoming niche consumers of diverse media forms (Anderson, 2003; Misztal, 2003), as national media constitutive of identity and political legitimacy suffer a falling share of the market. Internet use is reducing the use of all other media forms and politicians' recourse to the web remains limited. Politicians' personal web sites, publicly available email addresses and e-governance more generally appear to aim to increase participation in an existing system, failing to recognise public disengagement. Withdrawal has been a weapon of the subaltern throughout history – and withdrawal of symbolic legitimacy can undermine even the most authoritarian of regimes (Loveman, 2005). Public quiescence within periods of withdrawal becomes a contingent phenomenon subject to rebellious outbreaks.

186 *The Politics of Unsustainability*

The UK fuel protests of 2000 reportedly came close, within three days, to bringing the country to a virtual standstill (Urry, 2003), something not achieved by months of picketing by miners during the 1980s. The important point here is that the anatomy of media forms has changed significantly over a relatively short period of time. The cultural and political implications of such changes, in terms of social order and the credible ritual performances underpinning symbolic legitimacy within formal politics, are an area for further research. The constitutive role of the media in forming national collectivities (Anderson, 1989) is significantly attenuated in the face of global flows of information and niche uses of emergent media forms. In short the systems of representation mediating social order, including environmental orderings, have multiplied increasing complexity.

In the face of increasing complexity, political and security states have responded through well-established habits of mind attempting to reduce complexity by policing and security measures. There is nothing novel in states acting against troublesome environmental movements, including the use of extreme force in cases like the sinking of the *Rainbow Warrior*. Environmental activists have also been linked to external threats before, notably in claims that Russian gold was financing anti-nuclear movements during the 1970s (Welsh, 2000).[9] What is distinctive about the present is the extent to which analogous linkages between terrorism and activism have been codified in law and the pervasive implications of these laws for a wider range of citizens. This form of environmental ordering – in defence of civilisation – is accompanied by other administrative measures addressing environmental ends, such as recycling, which are accompanied by surveillance measures and fines, prompting public resentment and incredulity. The administrative measures buttressing neo-liberal globalisation have assumed far greater reach than previously witnessed within liberal democracies, extending far into the interstices of civil society.

Conclusions: Civilisation and Environmental (Dis)ordering

As argued above, Bateson regarded technology as central to the success of any civilisation, and new technology remains a prominent feature of US responses to climate change, particularly in the area of transport. It is salutary to recall a similar initiative. A year after Rio, then US President Bill Clinton announced a billion dollar partnership between US space and defence laboratories, Detroit and the Auto Workers Union to develop fuel cells creating the 85 miles per gallon car. Symbolically, the project was declared a 'terrestrial equivalent of President Kennedy's Apollo project' (*Guardian*, 'Clinton backs 85mpg car', 30th September, 1993: 1). More than 10 years later the promised technology barely registers within the US car market whilst consumers receive tax relief on gas guzzlers (Roberts, 2005). Given the contribution to climate change originating from internal combustion engines, this example underlines the incredibly slow pace of innovation within established sectors with significant fixed capital assets.[10]

It is illuminating to return to some of the inter-war literature discussing civilisation and technology and recall Mumford's caution that techno-scientific advance results in 'plateaus', steady state interregnums lacking fundamental advances, and his emphasis upon the importance of symbiotically attuning technical development to secure 'equilibrium in the environment' (Mumford, 1934/1972: 430).[11] Climate change dynamics are underpinned by what Mumford saw as one of the key elements necessary to achieve a shift to an 'organic ideology' capable of balancing technical progress and human needs – recognition that the 'conversion of the sun's energies' represents 'the prime fact of all economic activity' (Mumford, 1934/1972: 368ff., 375). Contemporary calls for technological solutions to climate change reassert faith in techno-scientific civilisation, underestimate the time needed for such initiatives to have an impact and deny the need to recognise limits.

Writing in the same era as Mumford, Freud regarded the absence of flooding and the imposition of hydrological order as a key marker of civilisation (Freud, 1930/1963: 29). By this standard, civilisation in Europe and America is at risk as catastrophic floods, arising in part from the culture of control via the canalisation of rivers, become increasingly frequent. Freud and Mumford also emphasised the need for sensitivity to signs calling for social reordering. For Freud, it was important to recognise that 'revolt against some existing injustice ... may prove favourable to a further development of civilization' (Freud, 1930/1963: 33). Mumford's writing from this period argued that those dissenting from a prevailing technocratic order represent 'elements that cannot without danger be ignored or repressed' (Mumford, 1934/1972: 280–1).

The political discourse of civilisation and terror has done exactly the opposite of this by translating social forces seeking to change systems into social forces threatening systems. As Theweleit (1987) notes, flooding becomes a metaphor underlining fears of inundation by people crossing borders, a central feature of the AGM in its contestation of global summit meetings. Habermas also likens globalisation to 'images of overflowing rivers, washing away all the frontier checkpoints and controls, and ultimately the bulwark of the nation state itself' (2001: 67).

The rise of the AGM has perturbated environmental politics. In 2001 Greenpeace International considered itself 'outflanked' by the effectiveness of the global movements and embarked upon a five year rolling programme of internal debate, *Breaking Down the Walls* (Greenpeace, 2001). The proposals included action and deliberation to address its own democratic deficit and to broaden its focus of opposition.[12] In part, the impact of the AGM on environmental politics arises through the fusion of a critique of the prevailing economic orthodoxy, which, as I have argued here, forms the overarching axiomatic shaping governance and partnership initiatives, with environmental and social objectives. Theoretically this leads to a final paradox relating to

188   The Politics of Unsustainability

agency. As the death of the subject is widely proclaimed and the absence of a (textual) outside arguably reinforces self-referential autopoiesis, complexity theory increasingly recognises the importance of 'free acts' and that 'individuals matter' in terms of changing systems in far from equilibrium states (Eve *et al.*, 1997: xi–xxvii, 269–80; Urry, 2003; Chesters & Welsh, 2005, 2006). It is the capacity of the AGM – in defence of civilisation – to facilitate such free acts and insert images of their enactment within a range of media which has proven challenging to the social order advanced through neo-liberal institutional dominance. The other worlds declared possible by the AGM offer more rational order, not less, by insisting that the economic alone cannot orchestrate human activity and that other rationalities must be harnessed to this end. The academic challenge of working within such contexts is part of engaging with what we have argued here is a post-ecologist condition.

Notes

1. Widening inequalities in wealth and health are amongst the examples I have in mind.
2. This term avoids the negative connotations of the prefix 'Anti' which misses the proactive content of the movement of movements.
3. For a critique of this ideological position see Bauman (1999), Bourdieu (1998, 2004) and Gounari (2006).
4. The term axiomatic is intended to reflect Deleuze & Guattari's (2003) sense of the term as developed in *A Thousand Plateaus: Capitalism and Schizophrenia* throughout this contribution.
5. For an account of the systemic, multi-agency use of violence and terror by Italian forces against anti-capitalist protestors in Genoa, the subsequent promotion of key personnel involved and efforts to gain legal redress see Chesters & Welsh (2006, ch. 4: 'From carnival against capitalism to death at high noon: states fight back').
6. In this context also see Blühdorn (this volume) on the 'non-negotiable consensus of defence'.
7. Based on numerous email exchanges and conversations with US academics and activists.
8. Personal observation of those involved included individuals with longstanding involvement amongst prominent UK groups and those attending their first such event. Participants included those with academic training in art and performing arts and those with no formal training or experience in performance.
9. The kernel of substance in this claim within the UK lay in funds from Russian miners reaching the National Union of Mineworkers, which backed the formation of the Anti-nuclear Campaign, but the association was drawn with the anti-nuclear movement as a whole.
10. States have not seriously attempted to restructure such sectors by creating appropriate markets via legislation. Cities like London pioneered road charging, and California, which in 2003 had the fifth largest economy in the world (Chytry, 2006), is pursuing legal action against the car industry. Many examples of systemic engagement come from sub-state actors.
11. Mumford included the use of 'sun converters', heat exchangers utilising oceanic temperature gradients and 'new types of wind turbine', commenting that wind alone could supply all reasonable energy demands given some advance in battery technology. Advances in battery technology and solar battery chargers now make the hybrid car the most viable short term technical option for reducing emissions arising from vehicular transport. The capacity of market mechanisms alone to effect such a transition within relevant timeframes is limited.
12. Other responses included experimenting with applications of complexity theory by establishing cascading email lists generating an interactive depiction of alignments and interests within a variety of constituencies. Greenpeace thus remain tapped into global, bottom-up formalisations whilst maintaining their strategic distance from formal initiatives, a position easily misinterpreted as non-participation within international realignment processes (see Rootes, 2006).

In Defence of Civilisation 189

References

Anderson, A. (2003) 'Communication, conflict and risk in the 21st century: critical issues for sociology', *Sociological Research Online* 8(4). Available at: www.socresonline.org.uk/8/4/andersonhtml.

Anderson, B. (1989) *Imagined Communities* (London: Verso).

Bateson, G. (1973) *Steps to an Ecology of Mind* (London: Paladin).

Bauman, Z. (1999) *In Search of Politics* (Cambridge: Polity).

Bauman, Z. (2004) *Wasted Lives: Modernity and its Outcasts* (Cambridge: Polity).

Beck, U. (1997) *World Risk Society* (Cambridge: Polity).

Bourdieu, P. (1992/2005) *Language and Symbolic Power* (Cambridge: Polity).

Bourdieu, P. (1998/2004) *Acts of Resistance: Against the New Myths of Our Time* (Oxford: Blackwell).

Canadian Security Intelligence Service (2000) Anti-globalization – a spreading phenomenon, Report # 2000/08. Available at: http://www.csis-scrs.gc.ca/eng/miscdocs/200008_e.html (accessed 23 March 2001).

Castells, M. (1996) *The Rise of the Network Society, Vol. 1, The Information Age: Economy, Society and Culture* (Oxford: Blackwell).

Chesters, G. & Welsh, I. (2004) 'Rebel colours: "framing" in global social movements', *Sociological Review* 53(3): 314–35.

Chesters, G. & Welsh, I. (2005) 'Complexity and social movement(s): process and emergence in planetary action systems', *Theory, Culture and Society* 22(5): 187–221.

Chesters, G. & Welsh, I. (2006) *Complexity and Social Movement(s): Multitudes at the Edge of Chaos* (London: Routledge).

Chytry, C. (2006) 'California civilization: beyond the United States of America', *Thesis Eleven* 85: 8–36.

Costa, R. L. (2006) 'The logic and practices in Pierre Bourdieu', *Current Sociology* 54(6): 873–95.

Crooks, E. (2002) 'Top economists engage in bickering', *Financial Times*, 3 July 2002, p. 13.

Deleuze, G. & Guattari, F. (2003) *A Thousand Plateaus: Capitalism and Schizophrenia* (London: Continuum).

Doherty, B. & Doyle T. (2006) 'Beyond borders: transnational politics, social movements and modern environmentalism', *Environmental Politics* 15(5): 697–712.

Donson, F., Chesters, G., Tickle, A. & Welsh, I. (2004) 'Rebels with a cause, folk devils without a panic: press jingoism, policing tactics and anti-capitalist protest in London and Prague'. *Internet Journal of Criminology, Online*. Available at: http://www.internetjournalofcriminology.com/Donson%20et%20al%20-%20Folkdevils.pdf (accessed 12 June 2006).

Dryzek, J., Downes, D., Hunold, Ch., Schlosberg, D. & Hernes, H.-K. (2003) *Green States and Social Movements. Environmentalism in the United States, United Kingdom, Germany and Norway* (Oxford: Oxford University Press).

Edelman, M. (1971) *Politics as Symbolic Action: Mass Arousal and Quiescence* (Chicago, IL: Markham).

Edelman, M. (1997) *Political Language: Words that Succeed, Politics that Fail* (New York: Academic Press).

Elias, N. (1939/1994) *The Civilising Process* (Oxford: Blackwell).

Eve, R. A., Horsfall, S. & Lee, M. E. (1997) *Chaos, Complexity and Sociology: Myths, Models and Theories* (London: Sage).

Fischer, W. F. & Ponniah, T. (eds.) (2003) *Another World is Possible: Popular Alernatives to Globalization at the World Social Forum* (London: Zed).

Freud, S. (1930/1963). *Civilization and its Discontents* (London: Hogarth Press & Institute of Psychoanalysis).

Gounari, P. (2006) 'Contesting the cynicism of neo-liberal discourse: moving towards a language of possibility', *Studies in Language and Capitalism* 1: 77–96. Available at: http://languageandcapitalism.info (accessed 4 December 2006).

190   *The Politics of Unsustainability*

Granovetter, M. S. (1973) 'The strength of weak ties', *American Journal of Sociology* 78(6): 1360–80.

Greenpeace (2001) *Breaking Down the Walls* (London: Greenpeace).

Habermas, J. (1985) 'Civil disobedience: the litmus test for the democratic constitutional state', *Berkeley Journal of Sociology* 30: 95–116.

Habermas, J. (2001) *The Postnational Constellation* (Cambridge: Polity).

Hutton, W. (2002) *The World We're In* (London: Little, Brown).

Ilcan, S. (2006) Global governing organisations: order-building and waster management, *Current-Sociology*, 54(6): 851–72.

Jackson R. (2006) 'Genealogy, ideology and counter terrorism: writing wars on terrorism from Ronald Reagan to George W. Bush Jnr', *Studies in Language and Capitalism* 1: 163–93. Available at: http://languageandcapitalism.info (accessed 4 December 2006).

Jamison, A. (2001) *The Making of Green Knowledge: Environmental Politics and Cultural Transformation* (Cambridge: Cambridge University Press).

Jawara, F. & Kwa, A. (2004) *Behind the Scenes at the WTO: The Real World of International Trade Negotiations* (London: Zed).

Latham, R. (1999) 'Politics in a floating world: towards a critique of global governance', in M. Hewson & T. Sinclaire (eds.), *Approaches to Global Governance Theory*, pp. 23–53 (New York: SUNY Press).

Loveman, M. (2005) 'The modern state and the primitive accumulation of symbolic power', *American Journal of Sociology* 110(6): 1651–83.

Manners, I. & Lucarelli, S. (eds.) (2006) *Values and Principles in EU Foreign Policy* (London: Routledge).

Melucci, A. (1996) *Challenging Codes: Collective Action in the Information Age* (Cambridge: Cambridge University Press).

Misztal, B. (2003) 'Negative capability or dealing with the complexity of the Iraqi War', *Sociological Research Online* 8(3). Available at: www.socresonline.org.uk/8/3/misztal.html (accessed 3 June 2004).

Mumford, P. (1934/1972) *Technics and Civilization* (London: George Routledge & Sons).

Mumford, P. (1973) *Interpretations and Forecasts: 1922–1972. Studies, in Literature, History, Biography, Technics, and Contemporary Society,* (New York: Harcourt Brace Jovanovich).

Munck, R. (2004) 'Global civil society: myths and prospects', in R. Taylor (ed.), *Creating a Better World: Interpreting Global Civil Society*, pp. 13–26 (Bloomfield, CT: Kumarian Press).

Murphy, P. (2006) 'American civilization', *Thesis Eleven* 85: 64–92.

Norberg, J. (2003) 'Why we should fight anti-globalists', *Wall Street Journal Europe*, 27 October.

Notes from Nowhere (2003) *We Are Everywhere: The Irresistible Rise of Global Anticapitalism* (London: Verso).

Paye, J.-C. (2006) 'A permanent state of emergency', *Monthly Review* 58(6): 29–37.

Reiner, R. (2005) 'Be tough on a crucial cause of crime – neo-liberalism', *Guardian*, 24 November 2005, p. 32.

Roberts, J. M. (2003) *The Aesthetics of Free Speech: Rethinking the Public Sphere* (Basingstoke: Palgrave).

Roberts, P. (2005) *The End of Oil: The Decline of the Petroleum Economy and the Rise of a New Energy Order* (London: Bloomsbury).

Rootes, C. (2006) 'Facing South? British environmental movement organisations and the challenge of globalisation', *Environmental Politics* 15(5): 768–86.

Saul, J. (2005) *The Collapse of Globalism: And the Reinvention of the World* (London: Atlantic).

Schudson, M. (1989) 'How culture works: perspective from media studies on the efficacy of symbols', *Theory and Society* 18: 153–80.

Sen, J., Anand, A., Escobar, E. & Waterman, P. (eds.) (2004) *World Social Forum: Challenging Empires* (New Delhi: Viveka Foundation).

Solomon, W. S. (2000) 'More form than substance: press coverage of the WTO protests in Seattle', *Monthly Review* 52(1): 12–20.

Stiglitz, J. (2002) *Globalisation and its Discontents* (New York: Norton).

Theweleit, K. (1987) *Male Fantasies Volume 1: Women, Floods, Bodies, History* (Minneapolis, MN: Minnesota University Press).

Thompson, J. B. (1995) *Media and Modernity* (Cambridge: Polity Press).

Torgerson, D. (2000) 'Farewell to the green movement? Political action and the green public sphere', *Environmental Politics* 11(1): 133–45.

Urry, J. (2003) *Global Complexity* (London: Routledge).

Webster, A. (2002) 'The environmental lawyer', in J. Bennet (ed.) *Facing the Future: Listening to the Past* (Upper Basildon: United Kingdom Environmental Law Association).

Welsh, I. (1996) 'Risk, global governance and environmental politics', *Innovation* 9(4): 407–20.

Welsh, I. (2000) *Mobilising Modernity: The Nuclear Moment* (London: Routledge).

Welsh, I. (2004) 'Network movement in the Czech Republic: perturbating Prague', *Journal of European Area Studies* 12(3): 321–37.

Welsh, I. (2006) 'Values, science and the EU: bio-technology and transatlantic relations', in I. Manners & S. Lucarelli (eds.) *Values and Principles in EU Foreign Policy*, pp. 39–76 (London: Routledge).

Index

absurdities 155, 159
Acceptable Risk Calculator 162
accountability 173, 176
acid rain 102–3, 107
action replacement 72
activists 51, 53, 61–2, 86
  civilisation 178–9, 181–3, 186
  irony 163
  legislation 103
  self-deception 141, 148, 150
adaptation 60
addiction 14
administration 177
Adorno, T.W. 76
aesthetic politics 82
Africa 136
Agenda 21 6, 27, 119
agenda setting 24, 36, 41
Agricultural Ministers' Council 136
agriculture 35, 59, 121, 136, 141,
  145–6
Alaska 153
alibi legislation 94, 100, 102
alienation 76–8, 80, 85, 99, 155, 166
Alternative Globalisation Movement
  (AGM) 174, 177–8, 181, 184–5,
  187–8
alternative politics 77–8, 80–1
America 11–12, 25, 126
  civilisation 174–5, 180–1, 187
  exceptionalism 180
  GM 143, 145–7, 150
Amsterdam Treaty 120
anarchists 179, 181
Andersen, H.C. 41
Anglo-Irish 157
animal feed 137, 139, 143

animal rights 61, 181–2
Antarctica 37–8, 40
anti-capitalist movement 162
anti-environmentalism 8, 11–12, 29,
  32, 42–3
anti-globalisation movement 13, 61,
  177, 180
anti-imperialism 177, 179
anti-nuclear protests 182
anti-politics 77
Apollo 186
Argentina 137
Aristotle 159–60
Asia 37
asylum seekers 148–9
authentic politics 69, 73–5, 77, 80–6,
  154
Auto Workers Union 186
autonomisation 76

backstage 162
bad faith 156
Baker, S. 17, 25–6, 113–33
banking 162–3, 176
barbarians 180, 184
Barry, J. 29, 42
Barthes, R. 168
Bateson, G. 175–6, 186
Baudrillard, J. 69, 76, 83, 108, 154,
  164
Bauman, Z. 9, 138, 150, 177
BBC 182
Beck, U. 76–7, 115, 135, 138–9, 144,
  149–51, 167, 174
behavioural adjustment 50
Belém 33, 35
Berlusconi, S. 179–80

194   *Index*

bias 50, 99, 125
Big Brother 183
bio-economy 182
biodiversity 23, 33–6, 136, 146, 153, 175
biosphere 27, 118–19
biotechnology 136–7, 150, 162, 177
Blair, T. 8, 143, 183
Blauert, J. 48
Blok, A. 59
Blühdorn, I. 1–21, 28–9, 48, 51, 59, 63, 67–91, 108, 117, 129, 138–9, 144, 149, 154, 157, 159–60
Bourdieu, P. 174, 184
bovine spongiform encephalopathy (BSE) 142
boycotts 137
brain drain 136
Brazil 33, 35–6
Breaking Down the Walls 187
Bristol 143
Britain 6, 17, 134–6, 139–40, 142–8, 150–1, 182–3
British Medical Association 136
British Nuclear Fuels 163
British Petroleum 154
Brookes, R. 142
Brundtland Commission 26–7, 49, 53, 113–14, 117–21, 127–8
Buell, F. 11, 29
Bundestag 100–1, 103
bureaucrats 53
Bush, G.W. 8, 12, 180–1

Cabinet 142, 182
Cadbury-Schweppes 162
Callinicos, A. 159
Canada 34, 136–7, 181, 185
capital flight 136, 182
capitalism 2–3, 11, 14, 16
  civilisation 176, 185
  discourse 23, 26, 31
  ecological modernisation 115–16, 129–30

irony 153–5, 164, 168
  post-ecologism 52
  symbolic politics 67, 69, 76–7, 80–1, 84–6
Cardiff Process 124
Carey, J.W. 24
Carnival 162
Carnival against Capital 162
Carruthers, D. 5
case studies 30–2, 48, 100–8
catalytic converters 101
Catholics 157
Cenotaph 183
central banks 176
Centre for Development of Adult Education and Folkeoplysning 54
certainty 138–9, 144, 149–50, 166
character types 157
charities 135, 178
Charles, Prince of Wales 33
China 67, 136
choreography 71
Christian Conservative parties of Germany (CDU/CSU) 101
Churchill, W. 143
Cicero 161
citizen involvement 47–64, 135
civil liberties 7
civil society 12, 154, 167, 173, 177–8, 184, 186
civilisation 17, 172–88
Clandestine Insurgent Rebel Clown Army (CIRCA) 168, 185
Climacus 165–6
climate change 4, 7–8, 16
  civilisation 186–7
  discourse 23, 30, 33–4, 36–8, 40–1
  ecological modernisation 128
  irony 153
  self-deception 141
  symbolic politics 81
Clinton, B. 7, 179, 186
co-production 53, 62–3, 168
Cohen, M. 4

Index 195

collaboration 99, 174, 181
Collins, A. 165
colonialism 179
commercial mediators 48, 58–63
Commission of the European
  Communities (CEC) 120–3, 125–6,
  128
commitment 113–30, 160
common good 27–8, 31, 36–7, 42–3,
  50–1, 128
communicative irony 157–62
Communism 180
competitive advantage 121
complexity *see* issue complexity
compliance 97, 104
comportment 159–60, 163, 166
computer-mediated communication
  (CMC) 178–9
The Concept of Irony 165
conformity 177
conservation 22
Conservative parties of Germany
  (CDU/CSU) 101, 104
Conservative Party of UK 13
constitutions 120
constitutive politics 175
constructivism 9, 129
consultants 49, 60–1
consumerism 2–3, 5–6, 8
  civilisation 178
  discourse 23, 28, 36
  eco-politics 10–11, 14–16
  ecological modernisation 117
  post-ecologism 50
  symbolic politics 67, 69, 76–7, 80–2,
    84–6
  threats 77
Contested Natures 9
control 24, 26, 40, 78
  civilisation 187
  ecological modernisation 118
  irony 155
  self-deception 94, 138, 140, 144,
    148–51

symbolic politics 82
Copenhagen 122
Corinth 158
corporations *see* corporatism
corporatism 3, 7–8, 11, 27
  civilisation 179
  ecological modernisation 126
  irony 158–60, 162
  post-ecologism 154, 156
  self-deception 136
corrective irony 163
correspondence theory of truth 154
cost-benefit analysis 98, 105–7
counter-revolution 76–8
courts 93
crime 6
Criminal Justice and Public Order
  Act (CJA) 182
Critical Art Ensemble 162
critical theory 76, 82, 87
cross-pollination 136, 147
Cult of the New Eve 162
cultivars 136
cultural modernism 155–6, 164, 166
cultural sociology 24
Czech Republic 181

Daily Mail 139, 148–9
Daily Mirror 149
Dalton, R. 12–13
Danish Consumer Council 62
Danish Radio (DR) 30
Danmarks Naturfredningsforening
  (Danish Society for Nature
  Conservation) 53
Darwin, C. 155
de Certeau, M. 160
deception 73–5, 82, 84–5
  ecological modernisation 130
  post-ecologism 155–7, 159, 163
  societal 92–108
  symbolic inversion 134–51
declaratory politics 113–30
decoupling 119, 121–2

196 *Index*

delegation 77–8, 99
Delors, J. 122
delusive context 76
democracy 2–3, 7–8, 11
    civilisation 173, 175, 180, 182–4,
        186–7
    eco-politics 14–16
    ecological modernisation 115, 121,
        130
    grassroots 76
    management 54–5
    post-ecologism 47, 49–50, 63
    public choice theory 98–9
    symbolic commitment 118
    symbolic politics 67–9, 71, 74, 76–8,
        80–5
denial 163
Denmark 15–16, 22–66, 123, 156
depoliticisation 78, 83
Detroit 186
Devall, B. 12–13
developers 183
developing world 15, 26, 35, 41, 144,
    176–7
direct action 7, 182, 184
discourses 24, 26–8, 30
    changing 36–7, 42–4
    civilisation 173, 175, 180, 183, 187
    commitment 113–14, 117, 123–6,
        128, 130
    GM 137–8, 144, 147
    irony 161
    post-ecologism 49, 53, 57, 63
    reassurance 116
    symbolic politics 67–9, 71, 75, 83,
        85, 87
dispositional irony 157, 166
dissent 25, 180, 187
double dividend 122–3
double irony 163
Douglas, M. 25, 148
Dover 143
Dow Corporation 162
Downs, A. 99
dramatised irony 161

Dryzek, J.S. 25, 178
dualism 10, 85
Dunlap, R. 12–13
Dybkjær, L. 54

Earth 10, 35
Earth Summits 16, 23, 30, 33–4,
    37–41, 118, 121, 186
East Anglia 142
eco-authoritarianism 50
eco-fascism 50
eco-imperialism 36, 178
eco-politics 1–18
ecocide 153
ecological debt 6
ecological footprint 6
ecological mandarins 50
ecological modernisation (EM) 17,
    22–3
    declaratory politics 113–30
    demise 42–4
    discourse 25–7, 29–37
    post-ecologism 53–4, 57–60, 63
    symbolic politics 68
ecological rucksack 6
ecologism 9, 31, 36, 58
Ecologist 13
ecologists 3, 76–7, 82, 85–6
economic growth 2–3, 5–7, 10
    civilisation 173
    discourses 22, 26–7, 29, 32, 39, 41–3
    eco-politics 16
    ecological modernisation 113, 115,
        118–25
    post-ecologism 51
Economic Growth and the
Environment: Some Implications for
Policy Making 123
economic terrorism 183
economics 68, 77, 81, 106
    alternative 77, 80
    civilisation 174–6, 181
    ecological modernisation 115–18
    GM 146
economism 29, 43, 63

Index   197

economists 39–41, 58–9, 176, 179
ecosystems 29, 78, 102
Edelman, M. 69, 73, 75–6, 80–2, 85,
    87
Eden project 149
Eder, K. 9, 27–9, 43
education 6, 24, 54–5, 178
EEA 123
effectiveness 94–7
eironeia 159
Either/Or 159, 165
elections 7, 37, 59, 97–9, 103
electricity industry 52, 103, 106, 168
Elias, N. 174, 177
elites 63, 68, 72–3, 75
    civilisation 176, 179
    ecological modernisation 127
    legislation 107
    post-ecologism 159, 163
    symbolic politics 83–4
emancipation 51–2, 71, 74–6, 116
embedding 181
employment 6, 60, 122–3, 125–6
empowerment 49, 54–5, 62, 75
enabling function 114
The End of Nature 8
end of nature 2, 4, 8–9, 12–13
energy security 4, 8
England 135, 142, 157
English Channel 135
Enlightenment 74–5, 154–5, 173
entertainment 25, 63, 181
entrepreneurs 28, 119, 121, 177
Environmental Action Programmes
    (EAPs) 120–1, 123
environmental legislation 92–108
environmental policy integration
    (EPI) 115, 120–1, 124–5
environmental security 67
environmental sociology 1–2, 8, 12–
    15, 17–18, 177
*Environmental Technology for
    Sustainable Development* 123
environmentalism 1–2, 4–5, 13, 16
    citizen involvement 47

contested 37–42
discourse 22–3, 25–30, 32, 37–44
ecological modernisation 114, 116,
    125, 130
end 8–12, 130
irony 166–8
legislation 92
post-ecologism 62
environmentalists 9, 11–12, 15–16
    civilisation 186
    discourse 33, 35, 37, 41–2
    post-ecologism 48, 53, 59–60, 62–3,
    154–6, 166–7
epistemology 154–5, 164, 166, 177
ethics 51, 59, 74, 120–1, 162, 164, 166
Eurocentric civilisation 174
Europe 4, 11–13, 15, 25
    civilisation 173–5, 180, 187
    discourse 37–8, 40–1
    GM 135–6, 140–1, 148, 150
    post-ecologism 47, 61, 156, 164, 166
    symbolic politics 74, 78
European Commission 136
European Community 127
European Council Summit 122
European Parliament 123
European Social Forum 185
European Union (EU) 5, 17, 26
    discourse 37, 39, 41
    ecological modernisation 113–33
    Framework Programmes 122
    GM 135–7, 144–6, 148–9
    legislation 96
evironmentalism 25, 51, 164
evolution 62
exceptionalism 175, 180
exclusion 60, 63, 77, 81, 83, 149, 182
exhaustion 75–80, 82–6, 184
expertocrats 50
experts 39–40, 49–50, 52, 58, 77, 103,
    137
exploitation 175

facilitation 48
Fairclough, N. 24

198   *Index*

false consciousness 76
famine 136, 157
Federal Bureau of Investigation 181
field trials 139, 146
Fifth Environmental Action
   Programme (EAP) 120–1
financial press 185
Finland 62
Fischer, F. 49
flooding 148, 187
focus groups 60
folk devils 174, 178
folkeoplysning 49, 54, 58, 63
food 121–2, 134, 136–7, 139–40, 145,
   147–50, 176
Fordism 122
foreigners 147–9
fossil fuels 34
Foucault, M. 24
Fourth Environmental Action
   Programme (EAP) 120
France 135
Frankenstein crops 145
free acts 188
free market 2, 28, 78, 118, 127, 129,
   174
free players 56–7
free speech 183
free time 6
free trade 176, 179
Freud, S. 155, 187
Friends of the Earth (FoE) 4, 17
   Britain 140, 162
   Cymru 139
   England 135
   GM 139–40, 150–1
From Apocalypse to Way of Life 11
fuel protests 186
fundamentalism 175
funding 55, 58, 60
future-fitness 68

Galileo 41
Gandhi, M.K. 63
gene flow 135

general irony 164–7
genetic modification (GM) 7, 17, 62,
   134–52, 182
Genoa 179
geography 151
German Environmental Agency
   (Umweltbundesamt - UBA) 100
Germany 16, 94–5, 100–4, 123, 143,
   180
global dynamics 178
global warming 22, 29–30, 33–4, 38–9,
   160
globalisation 3, 6, 135
   civilisation 173, 176–7, 182, 186–7
   GM 138, 141–2, 146, 148–50
   irony 163
'GM-free Wales' 139
Gnosticism 166
God 155, 175
golden skeletons 162
Goldsmith, Z. 13
goodwill 160
Gorz, A. 2, 50
government involvement 53–8
Granovetter, M.S. 185
grassroots 11–12, 26, 31, 37
   civilisation 178
   decline 51–3
   democracy 76
   post-ecologism 48–9, 56, 60–2
   symbolic politics 71
Greco-Roman civilization 174–5
Greece 159–60
Green Backlash 11
green backlash 4, 8–12
Green Foundation 56–8
Green Guide Scheme (GGS) 56–8
green guides 56–8, 60
Green Municipality 54–5
Green parties 4, 13, 77, 101, 104, 118
green revolution 136, 144
greenhouse effect 34, 38, 40, 42
greenhouse gases 33, 38–9
Greenpeace 4, 52, 62, 143, 149, 162,
   182, 187

Großfeuerungsanlagen-Verordnung
(Ordinance on Large Combustion
Plants) 94, 101–7
*Growth, Competitiveness and
Employment* (White Paper) 122–3,
126
Die Grünen 101, 104
Guardian 148
gypsies 149

Habermas, J. 52, 74, 83, 184, 187
Hajer, M.A. 26–7
Haraway, D. 147, 151
Hardin's Law 164
Haw, B. 183
health 29, 31–2, 68, 101, 106–8, 121–2,
136
hegemony 2–3, 5, 7, 80
Heilbroner, R. 50
Heinberg, C. 50
Hendon 182
heritage countryside 145
hidden agendas 74, 93
hierarchies 97, 102, 125
Homer 159
House of Commons 183
House of Lords 183
Hovden, E. 125
Hughes, E. 17, 134–52
Hurricane Katrina 67
hyper-ecologism 2
hyperreality 154
hysteria 83

identity 77–8, 81, 86
civilisation 178, 184–5
ecological modernisation 127–8
GM 145, 148–9, 151
Ilcan, S. 177, 184
imaginative politics 151
immigration 148, 175
immune system 136
impersonal irony 161
imposition 62–3
impression management 160

inclusion 48, 63, 77–8, 127, 149, 173,
178, 181–2
incorporation 62
Independent 136, 143, 183
Independent on Sunday 139, 148
India 67
individualisation 6, 81, 150–1
individualism 5, 178
industrialisation 8, 26, 33
backstage 162
ecological modernisation 113,
115–16, 118–19, 122, 129
GM 141, 150
irony 155
post-ecologism 59, 61
symbolic politics 68, 76
Industry Council 124
inertia 48
inflation 176
information asymmetry 99–100, 107
information flows 186
Inglehart, R. 76
insecurity 77
Institute of Environmental
Assessment 59
instrumentalism 178
integration 60, 71, 75, 96, 104–5,
124–9
integrity 147, 160
intelligence agencies 178
intelligent solutions 68
intelligentsia 87
inter-generational equity 5
interest-group theory 98–100
International Energy Agency 8
International Monetary Fund (IMF)
5, 176–7
internet 185
interpretation 48, 63, 71, 129
intervention 175, 182
investment 59
Iraq 180, 183
Irish potato famine 157
Iron Age 146
ironic ecology 166–9

200   *Index*

irony 153–69, 185
Islam 180
Island Britain 143
issue complexity 100, 106–8, 174, 186, 188
issue-related substantives 95–6, 98, 102–7

Jackson, R. 180, 184
Jamison, A. 59, 177
Japan 108, 119, 126
Jessop, B. 167
job creation 122–3
Johannesburg 23, 30, 37–41, 121
Johnson, S. 156
justice 93, 121, 178, 181, 187

'Keep Britain GM Free' 135, 139–40
Kennedy, J.F. 186
Kierkegaard, S. 156, 159, 163, 165, 168
Kohl, H. 103
Kyoto 37, 39, 41, 175

labelling 168
labour 6, 126, 181
Labour Party Conference 2006 7
Læssøe, J. 15–16, 47–66
Lafferty, W.M. 125
LaFleur, W.R. 108
laissez-faire 63
Lancashire 182
landscape 145–7
Langhelle, O. 27
language 154, 158, 160–1, 163, 179, 184
Latham, R. 177
Latour, B. 166
law suits 11
Lefort, C. 114, 129
left wing 60
legislation 16, 92–108, 182–4
legislative intent 97
legitimacy 82
less developed countries (LDCs) 177

levelling 48, 63
Liberal Democrats of Germany (FDP) 101, 103–4
liberal irony 159
liberalism 50, 58–9, 63, 115, 186
libertarianism 77
life in fragments 5
lifestyle 5–6, 14, 28
  civilisation 182
  discourse 32, 37
  ecological modernisation 117–18, 120
  GM 151
  post-ecologism 57
  symbolic politics 78
limits to growth 23, 26–7, 31
  discourse 33–7, 40, 42–3
  ecological modernisation 118–20, 122
  symbolic politics 67
Lisbon Strategy 123–4
livestock 137, 142
lobbying 98
Local Agenda 21 6, 57, 60
Locke, S. 153
LØJ (Organic Farmer Organisation) 53, 62
Lomborg, B. 10, 37–8, 40–1, 58–60, 63
London 162, 181–2, 185
Los Angeles Times 179
Luhmann, N. 86–7

Maastricht Treaty 120, 126–7
McGlade, J. 124
MacIntyre, A. 157
McKibben, Bill 8–9, 12
MacNaghten, P. 9
macro-economics 116
mainstreaming 1, 11, 13, 16
  civilisation 174, 177, 179
  discourse 22
  symbolic politics 52, 69, 77–8
maize 148
managerialism 118

Index 201

marginal utility 76–7
marginalisation 12, 28, 48, 50, 60, 174, 178
market 2, 28, 78
  civilisation 174, 178
  ecological modernisation 118, 127, 129
  post-ecologism 50, 60
Martinez-Alier, J. 63
Marx, K. 155
Marxism-Leninism 177
mass extinction 33–4
master discourse 27–8, 44
materialism 52
May Day protests 182
Meacher, M. 136
Meadowcroft, J. 5
media 4, 17, 22–44, 50
  civilisation 179, 182, 185–6, 188
  GM 134–8, 141–3, 148–9
  legislation 98, 100, 102, 104
  post-ecologism 53, 58–9, 61–2
  symbolic politics 68, 70–3
mediators 48–9, 56, 58–63, 71
Merritt, C. 146
meta-narratives 129, 155
metaphysics 164, 166
Metropolitan Police Academy 182
Meyer, T. 75, 82–3
Miles, G. 145–6
militants 62, 179
military 50, 128
mind-sets 176
Ministry of Environment and Energy Affairs of Denmark 58
mockery 162
modernity 3, 10, 14, 27–9
  discourse 32, 37, 43–4
  ecological modernisation 115–17
  GM 135, 149, 151
  irony 155, 164
  symbolic politics 74, 78, 83, 85
A Modest Proposal 157–8, 161
Mol, A.P.J. 27
monopoly 30

Monsanto 139, 141, 146
morality plays 162
moratorium 137
Muecke, D.C. 156–61, 163–5
multinationals 141
Mumford, P. 187
Murphy, P. 173–5

nation *see* state
National Seed List 136
nationalism 135
naturalism 155, 167
naturalness 9, 12–14, 145
naturecultures 167
neo-authoritarianism 8
neo-classicism 58–9, 118
neo-conservatism 11, 175
neo-liberalism 2, 17, 60, 78, 129, 160, 173–86, 188
neo-materialism 77–8
networking 48, 51, 151, 173, 178, 181, 184–5
new environmental policy instruments (NEPI) 115, 124–5
new social movements 78, 86, 154, 161, 164, 178
New York 180–1
Newig, J. 16, 92–112
news stories 23, 30–1, 36, 136–9, 142–3, 149
Nice Treaty 120
niche consumers 185
niche media 186
Nielsen, E. 54
Nietzsche, F. 155
nihilism 160
NOAH 51–2
Nobel Prize 176
non-governmental organisations (NGOs) 4, 11–12, 35, 51, 53, 62, 151
Nordhaus, T. 11–12
normalisation 3
North 5–7, 33, 79–80, 118–19, 178–9
North America 146, 181

202 Index

North, S. 143–4
nuclear power 4, 7–8, 52, 61, 145, 162,
  167, 182–3
Nullmeier, F. 81–2
Numbskull Jack 41
Nyhederne 30

O'Connor, J. 164
Oedipus the King 157–8
OOA (Organisation for Information
  about Nuclear Power) 52
Ophuls, W. 50
opportunism 99–100
opportunity society 76–8
opting out 77
Ordinance on Large Combustion
  Plants *see GroBfeuerungsanlagen-
  Verordnung* 96
Organic Farmer Organisation *see*
  LØJ
organic farming 51
Organisation for Information about
  Nuclear Power *see* OOA
Orwell, G. 183
Other 9–10, 36, 80–1, 83–4
Our Common Future 54–5, 127
Our Future, Our Choice 121
outsourcing 60
overconsumption 33–7, 42
overpopulation 33
Oxborrow, C. 140, 144, 150–1
ozone levels 24, 29, 101–2, 107
Ozongesetz (Summer Smog Act) 94,
  96, 100–2, 104–8

paradox 155, 167, 187
Paris 185
Parliament 185
Parliament Square 183
participation 47–64
paternalism 178
pathology 93, 108, 178
Patriot Act 181
Paye, J.-C. 181
peace vigils 183

Pearce, D. 118
penalties 97
pensions 68
performative regeneration 82, 84–5
pesticides 136
Petersen, L.K. 15, 22–47, 58
phenomenology 163
placebo politics 72
plateaus 187
PLATFORM 162
pluralism 76, 86, 126, 167
Poland 148
policing 179, 182, 184, 186
political symbolism 71
political-strategic dimension 95–7,
  104
politicians 6–7, 53–4, 62
  civilisation 172, 177, 179, 182, 185
  GM 146
  legislation 93, 97–102, 104
  symbolic politics 80, 83
politics of simulation *see* simulative
  politics
Politik als Ritual 75
Politiken 59
pollen 135, 142
Pollock, C. 146
pollution 37, 51, 101
  civilisation 176
  ecological modernisation 116, 119
  GM 144, 147
  legislation 103–4, 107
  post-ecologism 153
populism 30, 63
Porritt, J. 3
Post Environmentalism 8
post-democracy 8, 76–8
post-ecologism 1–4, 7–14
  civilisation 174, 178, 188
  discourse 28
  eco-politics 17
  irony 153–69
  itinerary 16
  legislation 92
  participation 47–64

symbolic politics 69, 76, 78–82, 84–6, 88
post-environmentalism 2, 23, 25, 28–30, 42–3
post-industrialism 8
post-libertarianism 77
post-materialism 77
post-post-materialism 77
postmodern irony 159–60, 163, 166
poverty 26–7, 35, 38–42, 161, 176
power constellations 106
power relations 177–8
Prague 37–8, 179, 181
Prevention of Terrorism Act 182
principal-agent problem 99
privatisation 176
professionalisation 52–3, 60–3, 85–6, 92
profit 37, 42, 117, 123, 146, 162, 175, 179
proportionality principle 93
protest movements 61–2, 78, 158, 161–3, 168, 178, 182–4, 186
protest societies 78
prototypes 95, 104
psychology 93, 106, 108
public choice theory 94, 97–100, 106–8
public discourse 22–44
public-private partnerships 3, 8
puppets 162
Pusztai, A. 136

quantitative/qualitative irony 163

radicalism 10, 13, 15, 26
    discourse 29, 31, 44
    ecological modernisation 117–18, 129–30
    post-ecologism 58, 61–2, 167
    symbolic politics 76, 78, 80, 86, 88
Rainbow Warrior 186
rainforest 33–5, 40
Rasmussen, A.F. 38
Reagan, R. 180

reason 155
rebranding 154
Reclaim The Streets (RTS) 181
recycling 6, 141, 186
regulation 51, 58, 77
    civilisation 173, 176, 185
    ecological modernisation 121, 125
    GM 135, 137–40
    irony 160
    legislation 94–5, 97, 106–8
religion 50, 155, 164, 166, 175, 180
renewable energy 51
rent-seeking 99
replacement action 72
repression 73–5
republicans 50
research and development (R&D) 115, 122–4
resource shortages 81
retrofitting 104, 106
rhetoric 3, 28–9, 40, 43
    civilisation 173
    ecological modernisation 114, 125, 127
    GM 151
    irony 158, 160–4, 168
    legislation 106
    post-ecologism 58
    symbolic politics 68–9, 73
right wing 48, 58–9, 149
Rio de Janeiro 23, 30, 33–4, 118, 186
risk communication 25
Risk Society 135
risk society 76–7, 174
ritual 24–6, 28–9, 36, 41
    civilisation 184, 186
    symbolic politics 71, 73, 82
Romanticism 155, 165
Rome Treaty 124
Rootes, C. 61
Rorty, R. 159–60
Rosser, J. 139
Rowell, A. 11
Rowett Research Institute 136
ruling class 81
Russia 186

204   *Index*

sarcasm 161
Sarcinelli, U. 71, 82
Sartor, R. 71
satire 162
Saul, J. 176
Scandinavia 102
schizophrenia 81, 108
Schroder, G. 180
Schweppes 162–3
science 52–3, 59, 77
  civilisation 173–6, 184, 187
  ecological modernisation 122–3
  GM 135–6, 141, 146–7
  legislation 107
  post-ecologism 155–6, 162, 164,
    167–8
Scotland 142
Scottish Parliament 135–6
Seattle 162, 178–9
Second World War 108, 143
security 150–1, 178, 181–2, 186
Security and Intelligence Service 181
seeds 135–6, 144
Seery, J.E. 166
Self 10, 77, 80–1
self-deception 17, 32, 84, 92–108,
    134–51, 156, 163
self-disparaging irony 161
self-presentation 154
self-referentiality 81
September 11, 2001 172, 179
Serious Organised Crime and Police
    Act 183
seriousness 69, 80–7, 93
settler civilisation 175
Shell 163
Shellenberger, M. 11–12
show politics 82
silent counter-revolution 76–7
silent revolution 76
simulative politics 16, 28–9
  discourse 32, 42–3
  GM 151
  post-ecologism 154, 159–60
  simulation 67–88

Single European Market (SEM)
    124–5
situational irony 157–9, 161, 163–4
Sixth Environmental Action
    Programme (EAP) 121, 123
The Skeptical Environmentalist 10
sleepers 182
smog 100–2, 105–8, 139
Soames, N. 183
social change theory 114–16, 119, 130
The Social Construction of Nature 9
Social Democratic Party of Germany
    (SPD) 101, 103–4
Social Forum 185
social movements *see* new social
    movements
social theory 85–7
socialisation 76
socialists 117
societal communication 23–5
societal self-deception 17, 84, 92–108,
    135, 150
sociology 1–2, 8–10, 12–15
  civilisation 177
  discourse 24, 27
  eco-politics 17–18
  ecological modernisation 115–16
  symbolic politics 75, 82, 85, 87
Socrates 161, 165, 168
soil 33–4
solidarity 31, 36, 126, 159, 179
Solomon, W.S. 179
Sophocles 157
South 5, 7, 33, 118–19, 177–9
South America 136
Soviet Union 180
Soweto 38
soya 139, 148
special measures 180–1
speed limits 106, 108
stakeholders 26, 49, 56–7, 145
state 3, 7–8, 28, 31
  civilisation 173–5, 178, 181–4,
    186–7
  dissolving 134–51

ecological modernisation 120, 123, 126–7
GM 134–5, 137–42
homogenous 142–3
irony 154, 158–60, 164
island 143–4
legislation 101, 105
legitimacy 177
post-ecologism 50, 58, 60
pure 144–7
self-deception 149–51
symbolic politics 76
steering groups 56–7
Stern Review on the Economics of Climate Change 3
Sterne, L. 164
Stiglitz, J. 176–7
strategic action 52
Strong, M. 34
structural adjustment 124
students 51
subsidiarity 137
subsidies 146, 176
substantive issues *see* issue-related substantives
substitute politics 72
successful legislation 94
summit sieges 179
supermarkets 137, 143–4
supply chains 135
supranational governance 127
surrogate politics 72
surveillance 6, 78, 81, 181, 186
survivalism 31, 36–7, 42–3
sustainability 26–9, 31, 36
    discourse 42–3
    eco-politics 1–18
    limitations 5–8
    participation 47–64
    symbolic politics 68
sustainable development (SD)
    eco-politics 5, 17
    participation 49–51, 53–63
    symbolic commitment 113–30

A Sustainable Europe for a Better World: A European Union Strategy for Sustainable Development 121
Sweden 61, 123–4, 149, 168
Swift, J. 157–8, 161
symbolic politics
    civilisation 174, 179, 182
    commitment 113–30
    dimensions 70–3
    eco-politics 16–17
    ecological modernisation 126–9
    goods 24
    industry 144
    intervention 175
    inversion 134–51
    legislation 92–108
    legitimacy 177, 179, 185–6
    post-ecologism 154, 160
    registers 178–9, 185
    simulation 67–88
    stakes 184–6
synergy 135
systems theory 9
Szerszynski, B. 17, 153, 179, 185

tactics 158–64, 168
taxes 40–1, 122, 126, 186
technocrats 49–50, 184, 187
technology
    civilisation 175–6, 186–7
    commitment 115, 118–25, 128
    discourses 22, 26, 29, 32, 35, 37, 39, 42
    eco-politics 2–3, 5–6, 8, 10, 14
    GM 136, 141, 145–6, 150
    irony 162, 165, 167
    legislation 106, 108
    post-ecologism 48–9, 51, 53–4, 57–8
    symbolic politics 68, 77–8, 81
television 23, 30, 42
terrorism 4, 7, 17, 172–88
Terrorism Act 182
Thatcher, M. 148
Theophrastus 159–60, 163, 165
Theweleit, K. 187

206 *Index*

think globally - act locally 54–5
Third World 117, 119, 122, 128
Thompson, J.B. 23, 184
threats 77, 81, 103
  civilisation 175, 177, 180, 186–7
  GM 144, 147–50
  post-ecologism 157
timing 97, 102
Titanium Dioxide Ordinance 95
Torgerson, D. 175
tourism 146, 183
Towards Sustainability 120
toxins 24, 27
trade disputes 137
traffic restrictions 101–2, 106–8
transaction relations 126
transboundary flows 135
transformation 114, 116, 185
transnational problems 139
Treasury of UK 3
tree-huggers 39
trespassing 182
Trident 183
Trilling, L. 159
Tristram Shandy 164
True Spies 182
trust 7, 138, 168, 184
truth 130, 154, 161, 168–9, 183
TV2 (Danish TV channel) 30–1, 36,
  42
TV-Avisen 30
Twyford Down 182

uncertainty 77, 138–9, 149, 155
unemployment 126, 176
Unesco 177
United Kingdom (UK)
  eco-politics 3, 13, 17, 175, 181–4,
  186
  GM 134–8, 140–1, 143, 145–9
  post-ecologism 162
United Nations Conference on
  Environment and Development
  (UNCED) 114, 117, 125
United Nations (UN) 33, 53, 114, 128

Millennium Development Summit
  177
  summits 23, 30, 121, 177
  World Summit on Sustainable
  Development 121
United States (US)
  civilisation 173–4, 179–81, 186
  discourse 29, 33–4, 37–8, 41
  eco-politics 4, 7, 11–12, 17
  ecological modernisation 128
  exceptionalism 175
  GM 136–7, 147–8
Urry, J. 9

values 9, 12–13, 27, 33
  civilisation 173, 177
  ecological modernisation 116,
  127–8
  GM 138, 141
  irony 163, 166, 168
  legislation 95, 107
  post-ecologism 48–9, 52, 56–7, 59,
  62–3
  symbolic politics 68, 71, 75–6, 78,
  81, 86
Vanity Fair 183
verifiability 85–6
vested interests 44
Vidal, J. 150
violence 61, 182
vocabulary 160
'Vote Blue Go Green' 13

Waldsterben 105, 107
Wales 139, 142
war on terror 4, 172, 174, 179–80,
  184
Washington 180–1
Washington Consensus 176
waste 6, 8, 26, 116, 119, 121, 177
watersheds 1–5
weak ties 185
wealth accumulation 2–3
weapons of mass destruction 180
weather 37, 107

websites 142, 144, 177, 180–1, 183, 185
Webster, A. 182
welfare 68, 77, 99, 117, 127
Welsh Assembly 135–7
Welsh, I. 1–21, 51, 59, 117, 139, 145, 148, 172–92
West
  civilisation 173–4, 176
  eco-politics 2–3, 5–6, 8, 11, 14
  ecological modernisation 113, 116–17, 120, 122
  GM 141, 148
  symbolic politics 67
Westminster 135
Whitehall 182
Wildavsky, A. 25
wildlife 11
withdrawal 185
workshops 61

World Bank 5, 176–7
world relation 163–6, 168
World Social Forum 179, 184
World Trade Organization (WTO) 10, 68, 135, 137, 141, 144, 162, 176–9
World War II 108, 143
World Watch 33
World Wide Fund for Nature (WWF) 37–42, 53
World Wildlife Fund *see* World Wide Fund for Nature

Yearley, S. 12–13
Yes Men 162–3
Young, J. 8

Zadek, S. 48
Zeitgeist 10, 78, 86, 88